The Life

Florence May

Alpha Editions

This edition published in 2022

ISBN : 9789356900264

Design and Setting By
Alpha Editions
www.alphaedis.com
Email - info@alphaedis.com

Contents

CHAPTER XII
1862-1864

Vienna—Musical societies—Leading musicians—The Prater—Brahms' appearance at a Hellmesberger Quartet concert—Brahms' first concert in Vienna—Conductorship of the Hamburg Philharmonic—First Serenade at Gesellschaft concert—Brahms' second concert—Richard Wagner—Second Serenade at Vienna Philharmonic concert—Return to Hamburg—Brahms elected conductor of the Vienna Singakademie—Return to Vienna—Singakademie concerts under Brahms.

It would be interesting, on accompanying Johannes Brahms in imagination on his first visit to Vienna—a visit that was to lead to results scarcely less important to his career than those of the first concert-journey through the provincial towns of Hanover undertaken nine years and a half previously—to describe the gradual change which had taken place in the musical life of the imperial city since the times when it had counted Haydn, Mozart, and Beethoven in turn among its inhabitants. It would, however, lead too far from the purpose of this narrative to follow the course by which the art of music, from being a luxury to be enjoyed chiefly by the rich—and in Vienna, perhaps, especially amongst the great capitals of Europe—had been opened to the cultivation of the masses of citizens. Suffice it to say that in the autumn of 1862 the conditions of musical activity in the Austrian capital were essentially the same as we know them in 1905.

The Court Opera, the home of which was the Kärthnerthor Theater, was conducted by Otto Dessoff, who had been a distinguished pupil of the Leipzig Conservatoire, and had succeeded the celebrated capellmeister, Carl Anton Eckert, on his resignation of the post in 1860. In intimate though not official connection with the opera were the Philharmonic concerts given in the same building. These, started in 1849 by the orchestral musicians of the opera as their own undertaking, had, after a period of varying fortune, entered upon a flourishing phase of existence. They were conducted by Dessoff in virtue of his position as capellmeister of the opera, and though his rather cold style at first prevented his winning Austrian sympathy, he by-and-by succeeded in making good his footing by his musicianship and thoroughness, and by the perfect finish of rendering that was attained by the orchestra under his direction.

The annual orchestral concerts given by the great Gesellschaft der Musikfreunde (Society of Music-lovers), founded in 1813, took place in the Redoubtensaal, and, though given under the Society's own 'artistic director,' had, during the eight or nine years preceding the appointment of Johann

Herbeck to this post (1859), been dependent on the services of the opera orchestra. Herbeck, feeling the inconveniences of such an arrangement, determined to form an orchestra of his own, and, whilst successfully carrying out his project, sought to make amends for the first inevitable lack of complete finish in his performances by cultivating a liberal spirit in the choice of programmes, and introducing from time to time unfamiliar works by the best modern classical composers. From this period the Gesellschaft and the Philharmonic concerts came more or less to represent severally the liberal and the conservative spirit of classical art, though it must be added that Dessoff cherished the wish to educate his audience to wider powers of appreciation, and sometimes included the name of Schumann in the Philharmonic programmes, which, before his advent, had been closed to works of more modern tendency than those of Mendelssohn.

Parallel with these two institutions for the performance of instrumental music were two choral societies, both supplied by amateurs. The Singverein, a branch of the Gesellschaft der Musikfreunde, which in 1862 was, like the orchestra, under Herbeck's direction, occupied itself with every kind of classical choral music in turn, and, occasionally giving concerts independently, often joined forces in public performance with the orchestra. The Singakademie, founded in 1858 by a circle of amateurs, made a special point of early church music, and of *a capella* singing, but usually devoted one of its three or four annual concerts to the performance of an oratorio or other great work, when, of course, the services of an orchestra were engaged. Under the direction of its first conductor, F. Stegmayer, the Singakademie gave the first performance in Vienna of portions of Schumann's 'Faust' (January 6, 1861) and of Bach's 'Matthew Passion' (April 15, 1862).

Occupying a position in Vienna at the very top of his profession, partly in virtue of the musical prestige attaching to his family name, but mainly as the result of his personal gifts and attainments, was the violinist Josef Hellmesberger, director and professor of the conservatoire (itself another branch of the great Gesellschaft der Musikfreunde), concertmeister of the opera, and therefore also of the Philharmonic concerts, late artistic director of the Gesellschaft (1851-1859), leader of the only resident and justly celebrated string quartet party called by his name, and accomplished virtuoso. Hellmesberger's playing lacked broadness of tone, but was distinguished by grace, poetic sentiment, and a facile instinct for his composer's intention. He possessed a good knowledge of the orchestra, and was a fair pianist.

Of other musicians resident in the Austrian capital in 1862 are to be mentioned the great contrapuntist Sechter, nearly approaching the end of his career, who, in his position of professor of composition at the conservatoire, had in his time taught several of the younger men next to be referred to; Nottebohm, professor of counterpoint at the conservatoire, known to the world by his writings on music, especially those on Beethoven's sketch-books; Rudolph Bibl, organist of the cathedral, and later, of the imperial chapel; Julius Epstein, professor of the pianoforte at the conservatoire, distinguished pianist and widely-reputed teacher, and esteemed, not only on account of his professional standing, but also by reason of his kindness to all persons having any sort of claim on his courtesy.

The composer Carl Goldmark, who has since attained European reputation with his opera 'The Queen of Sheba,' had been almost entirely resident in Vienna since his sixteenth year, and now at thirty was rising to fame. Peter Cornelius, composer of the comic opera 'The Barber of Bagdad,' and already mentioned in our narrative as a disciple of Weimar, was living at this time in the Austrian capital. Anton Brückner was favourably esteemed by some of the first resident musicians, though he had not yet been called there. Carl Tausig, one of the greatest of pianoforte virtuosi, whose sympathies were much with the New-Germans, settled in Vienna for a few years from 1861, and gave occasional concerts there which were but partially successful.

Of writers and critics, Edward Hanslick, Carl Ferdinand Pohl, and Selmar Bagge, all believers in the art of tradition and in its modern development as represented by the name of Schumann, were in the flower of their activity. Bagge's name is interesting in the history of Brahms' career on account of the sympathetic and detailed reviews of the composer's works which appeared from time to time in the *Deutsche Musikzeitung*, a paper founded by him in 1860. It became defunct at the close of 1863, when Bagge left Vienna to take up the editorship of the *Allgemeine Musikzeitung*, which he retained for two years. Very able articles were published in this periodical of Brahms' works as they appeared, some of them written by Bagge himself, and others by Hermann Deiters, a musical scholar and critic of exceptional insight and power of happy expression. Bagge remained just long enough in Vienna to witness the interest aroused by Brahms' first appearances there, to which, very likely, the remembrance of the articles of the *Deutsche Musikzeitung* gave additional stimulus.

Of publishers, the name of C. A. Spina should be gratefully remembered as that of the man to whom the world is indebted for the publication of many great and long-neglected works of Schubert. A large number of the master's half-forgotten manuscripts—those of the Octet, the C major Quartet, the B flat and B minor Symphonies amongst them—were found by Spina when he took over the business of his predecessors, the firm of Diabelli, and were gradually placed by him in the possession of the world.

On his arrival in Vienna, Brahms put up at the Hôtel Kronprinz in the Leopoldstadt, moving soon afterwards into a room at 39, Novaragasse, of the same inexpensive quarter, then called the Jägerzeil. Several of his old friends were fortunately at hand. Grädener had given up his position in Hamburg the preceding year to try his fortune in Vienna; Frau Passy-Cornet, whose name calls the concert of 1848 to remembrance, was now a professor of singing at the Vienna Conservatoire; and, a very few weeks after Brahms' arrival, Arthur Faber, lately married to Fräulein Bertha Porubszky, brought his bride to their home in the imperial city. His house was, of course, open to Johannes, who spent many, and especially Sunday, evenings with these friends. Amongst the most treasured memories of their early wedded life are those of performances of his compositions, played as he could play when quietly at ease with a few sympathetic friends for all audience.

From the first he felt at home in Vienna. The good-natured, easy-going Austrian people attracted him, and he at once conceived an affection for the Prater, in the immediate vicinity of which his hotel was situated. This great park of the Kaiserstadt contains, indeed, attractions to suit every variety of taste. There is the Hauptallée, with its broad drive and shady walks, its open-air cafés and music of military bands, which play waltzes and various dance movements as they are played in no other city. There is the Würstelprater, the playground of children and other simple folk, where, in the fine-weather season, a continual fair goes on with shows and games and entertainments of every kind likely to attract the patronage of the multitude, and where in the Hungarian restaurant, the 'Czarda,' real gipsy music played by a real gipsy band may daily be heard. There is the wild portion, bounded on one side by the Danube canal and stretching for some little distance beyond the town, where the solitary walker may fancy himself in a forest far from human habitation. Brahms, on this occasion of his first visit to Vienna, particularly attached himself to the Würstelprater, for which he ever after retained his partiality. The motley life to be seen there amused and interested him. He came to be a frequent listener at the 'Czarda,' and it is whispered that the spirit of fun has occasionally prompted him, when at the height of his fame, to prevail upon a party of friends to take a turn in his company on the curvetting horses of one or other of the 'carrousels' which are amongst the most popular attractions of this part of the grounds.

One of Brahms' first visits was to Julius Epstein. He did not send in his name, and, as the professor was engaged with someone else at the moment, was not admitted. A second call was successful. 'My name is Johannes Brahms,' he said as he entered; and his simple manner at once attracted Epstein, who was well acquainted with his published works. An opportunity was arranged without delay for his introduction to some of the leading musicians of the city.

'Brahms in 1862 played the Quartets in G minor and A major with the members of the Hellmesberger Quartet (Hellmesberger, Dobyhal and Röver) at my house in the Schulerstrasse, in the first place,' writes Professor Epstein to the author. 'We were all delighted and carried away. The works were shortly afterwards played in public by Brahms with the same colleagues.'

The G minor Quartet was, in fact, included in the list of works announced by Hellmesberger for the ensuing season, and the immediate interest awakened in musical circles by the arrival of the composer is even more strikingly testified by the fact that on October 14, only five weeks after his departure from Hamburg, the name of the orchestral Serenade in D major appeared in the forecast of the Gesellschaft season published in the *Blätter für Theater, Künst und Musik*.

On Sunday evening, November 16, Brahms made his first appearance before his new public at Hellmesberger's Quartet concert, which took place, as usual, in the Vereinsaal (the concert-room of the Gesellschaft der Musikfreunde) before an audience that crowded every part of the house in anticipation of the debut in Vienna of 'Schumann's young prophet.' The first and last numbers of the programme of three works were severally Mendelssohn's String Quartet in E flat and Beethoven's in C sharp minor, Op. 131, Brahms' G minor Pianoforte Quartet occupying the place of honour between them. If we were to judge of the result by the press reviews of the day, which were either unfavourable or reserved, it would be impossible to chronicle a success, and yet that the work was essentially successful is established by the fact that the composer received overtures after the concert from more than one Vienna publisher, which, however, he declined. He had certainly made his mark in his own characteristic way even before the 16th. A private circle of admirers began to form round him, and he was sufficiently encouraged to venture on a concert of his own, which took place in the Vereinsaal on November 29.

On this occasion the Pianoforte Quartet in A major headed the programme, the composer being assisted in its performance by the three members of the Hellmesberger party with whom he had already appeared. The remaining instrumental numbers were pianoforte solos, the concert-giver's Handel Variations and Fugue, Bach's F major Toccata for organ, and Schumann's C major Fantasia, Op. 17.

As regards the general audience, the concert was an unmistakable success. The room was fairly filled, and enough money taken to cover expenses. This, however, by the way. The circumstance most worthy of record is that artist and public found themselves *en rapport.* The performer had the infallible instinct of having with him the sympathy of his hearers, and played his best, giving out what was really in him as he had probably never been able to do before his indifferent or sceptical audiences in Germany. A friendly reception was accorded to the quartet, which was followed with close attention. Enthusiasm could scarcely have been looked for on a first hearing of so original a work. The variations and fugue, however, called forth a storm of applause that was renewed after the performance of Schumann's fantasia, the divine last movement of which was given with ideal insight and noble inspiration. The press notices, though respectful, were disappointing in regard to Brahms the composer.

'The quartet by no means pleased us, and we are glad that the unfavourable impression it created was obliterated by the variations which followed....' Hanslick wrote (*die Presse*). 'Brahms' talent has hitherto been displayed at its best in variation form, which requires, above all, facility in inventing figures, and unity of mood.... The unsatisfactory features of his creative style are more apparent in the quartet. The first subject has not enough significance. The composer chooses themes rather with a view to their capacity for contrapuntal treatment than on account of their intrinsic merit, and those of the quartet sound dry and flat.... The quartet and others of the composer's works remind us of Schumann's last period; the early works of his first period; but none of Brahms' yet known compositions can take their place beside those of Schumann's ripe middle period.'

As a pianist, Brahms was mentioned in the papers in more decided terms of appreciation. Bagge says:

'We have to bestow high praise not only on the enormous technical acquirement, but also on a performance instinct with musical genius, on a treatment of the instrument as fascinating as it was original.'

The playing of Bach's organ toccata is especially mentioned in terms of high admiration; the touch employed for the passages written for the pedals 'gave the pianoforte the effect of an organ.' The performance of each number was musical through and through, and although 'he has not the unfailing certainty nor the outward brilliancy of the virtuoso, he reaches and fascinates his audience by other means.'

The delightful natural letter to his parents, published by Reimann, written after the concert, shows the pleasure derived by Brahms from feeling his audience in sympathy with him:

'DEAR PARENTS,

'I was very happy yesterday, my concert went quite excellently, much better than I had hoped.

'After the quartet had been sympathetically received, I had great success as a player. Every number was greatly applauded, I think there was real enthusiasm in the room.

'Now I could very well give concerts, but I do not wish to do so, for it takes up too much time so that I can do nothing else....

'I played as freely as though I were sitting at home with friends; one is certainly influenced quite differently by the public than by ours.

'You should have seen the attention and seen and heard the applause.... I am very glad I gave the concert. You are probably rid of your guests again now and will be able to find a moment of time to write to me?

'Tell the contents of this letter to Herr Marxsen and say also that Börsendorfer[1] will not be able to send a piano before the New Year as so many are required for concerts. Shall I see about another for him? I await orders....

'I think my serenade will be given next Monday.

'I should have liked to introduce some of my vocal things in my concert yesterday, but it gave me a terrible amount of running about and unpleasantness and that is one of my reasons for wishing to be quiet now.[2]

'Did you sit together on Wednesday over the egg-punch? Write to me about it and anything else.[3]

'The publishers here, especially Spina and Levi, have been pressing me for things since the quartet, but much pleases me better in North Germany and particularly the publishers, and I would rather go without the two or three extra Louis-d'ors that these would perhaps pay.

'Does Avé often go to see you? Has he told you anything particular about Stockhausen?

'How about the photograph of the girls' quartet? Am I not to have it? N.B. Every time I write I forget to ask about Fritz.... Is he very industrious? He ought to make up his mind to give Trio concerts in Hamburg next winter. I would help him in every way....

'Write soon and have love

'from your

'JOHANNES.

'Hearty greetings to Herr Marxsen, and do not forget about Börsendorfer.'[4]

The two Pianoforte Quartets were despatched to Simrock, and were published by the firm early in 1863—the first one in G minor, being dedicated to Baron Reinhard von Dalwigk, Court Intendant to the Grand-Duke of Oldenburg, a really musical amateur and a warm supporter of Brahms; and the second, in A major, to Frau Dr. Elisabeth Rösing of Hamm, in whose house it was written.

The tone of the above extracts tells how lovingly the composer's thoughts turned to his home at the moment he was feeling conscious of a real success; and the question about Stockhausen may be taken as an indication of the clinging wistfulness with which he was bringing himself to resign the hope of being able to settle near his family as conductor of the Philharmonic—a position he would at the time have been proud to accept. The decision of the committee was now almost a foregone conclusion, though it was not formally arrived at till the following year. What it was may be told in the following extract from a letter written to Avé Lallement on January 31, 1863, by Joachim, whose influence with the committee had been energetically exerted in favour of his Johannes:

'... What can I say further about your plan with Stockhausen? You know how highly I esteem his talent, and he is certainly the best musician among the singers, but how anyone, having to choose the director of a concert institution between him and Johannes, can decide for the former, I, with my limited musical understanding, cannot comprehend! It is precisely as a man upon whom one can rely that I regard Johannes so highly, with his gifts and his will! There is nothing he cannot undertake, and, with his earnestness, overcome! You know that as well as I, and if all of you in the committee and orchestra had met him with confidence and affection (as you, his friend, always do in private) instead of with doubt and airs of protection, it would have removed the asperity from his nature; whereas it must constantly make him more bitter, with his touching, almost childlike patriotism for Hamburg, to see himself put second. I dare not dwell on the thought, it would make me too unhappy, that his narrow compatriots have deprived themselves of the means of making him more contented and gentle, and happier in the exercise of his genius. I should like to give the committee a moral cudgelling (and a bodily one too!) for having left you in the lurch with your plan. The slight to Johannes will not be forgotten in the history of art! But basta!'[5]

To the advertisement of the Hamburg Philharmonic programme of March 6, 1863, the words were added, 'Herr Julius Stockhausen has kindly undertaken to conduct the second and third numbers'; and a fortnight later Stockhausen's appointment as capellmeister to the society for the following season, 1863-64, was announced.

Meanwhile Johannes in Vienna may still, in the beginning of November, 1862, have clung to hope in view of the forthcoming performance of his serenade at the Gesellschaft concert of the 14th under Herbeck. The reception of the work proved, in fact, as favourable as might reasonably have been expected. It was listened to with respect by public and critics, and some of its parts, notably the first minuet, were greeted with manifestations of decided approval.

'The serenade, a fine, interesting, and intellectual work, deserved warmer acknowledgment,' wrote Speidel in the *Wiener Zeitung*. Hanslick, in the *Presse*, pronounced it one of the most charming of modern orchestral compositions, but took exception to the first subject of the opening movement, as he had objected to that of the A major Quartet, as being workable rather than original or significant.

'The first minuet seems to us the pearl of the work and perhaps the prettiest movement as yet written by Brahms. The instrumental colouring and the grace of the melody give it the characteristic of night music, and it is full of moonlight and the scent of lilac.'

A remarkable review—remarkable from its admirable appreciation of Brahms' creative personality—was despatched to Leipzig by the Vienna correspondent of the *Neue Zeitschrift*, who signs himself 'S.,' and appeared in the Vienna résumé contained in the paper's issue of March 23:

'As regards Brahms' serenade which has been favourably received, albeit in my opinion too severely criticised, only thus much; it is one of the most charming examples, not only of the class of composition from which it has sprung, but of all that has followed Beethoven up to the comprehensive conquests, as to contents and form, of the rising New Germany.

'It is fresh and rich in themes of which nearly every one is pervaded by a rare grace, and a brightness of tone becoming every day more unusual. The score convincingly exhibits, moreover, one of the most prominent sides of Brahms' musical individuality. I would call this a power of refashioning, in the best spirit of the present day, the contrapuntal forms of canon and fugue and of their degenerate and inferior representatives. Brahms succeeds in this, as in the majority of his works, in reconsecrating and carrying on the spiritual treasure inherited from Bach, Beethoven and Schumann, in the light of modernity. This fundamental characteristic is still more striking in a second great work of the composer, for the hearing of which opportunity is promised. I will therefore go on to remark on the orchestral colouring of the serenade, which, without being exaggerated, is, throughout, fresh and significant of youthful power. I should find it very difficult to express a preference for either of the six movements, whilst to speak of either of the several parts of this, in its way, masterly whole as inferior in excellence to others, appears to me utterly impossible. The *vox populi*, however, with which the principal journals here coincide on this occasion, has pronounced in favour of the first minuet and scherzo and the certainly wonderfully tender slow movement.'

Brahms appeared on December 20 at Frau Passy-Cornet's concert in the Vereinsaal, playing Beethoven's E flat Sonata for pianoforte and violin with Hellmesberger, and some Schumann solos (Romance and Novelette), and, in spite of his frequently avowed distaste for public appearances, gave a second concert on January 6, 1863, in order to bring forward some of his songs. On this occasion he played Bach's Chromatic Fantasia, Beethoven's C minor Variations, his own Sonata in F minor Op. 5, and Schumann's Sonata in the same key Op. 14, with omission of the scherzo.

'Brahms' playing,' wrote the Vienna correspondent of the *Signale*, 'is always attractive and convincing. His rendering of Bach's Chromatic Fantasia and of Beethoven's Variations was of the highest interest.... After repeated recalls Brahms treated his audience to another piece, a four-hand march by Schubert arranged for two hands. The delightful freshness of this composition gave no little pleasure.'

Frau Wilt, one of the first resident singers, performed several of the concert-giver's songs, amongst them being 'Treue Liebe' (Op. 7, No. 1), 'Parole' (Op. 7, No. 2), and 'Liebestreue' ('O versenk,' Op. 3, No. 1).

'This new experience was most agreeable and welcome to the whole public. All these songs breathe a fine sensibility, and are full of truth to life and nature.'

This second concert, indeed, stamped Brahms' visit to Vienna with the seal of decisive and permanent success—a success not immediately wide or popular, but which marked the beginning of a new epoch in the musical life of the city. Though he could not stoop to the attempt to dazzle his public by phenomenal feats of virtuosity, the grace, tenderness, and truth of his musical nature appealed to his southern audience, whilst the significance of his genius dawned on the perception of one or two discerning musicians. In a word, he had found a public which partially understood him; and a performance of the second serenade was announced for one of the Philharmonic concerts.

Before the opening of the New Year, musical attention in Vienna was turned to Richard Wagner, who conducted three concerts devoted to selections from his own compositions, and was received and discussed with the extremes of enthusiasm and disapproval that usually attended his appearances and the early productions of his works.

'One evening,' writes Hanslick many years later,[6] 'when we listened to Brahms' sextet after attending a concert of excerpts from Wagner's "Tristan" in the afternoon, it was as though we were suddenly transported to a world of pure beauty.[7] ... The general impression made in public by the two men was almost as different as that of their music. Brahms approached the conductor's desk with almost awkward modesty; he responded reluctantly and doubtfully to the most stormy calls and could not disappear again quickly enough.'

The attraction felt by Hanslick for Brahms' art increased with each opportunity of becoming acquainted with it. He secured his services as pianist at a lecture on Beethoven—one of a series—given by him in January, when Johannes, whose pianistic répertoire was almost inexhaustible, performed the thirty-three Variations on a waltz by Diabelli.

Wagner remained at Penzing, a suburb of Vienna, until the spring, and Brahms, who was on cordial terms with Tausig and Cornelius, paid him a visit in Tausig's company. He was much pleased by Wagner's reception of him, and spoke heartily of the pleasure he had found in his society. There was no future personal intercourse between the two composers, who were too widely separated by disposition, tastes, and artistic faith to grow into intimacy, though it should never be forgotten that Brahms felt, from first to last, immense respect for Wagner's gifts and achievement.

One of our composer's engrossing occupations during his nearly eight months' stay in Vienna was the study of Schubert's manuscripts, which Spina was delighted to show him, generously allowing him to copy from them for his own pleasure as he felt inclined. Shortly before his return home he sent some of the treasures thus obtained for Dietrich's perusal.

'... It occurs to me that I can send you my Marienlieder and Variations for four hands which arrived lately, and I enclose with them some extracts from an Easter cantata of Schubert's which I copied from the manuscript. They are not specially selected portions of Lazarus. By no means; I merely wrote the beginning and end of the first part. The music is as fine throughout; Simon's aria—oh, if I could send you the whole, you would be enchanted with such loveliness!...'

He decides to send in the same parcel, for Albert's inspection, the string quintet which he had taken to Vienna to get quite to his liking.

The second Serenade was announced for the Philharmonic concert of March 8 as the opening number of the programme, to be followed by Joachim's Hungarian Concerto, with Laub as solo violinist, and this by a new symphony by M. Kässmeyer—an astonishingly progressive list, which was due to Dessoff's influence and was approvingly remarked upon by

Hanslick in his review of the 11th of the month. Meanwhile difficulties presented themselves.[8] The discontent of the members of the orchestra was apparent during the first rehearsals of Brahms' work; complaints were heard of the great difficulty of performing many of the passages, and at the general rehearsal open mutiny broke out. The first clarinettist suddenly rose, and, in the name of the body of instrumentalists, declared their refusal to perform the composition. Dessoff, white with agitation, instantly replied by laying down his bâton and announcing his resignation of the post of conductor; Hellmesberger, as concertmeister, followed suit, and the first flutist, Franz Doppler, a celebrated performer, joined them. This decided matters. The malcontents gave way, the rehearsal proceeded, and the performance on the 8th was so greatly appreciated by the public that R. Hirsch, who made his début as Brahms' critic in the *Wiener Zeitung* in connexion with the occasion, and who for many years systematically (and perhaps conscientiously) decried his works, could find nothing worse to say than that the serenade would find many friends amongst those able to content themselves with modest gifts.

'Brahms should be on his guard against excess of things. The exorbitant applause raised by his friends had the effect of procuring him very loud hisses from other parties.'

'If either of the younger composers has the right not to be ignored, it is Brahms,' wrote Hanslick. 'He has shown himself, in each of his lately-performed works, as an independent, original individuality, a finely-organized, true, musical nature, as an artist ripening towards mastership by means of unwearied, conscious endeavour. His A major Serenade is the younger, tender sister of the one in D lately produced by the Gesellschaft and is conceived in the same peaceful, dreamy garden mood.... The work had an extremely favourable reception. The hearty applause became proportionately greater at the close as the modest composer made himself ever smaller in his seat in the gallery.'

Hanslick pronounced the Hungarian Concerto

'a tone-poem full of mind and spirit, of energy and tenderness. One might almost regret Joachim's achievements as a virtuoso, which must be the only cause that his powers are so seldom concentrated on the composition of a great work.'

The music season was now coming to a close, but the many attractions of Vienna—and not least among them its beautiful neighbourhood, with which Brahms' frequent long walks with Nottebohm, Faber, Epstein, and others gradually made him familiar—inclined him to stay on for some weeks longer; and it was not until the spring had well set in that he set out for Hanover *en route* for Hamburg, carrying with him many new possessions as mementoes of his visit, engravings of some of his favourite pictures in the Belvedere Gallery,[9] and the entire collection of the then published works of Schubert, presented to him by Spina, being the principal. He had a particular reason for wishing to pass a day or two with his friend. He was to be introduced to Fräulein Amalie Weiss, to whom Joachim had lately become engaged. This lady had entered into a three years' engagement as first contralto on the stage of the Hanover court opera in the spring of 1862, and it was not long before her gifts attracted the enthusiastic interest of the celebrated court concertmeister of the same capital. The two artists were betrothed in February, 1863, and the birthday of the Queen of Hanover, April 14, was celebrated by a festival performance of Gluck's 'Orpheus,' conducted, by Her Majesty's express desire, by Joachim, in which Fräulein Weiss appeared with brilliant success in the title-rôle. Brahms, on his arrival a little later on, was a delighted witness of a repetition of the opera. Frau Amalie Joachim, who retired from the stage on her marriage (June, 1863), gradually acquired a very great reputation as a concert-singer, and was a much-admired interpreter of Brahms' songs.

Brahms returned to Hamburg on May 5, and, after passing his thirtieth birthday with his family, took a lodging at Blankenese, on the Elbe, where an unexpected meeting with some of the former members of his Ladies' Choir agreeably reminded him of the charming society that had now quite fallen through, having served its purpose in the composer's course of self-training. Various plans for work and recreation for the summer and autumn months were under consideration, but were to be set aside. Before the month was out, Brahms received a convincing proof of the impression his visit had made in Vienna by getting a call to return there. The post of conductor to the Singakademie had fallen vacant by the death of Stegmayer, and, at the general meeting of the society in the course of May, Brahms was elected successor to the post. There was a severe competition between two sections of the members, a large and influential party, led by Prince Constantin Czartoriska, being strongly in favour of the election of Franz Krenn, an excellent musician of the old school, who belonged to Vienna as choir-master of the parish church of St. Michael, and professor of composition at the conservatoire, and who had conducted one of the Singakademie concerts during Stegmayer's illness. It happened, however, that amongst those members of the committee who desired that the practices and performances of the society should be placed under the direction of a young, resolute, and energetic musician, were several gentlemen belonging to the circle of enthusiastic admirers of Brahms' art which had sprung into existence almost simultaneously with his first appearance in Vienna, and had increased with each opportunity that had offered itself there for the hearing of his music. Amongst them were Dr. Scholz, a surgeon; Herr Adolf Schultz, a merchant; and Herr Franz Flatz, an insurance official of Vienna; and at their head Dr. Josef Gänsbacher, son of the distinguished musician and church composer Johann Gänsbacher, the pupil of Vogler and Albrechtsberger, acquaintance of Haydn and Beethoven, friend of Weber and Meyerbeer, and capellmeister of the cathedral from 1823 until his death in 1844.

Dr. Josef Gänsbacher, whose name has become known in the musical world of many countries by its appearance on the title-page of Brahms' first sonata for pianoforte and violoncello, was, in 1863, a young doctor of jurisprudence and advocate's draughtsman. Later on he adopted music as a profession, and became a valued teacher of singing, professor at the conservatoire, and violoncellist. He was one of Brahms' earliest and truest friends in Vienna, and became a devotee of his art even before making his personal acquaintance. He had considerable influence with the members of the Singakademie, and representatives of both sections of the committee called on him at his bureau to solicit his help, Prince Czartoriska presenting himself in person in Krenn's favour. Gänsbacher's sympathies, however, were all the other way; and, being selected by his party to make a speech at the general meeting in Brahms' interest, he used such forcible arguments as to bring over several of Krenn's supporters and to win the election for his own side by a majority of one.

It was in every way characteristic of our composer that he could not at once decide either to accept or reject the offer of the appointment, and was only at length brought to a resolution by a telegraphic request for his final answer.

'The resolve to give away one's freedom for the first time is exceptional,' he wrote to the committee, 'but anything coming from Vienna sounds doubly pleasant to a musician and whatever may call him thither is doubly attractive.'[10]

Something of what it cost Brahms to send his affirmative decision may be perceived in a letter to Hanslick, which indicates, also, the quick advance of friendship between the two men:

'DEAR FRIEND,

'You will wonder that most glad and grateful reply has not arrived sooner to yours and many other kind letters received by me. I seem to myself as one who has been praised beyond desert, and should like to creep into hiding for awhile. I resolved, on receipt of the telegraphic despatch ... to be content with such a flattering summons and not to tempt the gods further ... and since nothing more is in question than whether I have the courage to say "yes," it shall be so. Had I refused, my reasons would not have been understood by the academy or by you Viennese generally....'

These occurrences put an end to the various holiday projects which Brahms had been considering. 'I cannot make up my mind to deprive my parents of any of our short time together,' he wrote in answer to Dietrich's pressing invitation, and remained quietly near and at Hamburg. He began at once to occupy himself with plans for his programmes, and begged Dietrich's advice 'as a very experienced and learned court-conductor' on matters connected with his new duties. 'I feel enormously diffident,' he says, 'about trying my talent for these things in Vienna.'

Allowing himself but three days *en route* for a visit to beautiful Lichtenthal, a suburb of Baden-Baden, where Frau Schumann had purchased a house the previous year on giving up her residence in Berlin, Brahms was back again in Vienna by the last week of August, and soon engaged with characteristic earnestness in work connected with his new appointment. His scheme for the weekly practices of the Singakademie season included works by Bach, Beethoven, Mendelssohn, Schumann, and masters of the earlier period whose music was a speciality of the society. The first concert of the season 1863-64, given on November 15 under his direction, presented the following programme:

1. Bach:	Cantata, 'Ich hatte viel Bekümmerniss.' (First time in Vienna.)
2. Beethoven:	'Opferlied.'
3. H. Isaak (late 15th cent.):	Three German Folk-songs— *a.* 'Innsbruck ich muss dich lassen.' *b.* 'Es ist ein Schnitter heisst der Tod.' *c.* 'Ich fahr dahin wenn es muss seyn.'
4. Schumann:	'Requiem für Mignon.' (First time in Vienna.)

The co-operating artists were Frau Wilt and Frau Ferrari; Herr Danzer, Herr Dalfy, and Herr Organist Bibl. No doubt could be felt at the close of the performances of Brahms' gifts as a conductor.

'The concert was not only excellent in itself, but was, with exception of the first performance in Vienna of Bach's "Matthew Passion," by far the most noteworthy achievement in the record of the Singakademie, and gave us the opportunity of recognising Brahms' rare talent as a conductor.'

Bach's cantata was rendered 'with splendid colouring and spiritual insight'; the three delightful Volkslieder 'opened all hearts.' These were received with such stormy applause that a fourth, not less acceptable, was added. Considerable surprise seems to have been excited, not by the conductor's inspired conception of the works performed, but by the precision and clearness of his beat, which, remarks one critic, 'could hardly have been expected of an artist who has shown himself, in his creations and performances, so essentially a romanticist and dreamer.'

These last words sound strange as coming from a writer in Vienna who may be supposed to have gained some knowledge of the serenades, the B flat sextet, and the two pianoforte quartets, and they are quoted, not because of their aptness, but as illustrating a difficulty which the composer's individuality, reflected in his works as in a mirror, caused for many a long year to some of his less competent, even though friendly, critics—the difficulty of knowing how to classify him. From an early period his determination was strong to bring the womanly tenderness and dreamy romance that were in him under the complete control of his energetic will, to give supreme dominance in art, as in life, to understanding rather than to emotion, to possess and be master of his powers; but, during the earlier years of his activity, the subtle poetic charm dwelling within his works made itself felt by many sympathetic listeners who could not immediately follow their closely-woven texture, and who were puzzled by his independent treatment—at times almost amounting to a re-creation—of traditional form. Hence, he has not seldom been spoken of as essentially a romanticist long since his position as the representative descendant of Bach, Mozart, and Beethoven was recognised by those most competent to judge.

Meanwhile his art was gradually spreading through Europe. On November 10 the first serenade was given at Zürich under Fichtelberger, the conductor of the subscription concerts. The work deserved a warmer reception than was accorded it, in the opinion of the *Neuer Zürcher Zeitung*, whose critic recognised in Brahms a composer, not only of profound knowledge, but of inborn genius. He did not commit himself to pronouncement as to whether the composer's creative power would be of sufficient force to discover really 'new paths,' or would prove better qualified for making further developments within the already conquered domain of musical art, but thought the serenade pointed to the latter probability.

The B flat Sextet was performed at a concert given in Hamburg in November by Rosé and Stockhausen, whose friendship with Brahms had not been allowed to suffer by the action of the Philharmonic committee. The composition was given in Vienna at the Hellmesberger concert of December 27, when it awakened extraordinary interest and sympathy. In the Austrian capital, as elsewhere, it was the first of the composer's important works to become popular.

Christmas Eve was passed with the Fabers, Brahms being, as ever, the most cordial, happy, childlike guest. He continued, during the first years of his subsequent residence in Vienna, to spend the festival with these friends, who took pains to invite his favourite companions to meet him. Nottebohm was always of the party. Amongst his presents one Christmas for the gift-making ceremony at home in Hamburg, was a sewing-machine for his sister, who had expressed a wish for such a possession as a help in her employment. After the lapse of a few seasons, however, Brahms for a great many years habitually declined all invitations for Christmas Eve, only breaking his rule by occasionally spending it with Frau Schumann. Within the last decade of his life he again changed his custom, and passed the evening regularly in the happy home circle of some friends to whom the reader will be introduced in a later chapter.

The second and third concerts of the Singakademie took place on January 6 and March 20, with the subjoined programmes:

PROGRAMME OF JANUARY 6.

1. Mendelssohn:	Eight-part Motet.
2. Joh. Eccard (1553-1611):	'The Christian's Easter Day Song of Triumph' (double chorus).
3. Heinrich Schütz (1583-1672):	'Saul's Conversion' (triple chorus).
4. Giov. Gabrielli (1557-1613):	'Benedictus' (double chorus).
5. Giov. Rovetta (1643-1668):	'Salve Regina.'
6. Beethoven:	'Elegischer Gesang' (chorus with string accompaniment).
7. Three German Folk-songs.	
8. J. S. Bach:	Motet, 'Liebster Gott wann werd' ich sterben.'

PROGRAMME OF MARCH 20.

J. S. Bach:	Christmas Oratorio. (First performance in Vienna.)

With the assistance of the Imperial and Royal Court-Opera Orchestra.

They do not seem to have been so successful as the first. The public found the programme of January 6 monotonous. Hirsch, in his notice of the concert in the *Wiener Zeitung*, goes so far as to speak of 'shipwreck,' while Hanslick himself owns that the performance of the earlier numbers had the 'character of an improvisation or a practice rather than a concert production.' The three German folk-songs (the two last harmonized by Brahms) were so warmly received that the conductor's Minnelied, 'Der Holdseliger' was given in addition. The success of the Bach cantata was injured by a contretemps. The Börsendorfer piano, sent in the absence of an organ, was too high in pitch and therefore unavailable.

The concert of March 20, at which the Christmas Oratorio was given, seems to have been rather overshadowed by the performance of Bach's 'St. John's Passion' by the Gesellschaft forces at a somewhat earlier date.

The satisfaction and confidence extended to the conductor by the Akademie remained undiminished, however, by the falling-off in the success of the second and third public performances, and were expressed at the close of the subscription season by the arrangement of an extra concert devoted to Brahms' compositions. The instrumental numbers on this occasion were the B flat Sextet, played by the Hellmesberger party, and a Sonata for two pianofortes—in reality the arrangement in this form of the manuscript string quintet with two violoncelli, to which reference has already been made. Tausig, a great admirer of Brahms' genius, who took the Paganini Variations under his especial care later on, was the composer's colleague in the performance, for which, therefore, every advantage was secured; but Brahms had not yet, as it seemed, found the right medium for the expression of his thoughts. The sonata fell flat, making no impression on the audience. There were several vocal numbers, and amongst them was the charming 'Wechsellied zum Tanze,' No. 1 of the three Quartets for solo voices, Op. 31, which stand in an anticipatory relation to the 'Liebeslieder.' They show Brahms in his graceful, playful, genial mood. The 'Wechsellied' is in dance measure, and has two alternative melodies severally adapted to the character of Goethe's verses—the first in E flat, allotted to the contralto and bass, the 'indifferent' pair; the second in A flat, to the soprano and tenor, the 'tender' pair. Brahms has delightfully expressed the difference of mood animating the two couples, and, by the simple device of writing the first of the two little duets in imitation, the bass following the contralto at a bar's distance, has suggested a tone of bright enjoyment which contrasts effectively with the romantic spirit of the lovers' song. The four voices combine towards the close of the composition, which comes to an end in the key of the lover's melody.

ALTERNATIVE DANCE SONG

by Goethe.

THE INDIFFERENT PAIR.

Come, fairest maid, come with me to the dancing;
Dancing belongs to our festival day.
Though not my sweetheart, yet that may soon follow,
Follows it never, then let us still dance.
Come, fairest maid, come with me to the dancing;
Dancing belongs to our festival day.

THE TENDER PAIR.

Loved one, without thee what were there in pleasure?
Sweet one, without thee what joy in the dance?
If not my sweetheart, what care I for dancing?
Art thou it ever, then life is a feast.
Loved one, without thee what were there in pleasure?
Sweet one, without thee what joy in the dance?

THE INDIFFERENT PAIR.

Let them go loving and let us go dancing!
Languishing love careth not for the dance.
Circle we gaily amid the gay couples,
Wander the others in forest's dim shade.
Let them go loving and let us go dancing,
Languishing love careth not for the dance.

THE TENDER PAIR.

Let them go twirling and let us go wander!
Wand'ring of lovers is heaven's own dance.
Cupid is near, and he hears them deriding,
Certain and swift he will have his revenge.
Let them go twirling and let us go wander,
Wand'ring of lovers is heaven's own dance.

No. 2 of the same opus—'Neckereien' (Raillery), the text of which is a Moorish folk-song, is full of graceful fun. In this the tenors and basses alternate with the sopranos and contraltos; the youths court the girls, who will rather be transformed into little doves, little fishes, little hares, than have anything to do with them. The suitors, on the other hand, hint that such changes may be of small avail against little guns, little nets, little dogs.

No. 3, also set to a national text, this time Bohemian, is a charming four-part song, with a graceful accompaniment in waltz rhythm, and is developed from the melody used by Brahms in No. 5 of his set of waltzes for pianoforte. These quartets were composed at Detmold.

On May 10 the annual foundation concert of the Singakademie took place—as usual, before a private audience. The programme will be perused with interest by English-speaking readers:

1. Schumann:	First and second movements from 'Requiem für Mignon.'
2. Haydn:	Duet for Soprano and Tenor.
3. Schumann:	Stücke im Volkston for Violoncello and Pianoforte.
4. John Bennet (1599):	Madrigal (for chorus).
5. John Morley (1595):	Dance Song (for chorus).
6. Schumann:	Two Duets from the 'Spanisches Liederspiel.'
7. Brahms:	Two Songs for Soprano.
8. Schumann:	Fifth and sixth movements from the 'Requiem für Mignon.'

The fourth and fifth numbers of the programme were no doubt selected by Brahms from a collection of early English madrigals, edited by J. J. Maier of Munich.

Our composer's appointment as conductor of the Singakademie lapsed at the end of the season. By the rules of the society, election took place triennially, and Stegmayer's death had left only a year to run. Brahms' re-election was a matter of course, and was accepted by him, though not without doubt and hesitation; but his resolution failed him later on, and before the end of the summer he sent his resignation to the committee.

In the course of the year, Spina of Vienna (Cranz of Hamburg) published a setting of the 13th Psalm for three-part women's Chorus, with accompaniment for organ or pianoforte; and four Duets for Contralto and Baritone, dedicated to Frau Amalie Joachim. Breitkopf and Härtel issued two Motets for five-part mixed Chorus *a capella* (the first set to a verse of a church hymn by Paul Speratus, 1484-1551; the second to words from the 51st Psalm); a Sacred Song by Paul Fleming, 1609-1640 (set for two-part mixed Chorus, and written in double canon); and the three Quartets for Solo voices to which we have already referred as Op. 31.

Rieter-Biedermann published a set of nine Songs (Op. 32), No. 9 of which is the exquisite 'Wie bist du meine Königin,' one of the most fragrant love-songs ever composed; and a set of German Folk-songs, without opus number, dedicated to the Vienna Singakademie.

An Organ Fugue in A flat minor was published as a supplement to No. 29 of the *Allgemeine Musikzeitung*, edited, as the reader may remember, by Selmar Bagge.

CHAPTER XIII
1864-1867

Frau Schumann in Baden-Baden—Circle of friends there—Hermann Levi—Madame Pauline Viardot-Garcia—The Landgräfin of Hesse and the Pianoforte Quintet—Death of Frau Brahms—Concert-journey—The Horn Trio—Frau Caroline Schnack—Last visit to Detmold—First Sonata for Pianoforte and Violoncello—The German Requiem—Brahms at Zürich—Billroth—Brahms and Joachim on a concert-tour in Switzerland—Hans von Bülow—Reinthaler.

In the year 1864, or possibly at the end of 1863, the domestic troubles that had arisen from Jakob Brahms' early marriage with a delicate woman nearly twenty years his senior came to a crisis which Johannes, loving both father and mother with tender devotion, could no longer bear. By his wish the ill-assorted couple separated. Jakob had long since become fairly prosperous in a small way, holding a recognised position as a double-bass player amongst the orchestral musicians of Hamburg, and had even been appointed a member of the Philharmonic band since Stockhausen's election as the society's conductor. He now found quarters for himself in the Grosser Bleichen; the home in the Fuhlentwiethe was given up. Fritz, who, in spite of his want of energy, was doing well as a teacher, took lodgings in Theaterstrasse, and Frau Brahms and Elise removed to comfortable rooms in the Lange Reihe, Johannes, poor as he was, taking upon himself the sole responsibility of their maintenance. The time was still distant, in spite of the composer's steadily-growing fame, when his circumstances were to become prosperous. Had money-making been one of his immediate objects, he could certainly have attained it with little difficulty; but his aims were wholly ideal, and directly included pecuniary profit only so far as this was necessary for his own decent maintenance and for the exercise of ungrudging generosity to his family. His income, derived from the sale of his copyrights and from his public activity as a pianist—for he practically gave up teaching on going to Vienna—sufficed for these ends; he had learned from early youth to find happiness in the realities of life, and to treat as superfluities as many things as possible. The cultivation of happiness he viewed, not only as a part of wisdom, but as a duty. 'Let us, so far as we may, retain a fresh, happy interest in life, which we have at any rate to live' was not with him a mere phrase to be offered for the benefit of a friend in trouble, but one of the abiding principles by which he shaped his own daily existence.

No year would have been possible to Brahms without sight of his parents and he stayed near them for part of the summer, his first visit after embracing father and mother being, as usual, to Marxsen. Further plans were not difficult to arrange, and chief among them was that of a long visit to Baden-Baden. 'Johannes took us by surprise on July 30' is Frau Schumann's entry, in her diary, of his arrival. He stayed on for the remainder of the season, residing in a charming villa close to the grounds of the Kurhaus, which was placed at his disposal by Rubinstein, who had taken it for the summer, but left in August.

Frau Schumann's residence at Baden-Baden brought in its train results which are of much interest in the history of Brahms' career. The not-distant capital of the duchy of Baden, Carlsruhe, was to become, in the course of the next few years, an important centre for the cultivation of his art. It seems convenient, therefore, to mention at once the names of a few members of a group of friends belonging to Frau Schumann's circle who resided or stayed frequently in the neighbourhood, and with whom Brahms became more or less intimate.

Jakob Rosenhain (born 1813), a composer now forgotten, but esteemed in his day, and recognised both by Schumann and Mendelssohn, lived at Baden-Baden, and was sometimes to be met at Frau Schumann's house. His name heads the programme of Johannes' first public concert of 1848. The painter Anselm Feuerbach (1829-1880), a little-known and disappointed man in 1864, whose art has attained great posthumous celebrity, came annually with his mother to pass a few weeks there. The name of Frau Henriette Feuerbach appears on the title-page of Brahms' work 'Nänie,' which was composed soon after the premature death of her son. With the mention of Feuerbach must be associated that of Julius Allgeyer, introduced to our readers in an early chapter as a student of copperplate engraving at Düsseldorf, and now settled in Carlsruhe as a high-art photographer. Allgeyer had a genius for friendship. He was extraordinarily attached to Feuerbach, of whose art he made himself the apostle; but though his four years' residence in Rome (1856-1860) in close intercourse with the painter caused an interruption of his personal intimacy with Brahms, the two men remained in occasional correspondence, and held each other in cordial esteem. Now the old friendship was renewed, and it was not long before Brahms came to occupy a place in the engraver's affections second only to that of Feuerbach. The thought that he had known and loved both musician and painter through the period of their dawning fame was, in after-years, a source of satisfaction and pride to Allgeyer, whose name has become well known in Germany as that of Feuerbach's biographer.

In the middle of the sixties Carlsruhe, under the encouragement of its reigning Grand-Duke Frederick, occupied an exceptionally brilliant position amongst the smaller European centres of dramatic and musical art, to which it had been raised by the talents and devotion of Edward Devrient, the eminent stage-director of its court theatre, whose name may be familiar to some English readers as that of one of Mendelssohn's intimate friends. A man of wide general culture, the author of the standard work on its subject—'The History of German Dramatic Art'—playwright, singer, actor, possessed of an intimate knowledge of the best traditions of the German stage in the wide sense that includes opera, which had been derived from thirty years of professional association with the court theatres of Berlin and Dresden, Devrient was an ideal man for his post. His own sympathies remained faithful to the classical school of opera upon which his taste had been formed, but he did not allow his devotion to Gluck and Mozart and his interest in the revival of works of an early period to narrow the sphere of his activity. Taking a broad view of the duties of his position, he recognised the claim to hearing of the New-German school, and several of Wagner's musical dramas had been performed in the Carlsruhe court theatre by his permission, if not on his initiative, before his resignation of his post soon after the celebration of his artistic jubilee in April, 1869.

Not the least of his services to music was his choice of a successor to the post of court capellmeister at Carlsruhe, which fell vacant on the resignation of Joseph Strauss (not of the celebrated Vienna family) early in 1864. By recommending Hermann Levi (1839-1900) for the appointment, famous after the middle of the seventies amongst the famous Wagner conductors, and director of the first performances of 'Parsifal' (July-August, 1882), and by the generosity with which he permitted the youthful musician to profit by the fruits of his own ripe experience, he contributed in no small degree towards perfecting the technical education of an artist whose name will be remembered in musical history as amongst those of the great in his chosen branch of activity.

A gifted pupil of the Leipzig Conservatoire, Levi resolved, at an early age, to aim at achieving distinction as a conductor, and, on entering the service of the Grand-Duke of Baden in his twenty-sixth year, he had already laid the foundation of his future celebrity in successive posts at Saarbrück, Mannheim, and Rotterdam. He had a large and enthusiastic nature which caused him to reject the formal and stereotyped in art and to sympathize with what seemed to him genuinely progressive, and, becoming early in his career a great admirer of Schumann's music, he passed easily to a recognition of the genius of Brahms, with whom he had a slight acquaintance before settling at Carlsruhe.

The singer Hauser, the violoncellist Lindner, the hornist Segisser, the authoress Fräulein Anna Ettlinger—all resident in Carlsruhe—the learned Oberschulrath Gustav Wendt, called there in 1867, whose rooms were the scene of many distinguished gatherings, are to be included in our list; and of particular interest is the name of the violoncellist Bernhard Cossmann, of Weimar celebrity, who settled at Baden-Baden in 1870. Brahms was a willing and heartily welcome visitor at his house, and took part there in performances of his E minor Violoncello Sonata, and, with the hornist Steinbrügger, of the Horn Trio.

A noteworthy and picturesque figure, familiar in the artist circle, was that of Tourgenieff, who visited Baden-Baden annually from early in the sixties until the opening of the seventies. In conclusion is to be added the name of Pauline Viardot-Garcia, who settled at Baden in 1863, building a spacious villa in the Lichtenthaler Allée for her summer residence, which contained a gallery of fine paintings, chiefly of the Spanish and Netherlands schools. Amongst her possessions was Mozart's autograph score of 'Don Giovanni,' which she kept enshrined in a valuable casket. Madame Viardot was a musician in a very comprehensive sense of the word. Her triumphs on the operatic stage belong to the history of musico-dramatic art; she had been a pupil of Liszt on the pianoforte, had studied counterpoint and composition, and composed a good deal. Several of her operettas, for which Tourgenieff furnished the text-books, were performed privately by her pupils and children in her miniature theatre in Baden-Baden, where she was accustomed to entertain many of the celebrities of the time. One was given in German translation by Richard Pohl, as 'Der letzte Zauberer,' on the Court stages of Carlsruhe and Weimar. At the request of some of her girl pupils, Brahms composed a short choral serenade for her birthday one summer subsequent to our present date, and conducted its performance by the young ladies, outside her house, at an early hour of the morning. This pleasant incident of the seventies recalls that of the forties, when the youthful Johannes consented to fill the offices of composer and conductor at Winsen on the occasion of Rector Köhler's birthday.

Brahms was presented by Frau Schumann, in the course of this his first lengthened stay at Baden-Baden, to the Princess Anna, Landgräfin of Hesse on an occasion when the two artists performed his sonata for two pianofortes privately before Her Royal Highness. The work, which, as we have seen, had failed to win public sympathy when performed in a Vienna concert-room, made its mark on this occasion. It appealed strongly to the royal listener, who, at the close of the last movement, warmly expressed to the composer her sense of its beauty. Brahms, gratified and pleased at the Princess's unreserved appreciation, called on her the following day, and begged permission, which was readily granted, to dedicate the work to her;

and on its publication the following year in its final form—a quintet for pianoforte and strings—Her Royal Highness's name appeared on the title-page. The Princess acknowledged the compliment of the dedication by presenting Brahms with one of her treasures—the autograph score of Mozart's G minor Symphony. It passed after his death, as part of his library, into the possession of the Gesellschaft der Musikfreunde, Vienna.

An interesting reference to the dedication and the time is in the possession of the present Landgraf of Hesse, whose musical talent was recognised and encouraged by Brahms twenty years later, and is contained in a letter of thanks written by the master in 1892 on the dedication to him of a fantasia for pianoforte published that year by the Prince:

'YOUR ROYAL HIGHNESS
MOST GRACIOUS HERR LANDGRAF!

'Whilst I venture to express to Your Royal Highness my most respectful and hearty thanks for the dedication of the fantasia, very many and very pleasant recollections occur to me.

'The high and agreeable distinction, as which I regard the dedication, reminds me of the similar pleasure I experienced when I was permitted to inscribe my quintet to your highly-honoured mother, the Frau Landgräfin. That was in beautiful Baden-Baden, and it would be too tempting to go on chatting about the unforgettable music-hours and pleasant days; but much else crowds upon the memory: Meiningen, Frankfurt, Vienna, Baden, etc. I think that by my mere mention of these names Y.R.H. will know what a valued memorial your work and its dedication, by which I am so much honoured, will be to me of many pleasant times.

'With my hearty thanks for the valuable present, I unite the wish that our glorious art may bring to Y.R.H. many more hours as happy as those were of which this fantasia gives such convincing testimony.

'Your Royal Highness's deeply obliged

'JOHANNES BRAHMS.

'VIENNA, *Jan. 1892*.'

On September 12 Frau Joachim's first child was born, and there was no doubt as to what he should be called. Johannes must, of course, be godfather, and give his name to Joachim's boy. Brahms was not present at the christening, but he sent to the parents as his congratulatory gift the manuscript of the little song published long afterwards as No. 2 of Op. 91, the 'Geistliches Wiegenlied,' or, as it is called in the published translated title, 'The Virgin's Cradle Song.' The words are imitated by Geibel from a text of Lope de Vega, 'Die ihr schwebt um diese Palmen' (Ye who o'er these palms are hov'ring). The music, composed for contralto, viola, and pianoforte, is founded upon the melody of an old song,[11] which, given in Brahms' composition to the viola, serves as the basis for the contrapuntal treatment of the voice and pianoforte parts.

Brahms left Baden-Baden on October 10, and, returning to Vienna, passed the next few weeks in quiet pursuit of his ordinary avocations, happy at knowing himself in complete possession of his time, yet perhaps not without an occasional passing regret at the thought of the pleasure he had derived the previous season, as conductor of the Singakademie, from his association with choir and orchestra. The change he had advised in the family arrangements at Hamburg was not greatly to prolong for his mother the peaceful old age he had desired to secure for her. Frau Brahms had taken her last farewell of her dearly-loved son when he quitted Hamburg in the summer. Her health, which had for some time been growing weaker, continued to fail, and on February 2, 1865, she quietly breathed her last.

Johannes, who took the next train to Hamburg after receiving his sister's summons, arrived soon after all was over, and turned immediately towards his mother's bed-chamber. He had once before passed through a great sorrow, but in Schumann's case death had come in the guise of a friend. This was another kind of bereavement, and the loss of the dear, simply-loving old mother wrung his heart. 'Do not go in yet, Hannes,' said Elise, trying to prevent him, and, indeed, as he passed on into the room the sudden complete realization of the mother's tenderness gone from his life broke down his self-command on the instant. He knelt down by the quiet bed and sobbed aloud in uncontrollable grief. When he had somewhat collected himself he presently went out. Solitude, however, often welcome to him, was not what he wanted to-day, nor over-much sympathy, but affection—and affection of a kind that perhaps may have seemed to him something akin to the assured, unreasoning mother's love. He turned into kind Frau Cossel's and asked her to let him have a child. His own little goddaughter Johanna was most willingly at his service as a companion, and as soon as she was ready the pair walked away together hand in hand back to Elise, the little girl somewhat awed by the situation and the changed demeanour of the friend whom she was accustomed to regard as the merriest of her companions, but glad to be in his society on any terms. Leaving his godchild with Elise, Johannes almost immediately went out again, and returned after a while with his father, whom he drew with him into the adjoining room, accidentally leaving the door of communication a little open. The scene of the death-chamber was thus made visible to the frightened Johanna from her position in the parlour, and imprinted itself indelibly on her brain. She watched it spellbound, and was not too young a child to be penetrated and touched by what she saw.

The two men stood together by the bedside for a few seconds without stirring. Then Johannes, putting his hand on his father's arm, gently guided it towards the motionless figure, and, placing the husband's hand over that of the dead wife, kept both covered with his own in a last reconciliation. Kind friends came to the funeral, and true sympathy was at hand, but Johannes shrank in his grief from hearing the expression of condolence. 'I have no mother now: I must marry,' he said miserably when the service was over. Stockhausen and his wife insisted that he and Elise should dine quietly with them that day, and there is little doubt that Brahms was helped by the affectionate consideration shown on all sides, and was quietly grateful for it. He returned to his work in a few days, but the responsibility for the maintenance of Elise, who, having strongly felt the mother's side of the family difficulties, shrank from the idea of rejoining her father, remained entirely his.

The two first books of the 'Magelone Romances,' dedicated to Stockhausen, and the Pianoforte Quintet were published by Rieter-Biedermann early in the year. The version of the quintet as a Sonata for two Pianofortes was issued by the same house in 1872.

The Quintet in F minor, Op. 34, is unquestionably one of the greatest works of chamber music for pianoforte and strings ever written. Some distinguished writers go so far as to give it the first place amongst the composer's works of its class; and if regard be had to the largeness of its proportions, the stormy grandeur and the deep pathos of its ideas, its extraordinary wealth of thematic material, and the astonishing power with which this is handled, it must be admitted that there is something to be said in support of such a view. To the author it certainly appears impossible to select one of Brahms' works of this period and this class for preference as compared with the others. All are so great as, so to say, to defy future competition. They seem as unapproachable and secure on their own lines as the immortal '48' themselves in another category. The imaginative power which surges through the first movement of the quintet recalls the daring of the youthful Johannes, and is guided now by a master-hand. This movement dominates the whole work. Its contrasted tones of passionate splendour and scarcely less passionate mystery are reflected in the rich pathos of the 'andante un poco adagio,' in the weird fitfulness of the scherzo with its heart-gripping trio, and in the doubtful tranquillity of the finale, bursting in the coda into a rushing impetuosity which carries the movement to a triumphant conclusion. Few of Brahms' compositions contain more striking illustrations than this one of his power of fertilizing his themes and bringing new, out of previous, material, a power which gives to his works a coherence and solidity hardly equalled save in the compositions of Bach himself, and which has a certain artistic analogy with the secret force that governs all natural organic development.

The summer of this year was again spent near Frau Schumann. Brahms took lodgings—two small rooms well provided with windows—in Frau Becker's house, which was situated a little apart from the village of Lichtenthal in an idyllic spot amongst the hills. His plan of life, essentially the same wherever he fixed his summer residence, was to rise with the dawn, and, after making himself an early cup of coffee, to enjoy the fresh delights of early morning by going for a long walk in the surrounding forest. He then returned to work in his rooms until the time arrived for his mid-day dinner, taken usually in the garden of the 'Golden Lion'; for in these days he only dined occasionally, when accompanied by a friend, at the somewhat more expensive 'Bear.' By four o'clock he was generally in Frau Schumann's balcony for afternoon coffee and to pass an hour with her in music, conversation, or walking. More often than not he returned to supper at half-past seven, when his place was laid at table, as a matter of course, at Frau Schumann's right hand.

All the circumstances of his surroundings were favourable to his creative activity, which was unceasing, and the profound emotional experience that had recently moved and enriched his spirit had already caused in him the stirrings of the impulse that was to grow and gradually to dominate him until it had become embodied in a work which, had it been the only child of his genius known to the world, would have sufficed to immortalize his name.

Before Brahms' departure from Lichtenthal a communication from Hamburg added to his feelings of tenderness and regret the shadow of a grave family apprehension.

Having accepted engagements in Switzerland and Germany for the ante-Christmas concert-season, he remained on till the end of October in his quarters at Frau Becker's, and here, about a week before the commencement of his *tournée*, he received the news that his father had resolved to marry again, and had become engaged to a widow. The intelligence, such as it was, came direct from Jakob, but it contained no particulars whatever to soften the anxiety it aroused, no mention being made in it even of the name of the intended wife, and it threw the son into a state of the strongest agitation, in which the tender pang for the dear old mother may very possibly not have been the predominating element. Who could the wife-elect be? Would she make Jakob happy? Could the marriage state be happy except under the rarest combination of circumstances? Were there children of the widow's first marriage to be provided for? if so, by whom? Jakob's means could bear no additional burden. And yet, the dear, homely, uncultured father, often enough a butt for the wit of the younger musicians standing by his side in the Philharmonic orchestra; this musician without musical endowment, who loved his music and his instruments, as Johannes sometimes declared, if such affection were to be measured by proof given, better even than he himself loved his art; who had persevered doggedly through long years of privation and struggle in his endeavours to attain to some small place in the world of art, and had won it, his father—and it needs no prophet to realize the pathos of this thought to the loving heart of the great composer—did he not deserve happiness if happiness should follow the step? Johannes was that day capable of but two resolutions on the subject: first, that his father should be made happy if anything he could say or do could help to make him so, and, secondly, that as soon as his engagements should permit, he would go to Hamburg and judge for himself of the wisdom of Jakob's choice.

The first of Brahms' concert undertakings for the autumn was fulfilled on November 3 in the hall of the Museum, Carlsruhe, where he performed his Pianoforte Concerto at the first subscription concert of the season, accompanied by the grand-ducal orchestra under Levi. The work was received, for the first time, with every sign of approval. 'The people had the surprising kindness to be quite satisfied, to call for me, praise me, and all the rest of it,' he wrote to Dietrich.

Two of the vocal quartets, Op. 31, were included in the programme, and Brahms played some unaccompanied Schumann solos in the second part of the concert.

On the 6th of the month two new 'Magelone Romances' were sung for the first time in public by Krause, at a concert given in the same hall by Frau Schumann and Joachim; and before Brahms left Carlsruhe the first private performance took place of the newly-completed Trio in E flat for pianoforte, violin, and horn, a composition which has now long occupied a peculiar place in the affection of genuine lovers of his music on account of the tone of pure beauty that pervades it—beauty of sound, of mood, and idea. The noble simplicity of its themes and the spontaneous character which distinguishes their development hold the attention even of the unfamiliar listener from beginning to end of this inspired work, and the great musicianship of the composer has wrought it to a flawless example of its kind, in which no weak spot can be detected by deliberate examination. The adagio has the character of a lament, and can hardly be matched as an expression of profound sadness excepting by a few others of Brahms' and some of Beethoven's slow movements. The work was a favourite with the composer, and it is of interest to know from his own lips that its inception was due to an inspiration that came to him in the course of one of his walks near Lichtenthal. A year or two later than our present date, as he was ascending one of his beloved pine-clad hills in Dietrich's company, he showed his friend the exact spot where the opening theme of the first movement had occurred to him, saying: 'I was walking along one morning, and as I came to this spot the sun shone out and the subject immediately suggested itself.'[12]

From Carlsruhe Brahms proceeded to Switzerland, where he appeared at Basle, Zürich, and Winterthur. At Zürich he conducted his D major Serenade, given there two years previously under Fichtelberger, and performed the solo of Schumann's Pianoforte Concerto, and Bach's Chromatic Fantasia; and at Winterthur he gave a chamber music soirée in combination with his friend Theodor Kirchner and the young violinist F. Hegar. Of this Widmann, who saw and heard Brahms for the first time on the occasion, has given some account in his 'Recollections.'

'There was,' he writes, 'a something in his countenance which suggested the certainty of victory, the beaming cheerfulness of a poet happy in the exercise of his art.'

Returning to Germany, Brahms appeared next at Mannheim, and, on December 12, conducted his D major Serenade and played Beethoven's E flat Concerto at the fifth Gürzenich subscription concert of the season at Cologne. He had but little success on this occasion either as pianist or composer. The serenade was criticised as being too lengthy and its themes as too 'naïve' for his elaborate treatment of them. A different reception was accorded him at a soirée of chamber music held at the conservatoire, when he performed with Hiller his Duet Variations, Op. 23, and with von Königslow and his colleagues the G minor Pianoforte Quartet. Both works were received with acclamation, and the composer achieved a success worthy of his position in the world of art. Before leaving Cologne Brahms played at a meeting of the Musikverein to a private audience of the members, most of them professors and students of the conservatoire. Amongst the pieces chosen by him for performance on this occasion were Bach's great Organ Prelude and Fugue in A minor.

And now the anxious son found opportunity to hurry with beating heart to Hamburg to see his father and to make the acquaintance of his stepmother-elect. To find, also, every probability that Jakob had chosen wisely, and that his contemplated change of life bade fair to ensure a happy and peaceful close to a career that had been full of hardship and uncertainty.

Frau Caroline Schnack, a handsome widow who had already been twice a wife, was just turned forty-one, and therefore more than seventeen years the junior of her proposed third husband. She had an only child, her son Fritz, born of her second marriage, now a lad of about thirteen. Capable and managing, she kept an excellent public dining-room for single men not far from the musicians' 'Börse,' described in an early chapter of our narrative, and had a regular *clientèle* amongst the members of the Stadt Theater orchestra. Since the time when Johannes had thought it advisable for his parents to separate, Jakob had been one of her daily customers, and her good cooking and substantial capacity had gradually opened for her the way to his affection. Johannes, on his interview with Frau Schnack, was at once favourably impressed by her personality and gave his consent to the engagement, only insisting that full time for consideration on both sides should be allowed before the taking of the irrevocable step of marriage; and after a day or two in Hamburg he set out with a greatly relieved mind for Detmold, where he had arranged with Bargheer to spend the Christmas week and to reappear as composer and pianist on the scenes of his former activity.

The visit passed off most happily. The great composer, to whom, with some disappointment, much success and fame had come since his last sojourn in the little capital six years previously, was merry according to his wont when in the midst of familiar associates. Such changes as had taken place in the circle were for the better. Bargheer was married, Carl von Meysenbug engaged. The reunions of the former bachelor friends were enlivened by the presence of ladies—charming young married women and pretty girls—and Brahms was ready to abandon himself to any amount of fun, his almost extravagant buoyancy of spirits being no doubt assisted by the reaction from his late tension of mind in regard to his father's affairs. These social occasions were but the interludes between more serious pleasures. Every day there was music at the palace, the castle, or one or more of the private musical houses. Brahms conducted his A major Serenade and played Beethoven's E flat Concerto at an orchestral concert, and took part in a soirée at the palace, where, amongst other things, he performed the Kreutzer Sonata with Bargheer before the well-remembered sympathetic court circle. The visit, which was the last paid by him to Detmold, formed a fitting close to his association with Prince Leopold's court, to whose memory, and especially to that of the various members of the princely family, must ever attach the artistic distinction of their early recognition of the composer's genius and their appreciation of his personality.

Brahms' next destination was Oldenburg, where he arrived in time to celebrate the New Year's festival of 1866 with the Dietrichs. He played his own Concerto and an unpublished composition of Schubert at the subscription concert of January 5, and at the chamber music soirée of the 10th contributed some Bach solos to the programme and took part with Dietrich in a performance of Schumann's Variations in B flat, and with Engel and Westermann in the first public performance of his own Horn

Trio, which created a deep impression. It is important to add here that Westermann used the natural horn on the occasion by the particular desire of Brahms, who now and always insisted to the hornists of his acquaintance on the impossibility of securing a poetical interpretation of his work with the ventil horn.

'If the performer is not obliged by the stopped notes to play softly the piano and violin are not obliged to adapt themselves to him, and the tone is rough from the beginning.'[13]

The appearances at Oldenburg closed the *tournée.* Gratified as our musician declared himself to be with the results of his journey, which, if it had not brought him a series of triumphs, had at least demonstrated the fact that his works were gradually making their way through the musical circles of Europe, it was not, as we know, part either of his inclination or his aim to prolong his occasional artistic travels. He chafed at the restriction to personal freedom resulting from fixed engagements, and at the disturbance of mind inseparable from hurried journeys from place to place, and this year he had more than ordinary reason for desiring to be settled again to the quiet concentration of thought essential to all art-creation worthy to be so called. After a second and longer stay in Hamburg that confirmed the satisfaction with which he had lately contemplated the idea of his father's approaching marriage, he returned to Carlsruhe to pass the rest of the winter in Allgeyer's house in Langenstrasse, now known as Kaiserstrasse.

The first quarter of the year 1866 witnessed the publication of a long list of works. By Rieter Biedermann, the two sets of extraordinarily difficult and brilliant Paganini Variations for Pianoforte, which, when in the hands of a competent executant, are found to be full of original and striking effects, even if they be inferior in musical value to the composer's other achievements in this form[14]; the three Sacred Choruses, Op. 37, for unaccompanied women's voices, and mentioned in our first volume in connection with the Ladies' Choir. By Simrock, the second String Sextet in G major, worthy sister to its companion work, though it has not obtained quite so wide a popularity, and the Sonata in E minor, dedicated to Dr. Josef Gänsbacher. The Horn Trio was issued by the same house quite at the end of the year.[15]

The Sonata in E minor for pianoforte and violoncello, the earliest of Brahms' seven published duet sonatas for pianoforte and another instrument, all of which are characteristic examples of certain sides of his genius, is a valuable number in the comparatively short list of works of its class for the violoncello. The first movement is of graceful, expressive, delicately melodious character, rising at one point of the development section towards passion, but returning immediately to the dainty, dreaming mood by which the composer so often subdues his hearers to the spell of his imagination. The 'allegretto quasi menuetto' which follows is an exquisite example of a species of movement in the making of which Brahms stands unrivalled. It fascinates with irresistible certainty by its ethereal, playful, poetic fancy, to which the touch of seriousness in the trio offers just sufficient, not too pronounced, contrast. The finale is written *con amore* in the form of a free fugue, which, full of spirit and energy throughout its course, rattles to its close in a lively coda. Care should be taken not to exaggerate the pace of this movement in performance. If taken too quickly, the violoncello passages lose their due effect.

On his return to Carlsruhe, Brahms settled down to the actual writing of the German Requiem, with which he was occupied during the succeeding months, and it was one of Allgeyer's favourite recollections in later years that a portion of the inspired work had been put on paper under his roof.

It is well known that Brahms' nearest friends accepted the composition as his memorial of his mother. 'We all think he wrote it in her memory, though he has never expressly said so,' Frau Schumann told the author some years later. 'Never has a nobler monument been raised by filial love,' said Joachim, referring to the German Requiem in the course of his address at the Brahms Memorial Festival held at Meiningen in October, 1899; and we may at least say with certainty that the work, which must be regarded as the crowning point of much of the composer's previous activity, is, on the whole, a memorial of the emotions by which he was stirred during the period that immediately succeeded his mother's death, apart from the question of whether or not he had planned it at an earlier time. It is, however, a circumstance of great interest that the strains he had conceived in his grief for the tragedy of Schumann's illness recurred to him as appropriate for the solemn mourning march—one of the most vivid and extraordinary of his inspirations—of the Requiem,[16] and we cannot be wrong in assuming that the remembrance of his beloved friend was with him as he worked. Perhaps we may venture to think that two of the strongest affections and griefs of Brahms' life, associated with strangely contrasted objects—Schumann, the great genius and master, Johanna, the simple old mother—live together in this exalted music. There is no warrant for the statement of anything more precise as to the composer's intention excepting with regard to the fifth number, the soprano solo with chorus, which was added some time after the completion of the other movements. Of this it may be said definitely, as will presently appear, that whilst Brahms was engaged in writing it the thought of his mother was present in a special sense to his memory.

Jakob's marriage with Frau Schnack took place in March, rather more than a year after the death of his first wife. Johannes sent a substantial sum of money as a wedding present, and his great contentment in the anticipation of his father's happiness was a constant and favourite theme in his talks with Allgeyer, always an interested and sympathetic listener.

Frau Caroline's business was given up, and the newly-married pair settled into a comfortable flat on the fourth floor of No. 5, Anscharplatz, at the corner of Valentin's Camp, a respectable business quarter of Hamburg, where there was sufficient accommodation to allow Frau Caroline to turn her housekeeping talents to account by taking two or three men boarders. A large airy room, 'the corner room,' was reserved for Johannes, who was ultimately responsible for the rent of the flat, and to it were transferred his books, bookcase, and other belongings, from the apartments that had been his mother's in the Lange Reihe, whilst Elise arranged to live near an aunt in another quarter of the city. A photograph of Johannes, taken by Allgeyer, was sent to Jakob a few weeks after the wedding as a permanent souvenir of his son's felicitations on the occasion. It is still in existence, and is now in the possession of Herr Fritz Schnack, 'the second Fritz,' as Johannes caressingly called his quasi stepbrother.

Persuaded by Theodor Kirchner, who was at this time resident in Zürich, to spend the summer near him, Brahms, arriving in the middle of April, found a lodging in a small house on the Zürichberg which commanded a splendid prospect of lake and mountain. Here every facility was abundantly at hand for his enjoyment. Dividing his time, from a very early hour of the morning until noon, between musing in the open air and work in his room, he was usually to be met about twelve o'clock in the museum, which became a place of rendezvous for his friends. After the early dinner, always taken out of doors in fine weather, and a more or less prolonged sitting over newspapers, or in chat with acquaintance, in the open air, he would drop in at a friend's house, generally Kirchner's, pass an hour or two in informal sociability, and often make music with some of the resident musicians. It was at Kirchner's that he became acquainted with the celebrated Swiss writer and poet, Gottfried Keller, and with the distinguished Zürich professor of surgery, Dr. Theodor Billroth, who was some four years our composer's senior, and who, called subsequently to Vienna, became one of Brahms' most familiar friends. Billroth's love for music was second only to his devotion to his own great vocation. He had studied the violin under Eschmann, played at a weekly trio meeting at his house in Plattenstrasse, Zürich, and was sufficiently proficient to take part on the viola with professional musicians in private performances of Beethoven's quartets and Brahms' sextets. He could play the piano well, was a good sight-reader, and acted occasionally as musical critic to one of the Zürich papers.

'Brahms arrived here a few days ago,' he writes on the 22nd of April to his friend, Professor Lübke of Stuttgart. 'This morning he and Kirchner played some of Liszt's symphonic poems on two pianofortes. Horrible music!... We purged ourselves with Brahms' new sextet that has just come out. Brahms and Kirchner played it as a duet.'[17]

The composer became intimate, also, at the house of Herr and Frau Wesendonck, who had been Wagner's great friends during his residence at Zürich, and could not hear enough about the composer of the 'Meistersinger,' of whom the Wesendoncks possessed inexhaustible personal recollections and several valuable souvenirs. Amongst these was the master's autograph score of the 'Rheingold,' an object that was regarded by Brahms with a respect almost amounting to veneration.

Traits of habit and character similar to those with which the reader is familiar, and which recall the period of the Detmold visits, are described in Steiner's 'Recollections,' by Capellmeister F. Hegar,[18] who was the inseparable associate of Brahms and Kirchner:

'... We were no less impressed by his extraordinarily sound health. He could venture upon anything. How often has he passed the night on the sofa of my bachelor's quarters when he was disinclined to climb the Zürichberg in the late hours of evening. Once indeed, when an older friend less hardy than himself claimed my hospitality, he lay down underneath my grand piano, and declared next morning that he had slept splendidly.'

Hegar mentions that Brahms' musical memory and unusually rapid power of apprehension excited the astonished admiration of the Zürich musicians.

'When we played him our compositions for the first time, he would afterwards sit down and repeat long portions note for note from memory, pointing out the weak places.'

One or two reminiscences of the summer are to be found in the volume of Billroth's letters from which quotation has already been made. Amongst them is the description of a music-party at his house, at which Brahms was present to hear a performance of his lately-published Sextet in G major. The consciousness of the composer's presence so unnerved Billroth that he was obliged to ask Eschmann, who was amongst the listeners, to relieve him of his part of second viola.

'I have learnt never to play before a composer,' he wrote a few days afterwards, 'unless his work has been well rehearsed. As I was quite familiar with the composition, I could imagine the vexation Brahms must have felt, although he put the matter aside in the kindest way. Kirchner, Brahms and Hegar had been up late together the night before and were tired. Everything contributed to make the evening dull.'

Of the sextet he says: 'I think it wonderfully fine; so clear, so simple, so masterly.'

Brahms remained in Switzerland until the middle of August, and, arriving on the 17th of this month to stay for a few weeks at his old lodgings in Lichtenthal, surprised Frau Schumann by appearing before her for the first time with a beard. He did not at this period persevere very long in wearing the appendage, which changed his appearance in an unusual degree, but he adopted it a second time, and, as it proved, permanently, about fourteen years later.

The composer had worked steadily on at the German Requiem during the months of his residence in Zürich, and that he now completed it in Lichtenthal—save and excepting only the fifth number—is to be inferred from the inscription on the manuscript score—'Baden-Baden im Sommer, 1866'—now in possession of the Gesellschaft der Musikfreunde at Vienna. Great additional interest is given to this date by a short entry made by Frau Schumann in her diary early in September, which is, without doubt, the earliest written note upon the now famous work.

'Johannes has been playing me some magnificent movements out of a Requiem of his own and a string quartet in C minor. The Requiem delighted me even more, however. It is full of tender and again daring thoughts. I cannot feel clear as to how it will sound, but in myself it sounds glorious.'[19]

The extract has a double interest, as furnishing a new illustration of Brahms' caution with regard to publication, and especially in the case of works which constituted for him a new artistic departure. The String Quartet in C minor was not published until 1873, seven years from our present date.

About the middle of September Joachim appeared in Lichtenthal, and after a few days' stay there carried Brahms away with him. He had become a man at large through the political events of the year, by which the kingdom of Hanover became part of Prussia, having felt it impossible to accept the offer made him to retain his appointment after the deposition of King George, and was able to follow his inclination as to his arrangements for the autumn and winter season. These included tours in Switzerland and France, and it was ultimately arranged between the friends that Johannes should combine with him in some of his Swiss concerts.

Brahms spent most of the intervening time in Hamburg, and was so happy in his comfortable corner room in the Anscharplatz that he began seriously to entertain the idea of settling down again under his father's roof. Frau Caroline managed the household with careful but judicious thrift, and there was peace and contentment in the home. In his own way Jakob was as regular in his habits as his son. Every morning he went to the 'Börse' to inquire for work, and was generally successful in obtaining small engagements, often to act as substitute in the theatre orchestras. His position as bassist at the Stadt Theater had come to an end in the course of the fifties, owing to changes in the management, but he continued a member of the Philharmonic orchestra until a year before his death. He was proud and fond of Frau Caroline, always came home as soon as his work was done to enjoy the good plain fare which she had ready for him, and was perfectly happy as he sat in the kitchen with his pipe and a large cup of thin coffee, watching her movements. Once a week he amused himself by walking in the Jews' quarter of the city and inspecting the cheap second-hand wares with which the vendors sought to tempt his custom. His weakness for bargains was sometimes a source of embarrassment to his wife, in spite of her firmness in limiting his loose pocket-money to the sum of a few pence. Now he would send home to her a quantity of wardrobe hooks, another time many pounds'-weight of honey. 'Goodness, Brahms! what are we to do with it?' she would despairingly inquire. 'Yes, Lina, but I couldn't let it stand at the price,' he would answer. Johannes used to lecture his father on his weakness for spending money, telling him how careful he himself was obliged to be, and could be seriously vexed if he found that Jakob had been really extravagant or thoughtless. This, however, occurred but seldom.

A letter to Dietrich from the Anscharplatz mentions the Requiem, and evidently answers an inquiry from Albert as to the long-delayed Symphony in C minor of which we heard in the summer of 1862.

'DEAR DIETRICH!

'Before the summer is over you shall be reminded of me by a short greeting....

'Unfortunately I cannot wait upon you with a symphony, but it would be a joy to have you here for a day, to play you my so-called German Requiem.

'I have been till now living in Switzerland, in Zürich. I shall stay here a little and think of going then to Vienna....'[20]

The concert-journey with Joachim was very successful, and afforded Brahms quite unexpected evidence of the progress his music was making in Switzerland. This country was, in fact, one of the earliest in which his art met with general appreciation, and much of the credit of its acceptance there must be ascribed to the efforts of Theodor Kirchner, who, as the reader may remember, was one of the most gifted musicians of the Schumann circle, and who seized every opportunity that offered from the beginning of Brahms' career, to spread the understanding of his compositions. Kirchner filled an organist's post at Winterthur for nearly ten years before his removal to Zürich in 1862, and, whilst developing an active musical life in the little town, made his influence felt far beyond its limits.

The tour opened on October 24 in Schaffhausen, and included Winterthur, Basle, and finally Mühlhausen in Alsace. An interesting incident of the visit to Mühlhausen was the renewal of friendly relations, after ten years of estrangement, between Joachim and von Bülow, who was resident during the season 1866-67 at Basle, and gave Trio concerts there with Abel and Kahnt. No communication took place between the former Weimar intimates during the week passed by Brahms and Joachim at Basle, but Bülow's affectionate nature was strongly stirred by seeing his old friend again on the concert-platform and hearing his public performances, which he describes as 'ideal perfection.' The sequel may be told in the words of his letter to Raff, dated Basle, November 22.

'And now, a great piece of news. On Sunday the 10th I travelled to Mühlhausen for the Brahms-Joachim concert, and the relation of friendship between Joachim and me was renewed on French soil after ten years' interruption. This will lead to no results of a positive nature, but a stone has been taken from my heart, and from his also as he has assured your sister-in-law. For my sake Joachim returned to Basle for a few hours and then took the night train to Paris.'[21]

Some years were yet to elapse before Bülow could pretend to any cordiality of feeling towards the art of Brahms. In another letter of 1866 we read:

'I respect and admire him, but—at a distance. The Pianoforte Quintet seems to me the most interesting of his large compositions.... Kiel is much more sympathetic to me.'[21]

He prevailed upon himself, indeed, to play the Horn Trio at his Basle Trio concert of March 26, 1867, when his colleagues were Abel and Hans Richter, who commenced his artist's career as a hornist, and was at this time living in Switzerland in the enjoyment of Wagner's intimacy; and he included Joachim's Variations for viola and pianoforte in the same programme; but as late as 1870 he wrote to Raff:

'What do the Br.'s matter to me? Brahms, Brahmüller, Bruch, etc. Don't mention them again! Who knows whether a Riehl may not turn up in 1950 to beplutarch them as maestrinelli? The only one who interests me is Braff!'

The fact that von Bülow's critical faculty was subject to the disturbing influence of his capacity for warm friendship cannot lessen the admiration inspired by his talents and his generous nature. His severe animadversions on Brahms' works, together with his practical neglect of them up to a period when his opinion as to their merits had become very much a matter of indifference, may be pardoned by the lovers of our master's art, who remember that they were, for the most part, the outcome of his deep personal affection for Liszt, Wagner, and Joachim, and of his long-continued intimate association with the leaders and prominent disciples of the New-German school.

Brahms returned to Vienna, after about a year and a half of absence, immediately after his friend's departure from Mühlhausen, and spent the winter quietly at work in his room on the fourth story of No. 6, Poststrasse. The earliest event of any importance to his career that marks the opening months of the year 1867 is the first public performance of the Sextet in G major, which was given at the Hellmesberger concert of February 3. The reader will by this time hardly be surprised to learn that the work was received without enthusiasm.

'The composer was certainly called for and applauded,' says Schelle, Hanslick's successor in the *Presse*, and a loyal though unbiassed supporter of Brahms, 'but it was with a certain reserve. One felt distinctly that the public was not carried away by the work, but desired to do justice to so admirable an achievement.... Brahms may be called a virtuoso in the modern development of the quartet style, ... but only that can reach the heart which proceeds from the heart, and the sextet comes from the hand and the head, whilst the warm pulsations of the heart are to be felt only at intervals.'

So Bach's works were once spoken of, so Beethoven's in their day. So, it may almost be said, must be criticised all musical creative achievement that adequately expresses an original individuality. The composer of genius has to go through a long apprenticeship before he acquires a language of his own really capable of conveying his thoughts to the world. By the time he is master of it, he has, by the nature of things, placed himself outside the immediate comprehension of all but a few specially qualified listeners, and must be willing to wait for his reward until some of those to whom he speaks have had time to follow him a certain distance along his appointed path, and opportunity to become familiarized with his manner of utterance. Brahms was content to wait, and he waited almost with equanimity of spirit, never losing faith in the future, though he had something more pronounced to encounter than indifference. Hirsch, of the *Wiener Zeitung*, wrote apropos of the sextet:

'We are always seized with a kind of oppression when the new John in the wilderness, Herr Johannes Brahms, announces himself. This prophet, proclaimed by Robert Schumann in his darkening hours, who, for the rest, has his energetic admirers in Vienna—we mention this in our position, from pure love of truth—makes us quite disconsolate with his impalpable, dizzy tone-vexations that have neither body nor soul and can only be products of the most desperate effort. Such manifest, glaring, artificiality is quite peculiar to this gentleman. How many drops of perspiration may adhere to these note-heads?'

On the 25th of this same month of February, the earlier B flat Sextet, by this time almost popular in more than one Continental city, and long known in New York through Mason's concerts, was performed for the first time in England at the Monday Popular Concerts, St. James's Hall, London, by Joachim, Louis Ries, Henry Blagrove, Zerbini, Paque, and Piatti. The director, S. Arthur Chappell, printed a notice in the programme-books to the effect that he introduced the work by Joachim's desire. It made no impression, and the composer was not again heard at the Popular Concerts for five years.

If the recognition of Brahms' exact claims as a composer, even by his Austrian public, long remained dubious, his qualities as a pianist seldom failed to evoke unmistakable signs of their warm approval. With the arrival of March he prevailed upon himself this year to announce concerts in Vienna, Graz, Klagenfurth, and Pesth, and the success of his performances was unequivocal, in spite of the approach of spring and the unusual warmth of the season.

'At last a pianist who entirely takes hold of one,' exclaims Schelle, writing of the first concert; 'one only needs to hear his first few chords to be convinced that Herr Brahms is a player of quite extraordinary stamp. The musical critic of the *Wiener Zeitung* writes that Herr Brahms was cordially received by his "party." We may remark that Brahms was received, not by a "party," but by the entire very numerous public, with applause such as is seldom heard in Vienna concert-rooms. If, however, the audience of the evening is to be described as the "party" of the distinguished artist, it must be said that his party consists of the cultivated experts of musical Vienna.'

The instrumental numbers of the programme were Beethoven's Fantasia, Op. 77; Bach's G major Fantasia; Brahms' Scherzo; Schumann's Etudes Symphoniques; Brahms' Paganini Variations. The concert-giver played as an additional piece his own arrangement for the pianoforte of the fugue from Beethoven's String Quartet, Op. 59, No. 3,

'which,' says Schelle, 'claims almost more admiration even than his performance, for it is a most faithful reflection of the entire score which we meet unchanged in the effective costume.'

At the second concert in Vienna, which took place on April 7, after Brahms' return from the provinces, the programme included Bach's F major Toccata; Beethoven's Sonata, Op. 109; Brahms' Handel Variations and Fugue; Schumann's Fantasia in C, Op. 17; and short pieces by Scarlatti and Schubert. As an additional piece, an arrangement of a movement from Schubert's Octet was conceded. Vocal numbers were included in both programmes.

Brahms himself mentions the concerts in a letter to Dietrich.

'The result was so good in every respect,' he writes, 'that I must call myself doubly an ass for not having secured it earlier and taken the opportunity to get rid of my Requiem.'

He let the work lie for several months longer, however, without coming to any decision about it. On July 30 he again wrote to Dietrich:

'... In all haste: I start to-morrow with my father on a little tour through Upper Austria. I do not know when I shall be back. Keep the accompanying Requiem until I write to you. Don't let it go out of your hands and write to me very seriously by-and-by what you think of it.

'An *offer* from Bremen would be very acceptable to me.

'It would have to be combined with a concert engagement. In short *Reinthaler* must probably be sufficiently pleased with the thing to do something for it.

'For the rest, I am inclined to let such matters quietly alone, for I do not intend to worry myself about them.

'I am ready for anything from Christmas onwards. Joachim and I probably gave concerts here before.'

There is a trace of nervous anxiety in this letter which leaves little doubt that Brahms had within him the consciousness that in the German Requiem he had transcended all his previous achievements, and that he was even unusually anxious to ensure a favourable opportunity for the hearing of his new work. Until now it had been submitted to none of his companions, save, perhaps, Joachim, and it is evident that he did not easily bring himself to the resolution of sending it away even for Dietrich's sympathetic inspection, and that, whilst he hoped, he somewhat dreaded to hear the result of a communication with Reinthaler. We must postpone for awhile our account of the fortunes of the manuscript in order to follow our musician on his holiday journey, on which he no doubt started with a mind sufficiently relieved by the mere fact of his decision to be able to await with composure the next issues of fate.

Herr königlich Musikdirektor Carl Martin Reinthaler (born 1822), municipal music-director of Bremen and organist of the cathedral, to whom the manuscript is meanwhile to be submitted, was a distinguished musician and the composer of numerous works in very varied forms, vocal and instrumental. His oratorio 'Jepthah' was performed in London in 1856 under John Hullah's direction; several of his operas—'Käthchen von Heilbronn,' 'Edda,' etc.—composed later in his career, were given with success in Bremen, Hanover, and other towns; and his 'Bismarck Hymn' won the prize in a competition adjudged at Dortmund. By his talent and earnestness in his position as conductor of the orchestral concerts at Bremen, he did much to raise the standard of musical taste in the city.

CHAPTER XIV
1867-1869

Brahms' holiday journey with his father and Gänsbacher—Austrian concert-tour with Joachim—The German Requiem—Performance of the first three choruses in Vienna—Tour with Stockhausen in North Germany and Denmark—Performance of the German Requiem in Bremen Cathedral—Brahms settles finally in Vienna—Brahms and Stockhausen give concerts in Vienna and Budapest.

Our composer's invitation to his father to accompany him on a tour amongst the Austrian Alps had mightily gratified Jakob. The violinist, young Carl Bade, happening to call at the Anscharplatz on the day of his start for Vienna, found him carefully dressed for the journey, and in a high state of elation and delight. Wrapping himself in an air of mysterious mock dignity, he scarcely vouchsafed a word of greeting to his wondering young friend, but, drawing himself up to his full height, gravely adjusted his necktie and paced the room in silence. Then, coming to a standstill, he pursed up his lips and looked at Bade with an expression of sly significance. 'Min Hannes het mi inladt; ick reis mit min Hannes' (My Hannes has invited me; I travel with my Hannes), he said in answer to Bade's demands for an explanation. A glimpse of him on his arrival is afforded by the recollection of Dr. Josef Gänsbacher, who was to accompany father and son on their journey, and, calling to make last arrangements with Johannes, found Jakob with him. The manuscript of the beautiful song 'Mainacht,' which had that day been composed, was at hand, and at his friend's request Gänsbacher sang it then and there, and added the lovely 'Wie bist du meine Königin' for the benefit of the elder Brahms, who expressed himself, as in duty bound, pleased with the songs, and was undoubtedly gratified by the compliment paid him.

The route chosen by the travellers lay through Styria and Carinthia, regions abounding in grand and romantic scenery of mountain, lake and forest; but though Johannes, an inveterate optimist in many ways, talked afterwards of his father's enjoyment of the journey, it is to be feared that Jakob, who had scarcely quitted Hamburg since his arrival there as a youth of nineteen, did not develop any great appreciation of the beauties of nature. He managed the ascent of the Hochschwab, or part of it, on foot, but it was a great deal too much for him. He was too old and too heavy to begin an apprenticeship as a mountaineer, and on the next expedition of the kind made by Johannes and Gänsbacher he remained behind at the village of Wildalpen. He got on much better when walking on the even, but wisely made no attempt to emulate the indefatigable pedestrian powers of his son, who would frequently stride on until he was an hour ahead of his companions. Jakob was better able to appreciate those parts of the journey which were accomplished by carriage or boat, though even there he spoke but little, perhaps hardly knowing how to express himself. One day, however, when the three travellers were on the Grundlsee, one of the most secluded and romantic of the Austrian lakes, he stood up and looked slowly round him, as if impressed by the beauty of the scene. 'Just like the Alster at home in Hamburg,' he remarked at length, as he sat down again.

Johannes fell in with some parties of his Austrian friends during the expedition, and was plainly gratified by the consideration shown to his father by one and all. One enthusiastic lady went so far as to bestow a kiss on the old man—an attention which procured him some good-natured raillery from his son, and which he discreetly left unmentioned for some time after his return to the Anscharplatz. He went back by way of Heidelberg, stopping to see the castle and other attractions by the desire of Johannes, and, a little while after reaching home, received from Vienna a souvenir of the doubtful pleasures of his journey in the shape of some mountain charts of the districts through which he had travelled, with blue lines drawn to mark the summits he had been able to attain by mountain railways or other mechanical means of transit. The maps, carefully preserved by Jakob, remain as a memorial of the composer's loving thought of his father, whom he indulged and spoilt almost like a petted child at this period of his life.

The journey over, Brahms' thoughts reverted to the manuscript which he had confided to Dietrich's care, and as soon as he was back in Vienna he wrote to beg for its return:

'DEAR ALBERT,

'Please send my score back to me as soon as possible and turn the opportunity to good account by enclosing this and that—above all a long letter.

'I had the great pleasure of having my father with me for some weeks. We made a pleasant tour through Styria and Salzburg. Imagine what enjoyment my father's pleasure gave me, he had never seen a mountain....

'Now I think of remaining here quietly; it is unfortunately useless for me to make plans, for only that happens which comes of itself.

'Nevertheless I wish to have the Requiem in my own cupboard again, so send....'[22]

To this note Dietrich returned no answer, and Brahms, becoming impatient, applied for information as to the whereabouts of his work to Joachim, who wrote back that it was in Reinthaler's keeping. Possibly Brahms may have been a little startled at finding that Dietrich, in his eager friendship, had put such an elastic interpretation upon the mention of the Bremen director quoted in our last chapter as to pass over the injunction not to part with the manuscript; but however this may be, he cannot but have been gratified at finding, as the result, that the musician of his own selection had been so impressed by the work as to wish to produce it at the earliest appropriate opportunity in the cathedral of Bremen. It is known to some of Reinthaler's old friends that he suggested the enlargement of the work to the dimensions of an oratorio. That Brahms did not entertain the proposal is matter of history.

The first performance of the Requiem, as originally completed, to be given under Brahms' direction in Bremen Cathedral, was fixed for Good Friday, April 10, 1868. Meanwhile the composer's engagements kept him in Austria. The first three numbers of the new work were to be produced under Herbeck at the Gesellschaft concert of December 1, and a tour arranged with Joachim for the ante-Christmas concert-season included concerts in Vienna, Budapest, and various provincial towns. The journey, which opened at Vienna on November 9, was triumphantly successful. Joachim performed the great solos of his répertoire by Bach, Tartini, and Spohr, and shorter pieces by Schumann and Paganini, with all of which concert-goers are now familiar, appearing also on his own account in several great orchestral concerts. Brahms played works by Bach, Schumann, Schubert, and some of his own compositions. Together the concert-givers were heard in several of Beethoven's duet Sonatas, Schubert's Fantasia, Op. 159, and Rondo Brilliant, Op. 70, etc.

'When Brahms and Joachim play Beethoven, Bach, Schubert together, the conceptions are like living tone pictures,' says Billroth, who, called to Vienna about a year after his first acquaintance with Brahms at Zürich and settled there for good, had the delight of receiving and hearing his two great artist friends at his house several times during the two months of Joachim's stay.

The Gesellschaft concert of December 1 was devoted to the memory of Schubert, and the three first numbers of the German Requiem formed an appropriate first portion of a programme of which the second half consisted of a selection from Schubert's music to 'Rosamund,' given for the first time in a concert-room. The choruses were, of course, sung by the Singverein, and Dr. Pänzer, of the imperial chapel, was responsible for the baritone solo of the Requiem.

The performance of Brahms' movements did not result in a success, though the two first were received with some tokens of approval. At the conclusion of the third an extraordinary scene took place. The now celebrated pedal point,[23] on which the last section of this number is constructed, produced—partly owing to a mistake of the drummer, who drowned the chorus by playing the famous 'D' *forte* throughout—a condition of nervous tension in a portion of the audience, a longing to be relieved from the monotony of the one dominating sound; and when the composer appeared on the platform in answer to the calls of some of his hearers, unmistakable demonstrations of hostility mingled with the plaudits. It may, indeed, be confidently surmised, and cannot appear surprising, that but few even of those who supported him on this occasion had any clear conception either of the meaning or importance of his work. To Hanslick it appeared

'one of the ripest fruits in the domain of sacred music, developed out of the style of Beethoven's late works.... The harmonic and contrapuntal art learnt by Brahms in the school of Bach, and inspired by him with the living breath of the present, is almost forgotten in the expression of touching lament, increasing to the annihilating death-shudder.'

Of its reception he says:

'It is intelligible that a composition so difficult to understand, and which deals only with ideas of death, is not adapted for popular success and that it does not entirely answer to the demands of a great public. We should have supposed, however, that a presentiment of the greatness and seriousness of the work would have suggested itself even to those who do not like it and would have won their respect. This seems not to have been the case with half a dozen gray-haired fanatics of the old school, who had the rudeness to greet the applauding majority and the composer, as he appeared, with prolonged hissing—a requiem on the decorum and good manners of a Vienna concert-room which astonishes and grieves us.'

Schelle, after reviewing the first number sympathetically and the second almost enthusiastically, continues:

'Unfortunately the third is extremely inferior to it [No. 2]; the text demanded a strong increase of effect which the composer has been incapable of giving. The bass solo is not written gratefully for the voice and there is much that is obtrusively bizarre and unedifying in the chorus.... The movement was a failure....'

Hirsch did not fail to make use of his opportunity in the *Wiener Zeitung.* He speaks of the 'heathenish noise of the kettledrums,' and declares 'in the interest of truth' that the opposition party in the audience had an immense majority.'

The concert is mentioned by Billroth in a letter dated December 24:

'I like Brahms better every time I meet him. Hanslick says, quite rightly, that he has the same fault as Bach and Beethoven; he has too little of the sensuous in his art both as composer and pianist. I think it is rather an intentional avoidance of everything sensuous as of a fault. His Requiem is so nobly spiritual and so Protestant-Bachish that it was difficult to make it go down here. The hissing and clapping became really violent; it was a party conflict. In the end the applause conquered.'

It is characteristic of Brahms that his belief in the future of his work was not diminished by the untoward incidents of this occasion. He looked forward to the result of the coming performance in Bremen with a confidence that was even enhanced by the fact that he had gained experience with respect to the instrumentation of the third chorus.

He sent part of his manuscript to Marxsen with a letter from which the following quotation was first published by Sittard in his 'Studien und Charakteristiken':

'I send you some novelties and beg you, if time allows, to write me *one* or *many* words about them. I enclose also something from my Requiem and *on this I earnestly beg you to write to me.* It looks rather curious in places and perhaps, in order to spare my manuscript, you would take some music paper and put down useful remarks. *I should like that very much.* The eternal "D" in No. 3. If I do not use the organ it does not sound. There is much I should like to ask. I hope you have time and some inclination; then you will perceive at once what there is to ask and what to say.'

It is, as Hanslick observed, by no means unintelligible that the first part of the German Requiem was not immediately accepted by the general body of listeners assembled at the Gesellschaft concert of December 1, unprepared as they were for the new and important element underlying its conception. The title chosen by the composer was at the time, and has been occasionally since, demurred to as misleading, on account of the long association of the term Requiem with the ritual of the Roman Church. It should, however, be obvious that by the word 'German' departure is indicated from the practice of previous composers, which places the composition in a category of its own and gives to its message an applicableness beyond the limitations of creed. Brahms arranged his own words, and by the fact of doing so, by his inspired musical treatment of his texts, and his direct avoidance of giving to his work an association with a particular church service or a familiar musical form, requiem or mass, cantata or oratorio, has preserved in it, whether or not consciously, an element of personal fervour that constitutes part of the secret of its spell.

The texts, culled from various books of the Old and New Testaments and the Apocrypha,[24] have been chosen, with entire absence of so-called doctrinal purpose, as parts of the people's book, of Luther's Bible, the accepted representative to Protestant nations of the highest aspirations of man, and have been so arranged as to present in succession the ascending ideas of sorrow consoled, doubt overcome, death vanquished. That they open and close with the thought of love is not of necessity to be ascribed solely to the artistic requirements of the work, or the exigencies of its sacred theme. Whoever has studied Brahms' life and works with sympathetic insight will be aware that the suggestion of love triumphant runs through both like a continuous silver thread, and it is open to those who choose, to accept this as indicative of a faith dwelling within him, which was none the less fruitful for good because it knew nothing of the dogma of the Churches.

The opening chorus of the Requiem furnishes the key-note of its spirit:

'*Blessed are they that mourn, for they shall be comforted. He that goeth forth and weepeth, bearing precious seed, shall doubtless come again with joy, bearing his sheaves with him. They that sow in tears shall reap in joy.*'

What more reassuring prelude could prepare the human soul for encounter with its most dreaded foe than these inspired words, heard in the exquisite setting of consolation by which the composer has illumined their meaning? The tenderness of the benediction, the passion of the anticipation, the recurring mournful calm that dies away in the softest whisper of comfort, place the mind in an attitude of awed suspense which finds its solution in the opening bars of the solemn, mysterious march of the second movement. Here we are surely in the majestic presence of death incarnate, wrapped, however, in a haze of beauty, sorrow, tenderness, compassion, that betoken, not the ruthless enemy of mankind, but a deeply mournful messenger subdued to a Divine purpose. '*Behold, all flesh is as grass, and all the glory of man as the flower of grass,*' chant the altos and tenors in unison an octave above the basses, something of unearthliness in their tones, with the alternate repetitions of the march; and the delicate, evanescent harmonies of the answering phrase, '*The grass withereth, the flower fadeth,*' strangely deepen the impression of transitoriness conveyed by the text. Relief is given by a middle episode of somewhat more animated character: '*Be patient therefore, brethren, unto the coming of the Lord. Behold, the husbandman waiteth for the precious fruit of the earth, and hath, long patience for it until he receive the early and latter rain. Be ye also patient.*' The final ending of the march, which is repeated after the episode, is succeeded by the outburst of a transitional passage—'*God's word endureth for ever*'—leading to the vigorous gladness of the second section of the movement (fugato)—'*And the ransomed of the Lord shall return and come to Zion with songs and everlasting joy upon their heads: they shall obtain joy and gladness, and sorrow and sighing shall flee away*'—whose ringing, jubilant tones are checked only by the passing shade of sorrow, until it subsides into the more tranquilly happy mood in which the chorus terminates.

In the third number the vision alters. To exaltation succeeds abasement. We are shown the despondency, that is almost despair, of the soul prostrate before its Lord: '*Lord, make me to know mine end, and the number of my days what it is, that I may know how frail I am.*' The movement opens with a baritone solo, supported by basses, drums, and horn, which seems to crave nothing, hope for nothing. Words and melody are, however, immediately repeated in chorus with plain harmonies that somewhat relieve the first impressive gloom. Then there is a change. The final cadence of the solo[25] becomes, in the chorus, a surprise cadence upon which the baritone re-enters: '*Behold, thou hast made my days as an handbreadth, and mine age is as nothing before thee.*' The tension relaxes, and a note of pleading makes itself felt that is strengthened in the choral repetition of the phrase by the movement of the accompanying instruments. Through despondency, through resignation, through questioning, the soul gradually rises to hope: '*Verily man at his best state is altogether vanity. Surely every man walketh in a vain show, surely they are disquieted in vain; he heapeth up riches, and knoweth not who shall gather them. Now, Lord, what do I wait for?*' The pleading becomes importunity, and the crisis is reached with the reiteration of the last words, first in an increasing agitation, and finally in deliberate, hushed tones that seem to challenge the Lord. The effect that follows is, perhaps, unsurpassed in its pure loveliness throughout the domain of sacred music. With the passage '*My hope is in thee*' all doubt is resolved in a glow of warmth, reconciliation, and trust, and the perfect assurance of faith, '*The souls of the righteous are in God's hand*' becomes the subject of an accompanied choral fugue, constructed from beginning to end upon a tonic pedal point, which establishes the brief inspiration of the transition passage in a protracted expression of unshakable confidence, and forms, not only the climax of the movement, but the first climax of the entire work. In it the soul attains to an elevation of faith from which it does not again falter. Though sorrow may not yet be finally subdued, doubt is conquered, and the fourth number—'*How amiable are thy dwellings, O Lord of Hosts! My soul longeth, yea, even fainteth for the courts of the Lord: my heart and my flesh crieth out for the living God. Blessed are they that dwell in thy house; they will be still praising thee*'—is a clear, melodious choral song with a flowing accompaniment, harmonized simply, and with an occasional point of imitation, that expresses simple affection and trust, emphasized towards the close of the movement by the employment of increased contrapuntal resource.

The fifth number, added, as we have said, after the work was first finished, and not essential to its conception as a whole, may have been conceded to some need of contrast felt by the composer on hearing the completed six movements consecutively. It consists of a very beautiful soprano solo with chorus, of rather mystic character, to the words '*And ye now are sorrowful. As one whom his mother comforteth, so will I comfort you.*'

The sixth chorus opens with a dirge—'*For we have no abiding city, but we seek one to come*'—soon to be interrupted by the baritone solo: '*Behold, I shew you a mystery: we shall not all sleep, but we shall be changed.*' The words are repeated by the chorus with a heightening agitation of mysterious expectancy, that leaps suddenly at the clarion call to tumultuous exultation: '*In a moment, in the twinkling of an eye, at the trump: for the trumpet shall sound, and the dead shall be raised incorruptible, and we shall be changed.*' The wild agitation is stayed by the quiet message of the solo, '*Then shall be brought to pass the saying that is written,*' and a prolonged half-cadence leads to the re-entry of the chorus in a magnificently-sustained inspiration of triumphant joy: '*Death is swallowed up in victory. O death, where is thy sting? O grave, where is thy victory?*' The glorious movement, after mounting from height to height of power and splendour, suddenly, with an unexpected change of time and key, reaches its climax in a brilliant fugue, that seems, with its passion of never-ending praise, to reopen the door of heaven and to transport the soul of the hearer to the dazzling scene of the throne that is filled with the ineffable presence of God: '*Thou art worthy, O Lord, to receive honour and power, for thou hast created all things, and for thy good pleasure they are and were created.*'

The great work has now reached its final climax. The imagination of the modern seer, soaring beyond sorrow, doubt, death, has pierced for a moment through the mystery of things and shown us the unspeakable. But the vision is not yet at an end. As in the writing of the Revelation of St. John, so in the inspired music of the German Requiem. After the lightnings and thunders and all the manifold glory of the throne, the voice of the spirit: '*Blessed are the dead which die in the Lord henceforth; Yea, saith the Spirit, that they may rest from their labours, and their works do follow them.*' Confident, tender, majestic, the message floats through the seventh movement, a veritable requiem, a true song of peace, and, heard at length in the tones of the benediction with which the work opens, sinks into silence with reiteration of blessing.

It would be an attractive task to analyze the technical means that Brahms has employed to give musical expression to the varied ideas, all rooted in the central one of overruling love, which together form the subject of this exalted work. Whilst he has used the resources of classical art with a power and ease that recall the mastery of Bach and Handel, he has given warmth and life to his creation by availing himself of the harmonic development of musical means to which the genius of Schumann gave such strong stimulus. Wisely conservative, he was also modern in the best sense, nor could the German Requiem have attained the position it has won in the hearts of thousands of men and women to whom it has brought comfort in bereavement or solace in times of mental distress, if he had not understood and shared in the spirit, and answered to it in an idiom, proper to his time. This should not be forgotten in the performance of the great work, which is sometimes given with a cold, formal correctness supposed to be appropriate in the case of classical compositions. Brahms was not a pedant, but a poet and idealist, and the full beauty and fascination of his music is disclosed only when it is interpreted with the insight that is born of enthusiasm and imagination.

The Horn Trio was played in Vienna at the Hellmesberger Quartet concert of December 29 by Brahms, Hellmesberger, and Kleinecke. Kleinecke performed on the natural horn, and the beauty of his tone was remarked on by one or two of the critics. The trio was received not unfavourably, but with the reserve that usually attended the early performances of the composer's works in the imperial capital at this period of his career.

The publications of the year were but two in number—the set of sixteen Waltzes for four hands on the Piano, dedicated to Hanslick; and a book of five Songs for men's four-part Chorus, both issued in the spring by Rieter-Biedermann. Several, at least, of the waltzes date from the Detmold period, and were played by Brahms, and heard by Carl von Meysenbug, at the Hôtel Stadt Frankfurt. They are inimitable in their delicate, caressing grace, and possess a charm which perhaps exceeds that of any known examples of their kind. They were performed from the manuscript, as finally arranged for publication, by Frau Schumann and Dietrich at a music party given by the Grand-Duchess of Oldenburg in the autumn of 1866.

Joachim's prolonged visit to Austria came to an end in the second week of the New Year with a farewell dinner given in his honour by Brahms, Billroth, Hanslick, and other friends, and a fortnight later he removed with his family from Hanover to Berlin. His residence was permanently fixed in the Prussian capital in the course of the following year by his acceptance of the post of director of the Royal High School for Music (executive art), which was about to be founded by King William of Prussia (afterwards the German Emperor William I.), as an addition to the State department for Art and Science, and in the planning and practical arrangement of which Joachim actively participated. Under his devoted management, it quickly rose to the high state of prosperity for which it has long been famous, and now, after more than thirty-five years of existence, it still enjoys the high advantage and distinction of his personal labour and influence as director, conductor, and teacher. The occasion of the opening in 1902, by the

Emperor William II., of the spacious new buildings of the Royal Schools for Art and Science at Charlottenburg, of which the fine new music school is one, must have seemed to the great veteran musician, as he recalled the modest beginnings of his own special department in 1869, as one that included the crowning of much of the activity of his life.

Brahms quitted Vienna a few weeks after his friend to fulfil a series of concert engagements, most of them arranged with Stockhausen, for the months of February and March, by which he hoped to make his journey to North Germany on the business of the Requiem answer a practical as well as an artistic purpose. He took up his headquarters at his father's house, and it was the last time that he returned from Vienna to Hamburg as to his nominal home. The post of conductor of the Philharmonic had again fallen vacant in 1867 by Stockhausen's resignation, and again, though Brahms did not apply for the appointment, there was a strong conviction amongst his friends that he would accept it if it were offered him. But it was not to be. Admired and loved as he was in Hamburg by an ever-increasing circle of friends, it was by a circle only. He was not popular with the average musician or the general public, and the Philharmonic committee passed him over a second time, electing Julius von Bernuth as Stockhausen's successor. Brahms said little on the subject, but it is fairly certain that the mortification caused him by this repeated slight from the musical officialdom of his native city sufficed to lead him to the determination at which he soon afterwards arrived, to settle permanently in Vienna.

Brahms made several public appearances in Hamburg during the second half of February. He performed, at the Philharmonic concert of the 14th, Beethoven's G major Concerto and Schumann's Etudes Symphoniques, adding to the published version of the latter several variations contained in Schumann's original manuscript. On the same occasion Stockhausen sang Schubert's songs 'Memnon' and 'Geheimniss' to orchestral accompaniments arranged by Brahms, at his request, a year or two previously. The composer was able to spare a few days for Bremen, in order to make Reinthaler's personal acquaintance, though his numerous engagements for March obliged him to leave the work of preparation and rehearsal in the experienced hands of his new friend. He played at the Oldenburg subscription concert of the 4th,[26] and gave concerts with Stockhausen during the same week in Dresden and Berlin, appearing for the first time before the public of either capital. At the second concert in Berlin (March 7) Nos. 3 and 5 of the 'Magelone Romances' were included in the programme. On the 11th the two artists gave a soirée in Hamburg, when Stockhausen introduced Brahms' 'Mailied' and 'Von ewiger Liebe' from the manuscripts, and gave several folk-songs as an encore. At Kiel, where they appeared on the 13th, they made the acquaintance of Löwe, the famous ballad composer, now a man of seventy-two, with whose music Brahms proved to be thoroughly familiar. Their next destination was Copenhagen, where they had arranged to give four concerts. Stockhausen's selection on the first of these occasions included songs by Stradella, Schubert, and Boieldieu, all accompanied by Brahms, who performed as his solos a Toccata and Fugue by Sebastian Bach Andante by Friedemann Bach, two Scarlatti movements, Beethoven's Sonata in E flat, Op. 27, and, of his own compositions, Variations on an original theme and the early Scherzo in E flat minor. Both artists awakened a furore. Stockhausen 'electrified the house'; Brahms was 'enormously applauded,' especially after the performance of his own compositions. The second concert, given within the next few days, was equally successful. The concert-room was crowded, the audience extraordinarily enthusiastic, and the financial result brilliant beyond expectation. Then Brahms committed a *faux pas*, which put an end, so far as he was concerned, to further result of the triumph.

Being asked, at a party given by the Danish composer Niels Gade in his and Stockhausen's honour, if he had visited and admired the great Thorwaldsen Museum, of which the citizens of Copenhagen are so justly proud, he replied in the affirmative, and added that the building and its collection were so fine it was to be regretted they were not in Berlin. This unfortunate remark, made in a circle representative of educated Danish society, where the remembrance of the recent Prussian occupation of Schleswig-Holstein was still sore, produced an effect which the speaker had been far from intending. It was regarded as a deliberate insult to the country in which Brahms had been a fêted guest, and was resented so strongly as to make the composer's reappearance on a Copenhagen platform impossible. Pursuing the wisest course open, he embarked on the next boat for Kiel, leaving Stockhausen to make such arrangements as he could for the third advertised concert, and to pursue his success further by associating himself with Joachim, who was about to pay a short visit to the Danish capital.

Arriving at Kiel at a very early hour in the morning, Brahms proceeded to the house of Claus Groth, whose guest he had been on his outward journey, and, walking in the garden until the inmates were astir, was presently greeted by his friend from an upper window. 'Be quick and come out; I have made a heap of money,' he cried in answer, slapping his pocket. Coffee was soon served and a lively talk ensued, but, as no explanation was offered by Brahms of his sudden reappearance, Groth at length began to question him. 'What have you been about that you have, so to say, run away? Stockhausen has not returned, and you have had great success?' And thus brought to the point, the delinquent was obliged to relate his indiscretion. 'Brahms! how could you have said such a thing in a company of Danes!' cried Groth. 'I only meant,' replied Brahms, 'that it would be better if so fine a work, so many beautiful objects, were in a great centre where many people could see them.' 'But you might have supposed Danes would not put up with such a remark.' 'It did not occur to me,' answered Brahms. 'However,' he added after a moment, 'I have earned so much money I shall not want more for a long time; so the matter is indifferent to me.'

Brahms arrived in Bremen on the first day of April, to remain until after the 10th as the guest of Reinthaler, with whom he soon became intimate. Appreciation of his works had steadily grown in the artistic circles of Bremen since the musical life of the city had been under the leadership of the distinguished artist whose name will remain associated with the first performance of the then complete German Requiem; and the Good Friday concert of this year was anticipated with the interest attaching to an event of unusual importance, the more so as many distinguished visitors from far and near were expected to be present as performers or in the audience. To the gratification of the former members of the Ladies' Choir, Brahms expressed a wish that the old favourite society should be represented in the chorus, and four of the most enthusiastic and trusty of his quondam disciples—Fräulein Garbe, Fräulein Reuter, Fräulein Seebohm, and Fräulein Marie Völckers—answered to his summons, arriving at Bremen in time to take part in the last general rehearsal. The programme of the sacred concert, the proceeds of which were to be devoted to the Bremen musicians' provident fund, included the German Requiem (baritone solo, Stockhausen), between the first and second parts of which, some of the miscellaneous items were placed; movements by Bach and Tartini, and Schumann's Abendlied for violin (Joachim); 'I know that my Redeemer liveth' (Frau Joachim); air for contralto with violin obligato from Bach's 'Matthew Passion' (Frau Joachim and Joachim); and the 'Hallelujah' chorus. Brahms was to conduct his new work, Reinthaler the remaining selections. All the soloists gave their services.

The doors of St. Peter's Cathedral Church opened punctually at six o'clock on Good Friday evening, and during the next hour the visitors, many of them old acquaintances of the reader, streamed to their places. Frau Reinthaler and Frau Stockhausen were of course present. The Dietrichs, with their friend Fräulein Berninger, came from Oldenburg, the Grimms from Münster. The Hamburg contingent included Minna Völckers, the composer's former pupil and very stanch friend, now grown up into a young lady, and her father, who had invited Jakob Brahms to accompany them as his guest. Max Bruch, Schübring, and young Richard Barth were there. Switzerland was represented by the future publisher of the Requiem, Rieter-Biedermann; England by the enthusiastic John Farmer; and shortly before the time of commencement Frau Schumann walked up the nave on

Brahms' arm. She had arranged that her intention of making the journey from Baden-Baden with her daughter Marie should be kept a secret from the composer, and the two ladies surprised him with their greeting at the cathedral door.

No pains had been spared in the preparation of chorus and orchestra, and their difficult tasks were perfectly achieved.

'The impression made by the wonderful, splendidly performed work was quite overpowering,' says Dietrich, 'and it immediately became clear to the listeners that the German Requiem would live as one of the most exalted creations of musical art.'

The composer, the executants, and their friends, to the number of about a hundred, met for supper in the ancient Rathskeller close to the cathedral, and listened afterwards to a short address by Consul Hirschfeld and to about a dozen other speeches.

'It is with great pleasure and justifiable pride,' said Reinthaler, 'that I greet this distinguished assemblage of visitors, some of them gathered to perform, and others to hear, the new work of the composer who is staying in our midst. The circumstance that it has been performed for the first time here in Bremen gives me quite peculiar happiness. It is a great and beautiful—one may say, an epoch-making work, which has filled us who have heard it to-day with pride, since it has inspired in us the conviction that German art has not died out, but that it begins to stir again and will thrive as gloriously as of old.

'A gloomy, anxious period has intervened since our last dear master was carried to the grave;[27] it has almost seemed as though the evening of musical art had fallen upon us; but to-day we are reassured. In the German Requiem we believe that we have a sequel worthy of the achievements of the great masters of the past.

'That I have had the good fortune to contribute towards ensuring a not quite unworthy performance of the work gives me lively satisfaction. Everyone concerned, however, has supported me to this end. Each has brought cheerful good-will to his task, and devoted himself to it with active zeal and unmixed enthusiasm, for each felt it to be an elevating one.

'You will all certainly rejoice with me that the creator of the glorious work is present amongst us and will joyfully raise your glasses to the health of the composer, our Brahms.'

Brahms' answer was characteristically short and to the purpose:

'If I venture to say a few words to-night, I must premise that the gift of oratory is in no wise at my command. There are, however, amongst those present, many to whom I wish to say a word of thanks, many dear friends who have been kind and good to me, and this is especially the case with my friend Reinthaler, who has given himself with such self-sacrifice to the preparation of my Requiem. I place my collective thanks upon his head therefore, and call for three cheers for his name.'

It may surprise and interest English readers to know that their country was toasted on an occasion so peculiarly representative of German music and musicians. After the various artists who had assisted in the performance and one or two of the other distinguished guests had been duly honoured, John Farmer rose to his feet, and delivered himself of his sentiments in such German as he could command.

'I have come from a city,' he said, 'that is much larger than Bremen, in which there are many fine houses and many rich men. You, however, may be prouder than all the rich men in the big houses, who are, indeed, very unfortunate. They have no such beautiful music as you in Germany. If you were to come to England, and Brahms himself were to come with you, to perform the Requiem, they would not attend the concert, or if they were to attend it they would say, "Is the fellow crazy?" You can have no idea how fortunate you are in being able to understand all this beautiful music. Oh, I have observed and have perceived that each one has followed it with love and the whole energy of his soul! When I return to England, I shall relate what I have seen, and will hope that we may, before long, become as fortunate as yourselves and may be able to understand and perform German music as you do.'

England found its defender in Herr Lehmann, who immediately rose to reply:

'I would venture, nevertheless, to say a word in England's honour. So many artists have met with an encouraging reception or have found a happy home there; there are so many Englishmen who understand and sympathize with German art and German life, that I would beg leave to propose a glass to the honour of art-loving England.'

The feeling of satisfaction expressed in Reinthaler's speech that the distinction of the first performance of the German Requiem should have fallen to Bremen was generally shared by the musicians and amateurs of the city.

'Reinthaler has, with laudable judgment, concentrated his best powers upon the arrangement of a concert which has given to Bremen a distinctive artistic reputation,' says the critic of the *Bremen Courier*, and the sentiment was expressed practically, as well as verbally, in a communication sent to the composer a few days after his return to Hamburg. The work was repeated on Tuesday, April 28, in the hall of the Union, under Reinthaler's direction, when the baritone solo was sung by Franz Krolop.

It is pleasant to be able to associate with the musical events of 1868—the year which, by virtue of the occurrences now recorded, marked the beginning of a new period in Brahms' outward career and established him in the eyes of the musicians of Europe as the greatest living artist in his own domain—the name of an early friend whose skilled appreciation of his genius had cheered and encouraged him in the dark days of his youth. Frau Dr. Louise Langhans-Japha played the Quintet in F minor for pianoforte and strings at her concert in the Salle Erard, Paris, on March 24, and secured for it a very decided success. It is impossible actually to affirm that the work was heard for the first time in public in its final form on this occasion, but it is the first public performance of which the author has been able to find record.

Brahms stayed on in the north for several weeks after the Good Friday concert at Bremen, and found time to pay another, this time a holiday, visit to the Reinthalers, and to make the acquaintance of many of their friends. He derived particular pleasure from the society of some small playfellows who welcomed him to Frau Reinthaler's nursery, and struck up a special friendship with the eldest daughter of the house, little Henriette. Hearing the child, hardly out of baby years, practising the treble of a little pianoforte duet, he proposed to take the bass, and, amusing himself by striking a wrong note, was promptly rebuked by his colleague. 'You have played a wrong note,' said Misi, stopping short. 'Nun, we must do it again,' returned Brahms penitently, and recommenced. 'You have played another!' cried Misi; nor could the master be pronounced perfect in his part until after two more attempts. He stayed, too, for a few days in Oldenburg, and whilst there made several excursions in the neighbourhood with Dietrich and Reinthaler. Driving one day to Wilhelmshaven, the great northern war-harbour of Germany, he was unusually absent-minded and serious, and mentioned that he had been much struck with Hölderlin's poem, 'Hyperion's Song of Destiny,' which he had read in the morning for the first time. After inspecting the harbour and its sights, he withdrew to a distant part of the beach, where he was observed by his friends to be busy with pencil and paper. He was putting down the first sketches of his now celebrated setting of the work.

Brahms spent the remainder of the year in Germany and Switzerland. After attending the Rhine Festival held the last week of May in Cologne, he settled down for some months at 6, Kessenicherweg, Bonn, in order to be near Dr. Deiters, whom he met daily and admitted to his confidence on the subject of his work. He was occupied with the final preparation of the manuscript of the Requiem for the engraver, and played it through to his friend, who had already studied it from the manuscript, saying, in the course of the just-completed fifth number, '... *I will comfort you as a mother comforts*,' that here he had thought of his mother.[28] He was engaged again, also, with the C minor Pianoforte Quartet, which, as we have seen,[29] has associations with a very much earlier period, and played the sketches to Dr. Deiters, though the work was not finally completed until after the further lapse of several years. The music to Goethe's cantata 'Rinaldo' was in progress, and was finished shortly before he quitted Bonn. Deiters was fortunate enough to have the opportunity of listening, at his own house or in Brahms' rooms, to the composer's interpretation of some of his published works, and to hear his own opinion of many of his songs, which he estimated very variously. Amongst those of which he thought most highly at this time was the 'Von ewiger Liebe,' published later in the year as No. 1 of Op. 43.

Brahms was in happy summer mood throughout the time of his sojourn on the Rhine. The fondness for dumb pets that always characterized him, though he kept none of his own, was gratified by the confidence of some pigeons that used to fly into his room and come to him to be fed. He invited his father to join him during the last ten days of his stay, and pleased himself by showing him the Rhine country and introducing him to his friend. It was the only year of his life during which there was intimate personal intercourse between himself and Deiters, but the two men remained in correspondence, and the composer frequently sent copies of his new works as they appeared, with an autograph inscription, to the critic whose early appreciation through a period when their personal acquaintance had been of the slightest had awakened in him a strong feeling of regard and esteem. 'I feel under a great debt of obligation to friend Deiters,' he says in the course of a letter to Dietrich written in 1867.

Jakob Brahms was not allowed to return to Hamburg until he had a second time tested his capacity for enjoying the delights of mountain scenery by accompanying his son on a few weeks' journey in Switzerland; but though Johannes made all possible arrangements to spare his father fatigue, it became evident that he was very homesick. 'See, Johannes, here is a little blue flower like that which grows near Hamburg,' he said one day, lagging a little behind after he had walked some distance in silence. An incident of the tour which pleased him, perhaps, better than his pedestrian and driving experiences was the trial, at which he was present, of the new movement of the Requiem, which the composer wished to hear before delivering it for publication. This was arranged for at Zürich by Hegar. Frau Suter-Weber undertook the soprano solo, and orchestra and chorus were supplied by resident musicians. Jakob, on this, as indeed on all occasions, fully appreciated the distinction he derived from being his son's companion; but it is certain that he was much relieved when the day came for him to return to his quiet home and the unembarrassing society of his wife. 'Nu, Line, krigt mi Johannes nit wieder hin' (Now, Lina, Johannes will not get me again), he said, as he settled himself once more in his own chair; and he kept to his determination, though he compromised matters on one or two subsequent occasions by accepting his son's proposal that he should visit the Harz and other districts in Frau Caroline's company.

Of the many pleasant social events of the year, a gathering in the autumn at Dietrich's house in Oldenburg remains for mention. Frau Schumann, her daughter Marie, and Brahms enjoyed their old friends' hospitality during the last week of October, and the visit was signalized by the first performance from the manuscript, before a private audience, of the Hungarian Dances in their arrangement for four hands on the piano.

'Frau Schumann and Brahms played them with an inspiration and fire that transported everyone present,' says Dietrich.

Frau Schumann gave an evening concert in the hall of the Casino on the 30th, when her programme included her performance with the composer—probably the first before a public audience—of Brahms' Waltzes.[30]

Brahms and Stockhausen again united their forces in November, and gave several concerts together. At the first of two soirées in Hamburg, Brahms created a furore with some of the Hungarian Dances in their arrangement as solos. The programme included a performance by Stockhausen and his pupil Fräulein Girzik of two of the Duets, Op. 28, the second of which was rapturously encored. Brahms, as usual, accompanied his friend throughout the evening. He was received with acclamation at Bremen on the 30th of the month, when he played the pianoforte part of his A major Quartet at a concert of the excellent resident string quartet party led by Jacobsen, a fine player, and second concertmeister of the Bremen orchestra. On this, as on subsequent visits to Bremen, Brahms stayed, as a matter of course, with the Reinthalers.

Carl Bade, paying one of his frequent morning calls at the Anscharplatz about this time, was startled as he entered the house by the appearance of Jakob, who, coming towards him with finger on lip and laboriously treading on tiptoe, solemnly whispered, 'Hush!...' 'What is it, Brahms? Who is ill?' returned Bade under his breath, seriously alarmed. 'Hush!' repeated Jakob as mysteriously as before; '*he is dor*' (he is there); and, opening the door of the corner room, he pushed in the astonished Carl and shut the door behind him without another word, leaving him alone with his son, who was busy weeding out his library in readiness for the despatch of his Hamburg possessions to Vienna. 'See here,' said Johannes, after a kind word of greeting, giving Bade time to recover the composure of which Jakob's strange *coup* had for a moment robbed him, by pointing to a volume in his hand, 'Kuhnau was a capable musician!'

The relation existing at this time between the elder and younger Brahms, of which mention was made in an early chapter, was well illustrated during the homely 'second breakfast' for which the party soon assembled. Sociability was rendered impossible, in spite of the persistent efforts of Johannes, by the father's overwhelming consciousness of his son's presence. The awed feeling which possessed Jakob whenever he found himself face to face with the living embodiment of his own miraculous success in life was not unnatural, and can only inspire respect for the memory of the older man, in whose simple humility, rooted in the strongest and most legitimate pride, may, perhaps, be recognised some of the essential qualities which endeared the great composer to all who were privileged to call him friend.

Brahms returned to Vienna in December, and was, of course, present at several concerts given there before and after Christmas by Frau Schumann, who visited Austria after an interval of some years.

The list of publications belonging to this year is an important one, not only because it includes the German Requiem (Rieter-Biedermann), but because it is representative of the master in what may be roughly called the second period of his activity as a composer of songs. From beginning to end of his career he poured forth songs in many different forms—the simple strophic, the 'durchcomponirtes' Lied, the latter necessarily varying in structure with each fresh example.[31] This second period, however, is marked not only by the sure mastery which had long characterized Brahms' works in whatever domain he chose for the exercise of his powers; its spirit is generally distinctive, and is that of the poet's ripe manhood. Youth with its uncertainties is behind, age with its gathering shadows not yet in sight; the composer holds the present in firm grasp, and presents us with exquisite dream-pictures of life and nature, the children of an imagination penetrated with a sense of the beauty, the tenderness, the pathos of existence, and content in the exercise of its ideality. Each of the five books published in 1868 (Op. 43 by Rieter-Biedermann, and Op. 46, 47, 48, 49 by Simrock) contains such wealth of beauty that it is difficult to select either for particular mention. Perhaps the palm should be given to Op. 43, of which 'Von ewiger Liebe' and 'Mainacht' are Nos. 1 and 2; but then, Op. 47 contains 'Botschaft,' and Op. 46 'Die Schale der Vergessenheit.' Stockhausen, who stayed at Neuenahr in the summer of 1868, came over to Bonn one day, and sang the greater number of these songs from the manuscript, accompanied by the composer, to Deiters. Brahms seemed determined not to publish 'Die Schale der Vergessenheit,' declaring it to be too 'desolate,' but Stockhausen's enthusiasm prevailed to alter his decision. Some of the shorter numbers belong, by date of composition, to an earlier period, as Goethe's 'Die Liebende schreibt,' the manuscript of which, in the possession of Frau Professor Böie, bears the inscription 'Frl. Marie Völckers in kind remembrance' and the date 1863. The widely popular 'Wiegenlied,' Op. 49, No. 4, was composed for one of Frau Faber's children, and the accompaniment is reminiscent of a folk-song which Brahms heard from Fräulein Bertha Porubszky in the old days of the Hamburg Ladies' Choir. The manuscript bears the inscription 'For Arthur and Bertha Faber for ever happy use. July 1868'; and at the close 'Mit Grazie in infinitum,' and is in the possession of these old friends of the composer.

Now, as ever, Brahms returned with delight to the fresh naïveté of the folk-song, and numerous examples of his settings of texts obtained from German, Bohemian, Italian sources are to be found in these books, of which 'Sonntag,' Op. 47, No. 3, and 'Am Sonntag Morgen,' Op. 49, No. 1, are perhaps the best known. 'Gold überwiegt die Liebe' is a touching little lament (No. 4 of Op. 48). The text of 'Von ewiger Liebe' is itself a Wendic folk-song, but the composer's treatment has placed it amongst the finest works of German art in song-form. As a rule, however, Brahms set folk-songs as such, and his treatment of them was direct, and, so to say, unstudied. He has set for a single voice popular texts of more than twenty nationalities besides his own, and, as he found them, as they appealed to him, so he composed them, without attempt either to interfere with the frank naturalness of the words, or to give national colour to his music. Such musical references as he occasionally makes in his songs to the origin of his texts are so unobtrusive as to be hardly noticeable, excepting by a special student of the subject.[32] 'Vergangen ist mir,' Op. 48, No. 6, points back to the tonal system of the Middle Ages. Like 'Sehnsucht,' Op. 14, No. 8, it is composed in the Dorian mode.

The enumeration of the great song publications of 1868 is not yet at an end. The issue by Rieter-Biedermann of Books 3, 4, 5, containing in all nine numbers, of the 'Magelone Romances,' of which the first two books had appeared in 1865, completed a song-cycle which ranks among the few supreme achievements of its class, increasing to the number of four a special group of names which had hitherto included those only of Beethoven, Schubert, and Schumann.

The fifteen 'Magelone Romances' are extremely various in structure, and can hardly be classified categorically under any of the ordinary song-forms. Spitta expresses his sense of their importance by the word 'symphonic.' Brahms' own name 'Romance' sufficiently indicates their nature, however. Some are of great, others of smaller, dimensions. Some consist of several movements, others of one short movement in three sections, of which the last repeats the first; one is bound into a whole by the melody of a refrain.

They give vivid expression to a wide range of feelings: chivalric delight, progressive phases of passionate love, the despair of separation, reawakened hope, the confident bliss of reunion, certainty of the sacred power of love. Remembrance of the ideal performances of Stockhausen, to whom the cycle is dedicated, was indubitably present to Brahms' mind as he composed the songs, which, with the exception of Nos. 11 and 13, should be sung by a man. One may read and reread them, hear them and hear them again, but try in vain to decide on a favourite number. Each one places the listener in an enchanted world of noble beauty and romance, and in wealth and individuality of idea the cycle assuredly does not rank last amongst the few works of its kind.

The Songs and Romances Op. 44 mentioned in our first volume in connection with the Ladies' Choir were now also published by Rieter-Biedermann;[33] and Cranz of Hamburg issued the three Songs for six-part Chorus *a capella*, Op. 42, all of great charm. Its five-bar rhythm is an interesting feature of the second number, the lovely 'Vineta.' The text of No. 3, 'Darthula's Grabesgesang,' is a translation from Ossian, and is contained in Herder's 'Stimmen der Völker.'

'Brahms is here,' writes Billroth from Vienna on January 11, 'and is to give concerts with Stockhausen. He is going to bring out a cantata, Rinaldo, in February.... He is enthusiastic about thc text because it leaves so much to the composer.'

Goethe wrote his cantata expressly that music might be set to it by Capellmeister Winter, a respectable musician of his day, for the Prince Friedrich of Gotha, the possessor of an agreeable tenor voice, and a good amateur vocalist. It is founded on an episode in Tasso's 'Jerusalem Delivered,' and exhibits the conflict between weakness and strength in the brave knight Rinaldo—a fictitious personage introduced into his poem by Tasso—who is roused from his surrender to the witcheries of Armida by the arrival, at the islet on which he is living with her, of a party of knights, his friends—two only in Tasso's epic, but increased to a chorus by Goethe. The cantata opens at a point where the knights have succeeded in awakening Rinaldo from his dream of happiness, but are unable to nerve him to the resolution of departure. As a final resource, they hold up before him a diamond shield, which reflects his own image in its degeneracy. The shock of what he sees restores him to full consciousness, and he leaves the island in spite of Armida's lamentations, fury, and enchantments, and his own regrets, encouraged and supported by his friends. The final chorus with solo depicts the happy return voyage, and the safe arrival of the ship at the shore of the Holy Land.

Armida does not appear as a *dramatis persona* in Goethe's work, and Brahms' music is accordingly composed for tenor solo, men's chorus, and orchestra. The poem is short and concise, containing but one dramatic situation, but its very terseness has been advantageous to the composer, for the text has not fettered his imagination by detail, whilst it has supplied him with sufficient material for powerful and contrasted musical presentation in the enchantments of Armida, the storm raised by her to prevent the ship's departure, the calm, persuasive firmness of the knights, the vacillation of Rinaldo (expressed in the first instance in an impassioned scena), his pleadings with his friends, his final awakening and recovery from the intensity of passion. Of all these points Brahms has availed himself with force and warmth of imagination. Many interesting details of the composition tempt our notice, but we may only stay to direct the reader's attention to the conviction inspired by the choruses of the noble, lovable character of the knights; to the masterly means employed—so simple that only a master would have ventured to restrict himself to them—at the moment when the shield is displayed, which, in their place, convey, without any attempt at tone-painting, but with absolute distinctness, the impression of the friends' gentle determination with the shrinking Rinaldo; to the bright martial movement in which the knights encourage him by reminding him of the flashing lances, the waving pennons, the whole brilliant battle array, of the crusaders' army from which the allurements of Armida have too long detained him. In the final chorus a favourable wind swells the sails of the ship, which rides joyously over the green waves, breaking them into light foam as she passes, whilst Rinaldo and his companions amuse themselves by watching the dolphins at play in the water, and are filled with a light-hearted happiness that, as land is sighted, bursts into exultant shouting of the names of Godfrey and Solyma (Jerusalem).

The work was performed for the first time from the manuscript, under the composer's direction, on February 28, 1869, at a concert of the Akademischer Gesangverein, Vienna. The title-part was sung with great success by Gustav Walter, three hundred students well prepared by Dr. Eyrich, the society's conductor, were responsible for the choruses, and the orchestral accompaniments were performed by the entire body of instrumentalists of the court opera.

A series of three concerts, given in Vienna in February and March by Brahms and Stockhausen were phenomenally successful. The great baritone had not been heard in the Austrian capital for many years, and all tickets for the first concert were sold immediately after its announcement. Brahms' selection for the series included works by Handel, Bach, Couperin, Gluck, Beethoven, Schubert, Schumann, some of his own Variations—notably those of the B flat Sextet—and Hungarian Dances; and he accompanied his friend in many of the most celebrated songs of his répertoire. The wonderful performance by the two artists of Brahms' songs 'Von ewiger Liebe' and 'Mainacht' was one of the choice delights of the first concert. A feature of the second was the performance by Stockhausen and Fräulein Girzik of two of the composer's vocal duets. The enthusiasm excited by the concert-givers in Vienna was equalled in Budapest, whither they proceeded on March 10, in order to give a similar series; and it was, if possible, exceeded on their final reappearance in Vienna.

These concerts are of peculiar interest in Brahms' career, because the last of them closes the period of his activity as a virtuoso. For fourteen years, from the autumn of 1855 to the spring of 1869, circumstances had obliged, and happily permitted, him to earn his livelihood chiefly by the exercise of his powers as an executive artist; but his reputation as a composer had grown uninterruptedly throughout this time, and with the production of the German Requiem it attained a height that gave him future independence of action. Though years were still to pass before his circumstances became easy, they were not again straitened, and from henceforth he undertook concert-journeys only in the rôle of a composer, to assist at performances of his own works. The occasions on which he appeared additionally as pianist with one of Beethoven's or Schumann's great compositions became less and less frequent, moreover, as, with passing time, he felt increasingly out of regular practice. Brahms was, in later life, fond of illustrating the fact of his long struggle with poverty by referring to the manuscript of the Requiem. 'The paper is of all sizes and shapes, because at the time I wrote it I never had money enough to buy a stock.' The immediate impression created by the great work was, however, sufficiently widespread and profound to place the composer alone, among the musicians of his day, as the accepted representative of the classical art of Germany, and the prices commanded by his copyrights gradually increased accordingly. No long time elapsed before the German Requiem had made the round of the musical cities of Europe. It was given, for the first time after final completion and publication, at the Leipzig Gewandhaus concert of February 18, 1869, under Reinecke, and was performed in the course of the next few weeks in Basle (twice), Carlsruhe (twice), Münster, Cologne, Hamburg, Zürich, and Weimar, and, later in the year, in Dessau (twice), Chemnitz (twice), Barmen (four choruses only), Magdeburg, Jena, and again twice in Cologne. The complete work was not heard in Vienna until March 5, 1871, when it was given by the Gesellschaft der Musikfreunde under the composer's direction, with Frau Wilt and Dr. Krauss as soloists, but achieved no striking success. It was performed on July 7 of the same year (1871) for the first time in England, before an invited audience, at the residence of Sir Henry Thompson. Stockhausen conducted the rehearsals and performance, and sang the baritone solo, Fräulein Anna Regan the soprano solo. The chorus was composed of about thirty good musicians, and the accompaniments were played in their arrangement as a pianoforte duet by Lady Thompson and the veteran musician Cipriani Potter, then in his eightieth year. The first public performance in England which the author has been able to authenticate with precision is that of the Philharmonic Society in St. James's Hall on April 2, 1873, under the direction of W. G. Cusins, when the soloists were Mlle. Sophie Ferrari and Santley. The work was performed for the first time in Berlin, Munich and St. Petersburg in the spring, and in Utrecht in June, of the year 1872, and in Paris in 1874.[34]

Probably it was due to the impression created by the German Requiem that the Serenade in D, Op. 11, was performed for the first time in Berlin in November, 1869, at one of the concerts of the Symphony Orchestra under Capellmeister Stern.

'The reception showed that the public is beginning to understand and value the composer Brahms, one of the few living creative artists who are genuine and sincere,' wrote a Berlin critic.

In the earlier part of the same year Louis Brassin played the Handel Variations and Fugue in Munich with very great success. Brassin was one of the first artists to perform the work in public, and that he introduced it to a Munich audience is the more interesting since the musicians of the Bavarian capital had in 1869 shown scant, if any, recognition of our composer's art, which was too progressive for Franz Lachner, and too conservative for von Bülow, the successive leaders, up to that date, of the musical life of the city. The work was played by Bülow in November, 1872, in Carlsruhe, and from that time was heard at his concerts with increasing frequency.

CHAPTER XV
1869-1872

Brahms and Opera—Professor Heinrich Bulthaupt—The Liebeslieder—First performance—The Rhapsody (Goethe's 'Harzreise') performed privately at Carlsruhe—First public performance at Jena—Geheimrath Gille—The 'Song of Triumph'—Performance of first chorus at Bremen—Bernhard Scholz—The 'Song of Destiny'—First performance—Death of Johann Jakob Brahms—First performance of completed 'Triumphlied' at Carlsruhe—Summary of Brahms' work as a composer since 1862.

The theory that found wide acceptance during the lifetime of Brahms, and was discussed at length in a feuilleton of the *Strassburger Post* immediately after his death, that he never had and never could have seriously entertained the idea of composing for the stage, was long ago conclusively refuted by Widmann in his 'Recollections.' He shows that the master's wishes pointed at more than one period of his career in the direction of dramatic composition, and that he was prevented from following them by the same difficulty which proved insoluble to Mendelssohn—that of finding a libretto to suit his fancy.

'He was always particularly animated when speaking of matters connected with the theatre, as for instance when he once very decidedly demonstrated to me the vaudeville character of the first act of "Fidelio," which generally passes for a very good text-book. He possessed a genuine dramatic perception, and it gave him real pleasure to analyze the merits and defects of a dramatic subject.'[35]

The interest of this passage is enhanced by a few words that occur in an article on Brahms by Richard Heuberger:[36]

'We sat together the whole evening and I remember that Brahms spoke in detail of Mozart's "Figaro" and laid stress on the unparalleled manner in which Mozart has overcome the enormous difficulties of his text; "Mozart has composed it, not as a mere ordinary text-book, but as a complete, well-organized comedy."'

It would certainly have been matter for surprise if Brahms, who was peculiarly sensitive to the influence of really poetic dramatic effect, and whose interest in the drama furnished him with a source of frequent pleasure that did not diminish as he grew older—he rarely missed a première at the Vienna Burg Theater—had passed through life without feeling the inclination to test his powers as a composer for the stage, and this is very far indeed from being the case. Widmann's account of what took place between himself and Brahms on the subject of opera belongs to the late seventies, and we shall revert to it in its place; it points back, however, to an earlier time, which proves, as we might expect, to be that of the composer's intimacy with Devrient and Levi, with whose varied professional activity he manifested the warmest sympathy, and especially to the year 1869, when the publication of the German Requiem had left his mind at leisure for new important effort. Perhaps we may perceive the direction in which his wishes were moving in the fact that 'Rinaldo,' which contains the nearest approach to dramatic composition to be found in the catalogue of Brahms' works, was completed almost simultaneously with the Requiem; and it is possible that an indication of the obstacle that was to prove insuperable to their fulfilment may be read in Billroth's words quoted in the last chapter: 'Brahms is enthusiastic about [the text of] Rinaldo because it leaves so much to the composer.' However this may be, it is certain that he was strongly possessed at this period and on into the early seventies with the desire to compose an opera, and that he not only opened his mind unreservedly on the subject to his friends at Carlsruhe, but made repeated efforts in other directions to procure a libretto adapted to his views. Allgeyer furnished him with a completed text-book on Calderon's 'The Open Secret.' Through Claus Groth he obtained an unused text written for Mendelssohn by the poet Geibel, founded on the episode of Nausikaa in the 'Odyssey,'[37] and amongst others with whom he discussed the subject were Tourgenieff at Baden-Baden, who provided him with sketches, and, Heinrich Bulthaupt, then a rising young dramatic author and an intimate friend of Reinthaler's.

To Bulthaupt he proposed as a subject Schiller's fragment of a play 'Demetrius,' which he esteemed very highly, and, in a long conversation with this gentleman at his house in Bremen, he explained with precision his ideas as to the desirable treatment even of the minutiæ of dramatic action, taking as the theme of his exposition the libretto, written by Bulthaupt, of Reinthaler's opera 'Kätchen von Heilbronn.' Some of the peculiarities of his views which created for him unnecessary difficulties must be attributed to his inveterately logical habit of mind, which made it repugnant to him to take certain things for granted for the sake of stage exigencies. He went too far in a desire that the minor details of the drama should be visibly developed. Pointing to a scene in 'Kätchen von Heilbronn,' in the course of which three soldiers go into a drinking cellar, not to reappear, he inquired: 'What becomes of them?' 'It is assumed that they go away,' replied Bulthaupt; 'do you mean to say that you wish actually to see them come out again on to the stage?' 'I should like to do so,' Brahms answered. A moment's reflection would, of course, have shown him that the scene in question was, in fact, realistic, since the soldiers might in actual life have left the cellar by a back-door, unseen by those who observed them enter through the front one. The anecdote is, however, illustrative of a mental habit which must have confronted Brahms with countless difficulties so long as he merely contemplated the composition of an opera. The work of composing one, had he ever settled down to it, might probably have solved many of them.

The idea of 'Demetrius' fell through. Bulthaupt suggested to Brahms a consideration which, in no way applicable to Schiller's piece, seemed to him of importance in view of its adaptation as an opera. He thought that the necessity of introducing some amount of Russian colouring into the music of a drama having for its subject an episode of Russian history, not only might prove irksome to a composer so strongly imbued as Brahms with the sentiment of German nationality, but would be prejudicial to the tragic breadth of Schiller's play as it stands. Brahms, on thinking over the matter, probably felt the weight of his friend's remarks, for he did not return to his proposal.

Points of interest in the composer's suggestion of Schiller's 'Demetrius' for the subject of a tragic opera are that ambition and not love is the mainspring of its action, and that the feminine interest of the piece is centred neither in maiden nor wife, but in Marfa, the mother of Demetrius, in whom are exhibited powerful emotions arising from unerring maternal instinct and baffled affection. It recalls the period, moreover, when Brahms and Joachim shared each other's daily thoughts on all subjects. Joachim composed an overture to Hermann Grimm's play of 'Demetrius' in 1854, and, about the middle of the seventies, the well-known 'Marfa' scena for contralto and orchestra from Schiller's fragment. A similar association is presented in Brahms' favourite suggestion for the text-book of a serio-comic opera or operetta, of Gozzi's 'König Hirsch,' the work with which Joachim's 'Overture to a Play of Gozzi's' is to be connected. Arrangements by Brahms of both these compositions of his friend, as pianoforte duets, were found in his rooms after his death, and were published with the very few manuscripts that he allowed to survive him.

Brahms travelled to Carlsruhe in March in order to conduct the repetition performance of the German Requiem, but except for this journey spent the early part of the year 1869 quietly in Vienna. The advance of spring induced him to pay some visits in the north, after which he proceeded to Lichtenthal. The event of the season in Frau Schumann's private circle was the marriage of her third daughter Julie to the Conte Radicati di Marmorito. The legend of an attachment between Brahms and this lady has obtained sufficiently wide credence to demand mention in our pages. It is, perhaps, not unnatural that the composer's dedication to Fräulein Julie Schumann of his Variations for two pianofortes on her father's theme, published in 1863, should have led a few enthusiasts to draw their own romantic conclusions, and that such conclusions should have spread; the less so since Fräulein Julie was possessed of a graceful charm that made her interesting to all who were brought into near contact with her. Brahms was not an exception from others in his power of appreciating her attraction, but his admiration of his old friend's daughter at no time advanced into special intimacy. 'I have spent the summer at Baden, and am going to remain for Julie Schumann's wedding,' he writes to Dietrich. Brahms, Levi, and Allgeyer together presented the bride with an *objet d'art*, a bronze plate, and are represented contemplating it in a group in a photograph of the time. The Contessa Radicati di Marmorito was taken by death from her husband and children after a few years of happiness.

The completed musical fruits of Brahms' year were the Liebeslieder Walzer and the Rhapsody for contralto solo, men's chorus and orchestra. The 'Liebeslieder,' waltzes for pianoforte duet and *ad libitum* vocal quartet, composed to a number of verses from Daumer's 'Polydora,' translations or imitations of Russian and Polish folk-songs, are amongst the most popular of the composer's works, and are too familiar to need detailed comment. They show Brahms in his perfection of dainty grace and fresh, playful imagination, a mood in which he stands unrivalled. They were performed for the first time in public at the subscription concert of the Carlsruhe court orchestra of October 6. Frau Schumann, who played Beethoven's G major Concerto on the same occasion, and Levi, were the pianists, and Fräulein Hausmann, Frau Hauser, Herr Kürner, and Herr Brouillet, the singers. Published shortly afterwards by Simrock, they were heard in Vienna before the close of the year at the first Singakademie concert of the season; and were performed at Frau Schumann's concert in Vienna of January 5, 1870, by the concert-giver and composer and the singers Frau Dustmann, Fräulein Girzik, Herr Gustav Walter, and Dr. Krauss.

The Rhapsody was first heard privately at the rehearsal of the Carlsruhe concert of October 6, Levi having arranged a performance for the benefit of Frau Schumann and of Brahms himself. The solo was sung by Frau Boni. The composer, writing to Deiters in September, says:

'... I should like to make a request to-day. I remember to have seen at your house a volume of songs by Reichhardt (possibly Zelter) which contained a stanza from Goethe's Harzreise. Could you lend me the volume for a little while?

'I need hardly add that I have just composed it and should like to see the work of my forerunner. I call my piece "Rhapsody," but believe I am indebted also for the title to my respected predecessor.

'I shall hear it in a few days, and should I then decide not to print or perform the somewhat intimate music, I shall nevertheless show it to you.'[38]

It seems probable, from the circumstances of the first public performance of the Rhapsody, that Madame Viardot-Garcia was amongst the small audience on this private occasion. The work was given on March 3, 1870, soon after its publication, at the Academic Concerts, Jena, under the direction of the society's conductor, Dr. Ernst Naumann, when Madame Viardot sang the solo; 'Rinaldo,' with Dr. Wiedemann as tenor, being included in the programme.

Madame Viardot-Garcia, staying early in 1870 with Liszt, who had returned to Weimar in 1869 after an absence of many years, met at his house his devoted friend Geheimrath Gille, a distinguished musical amateur, who occupied an official post at Jena and employed the greater part of his leisure in the interest of the musical culture of the little university town. Gille had in his youth known Goethe and Hummel, and been on terms of close friendship with Henselt. His intimacy with Liszt dated from the commencement of the great man's residence in Weimar, and he soon became a warm supporter of the New-German party, received Wagner into his house at Jena on his flight from Dresden to Liszt at Weimar, and saw him safely over the German border. His sympathy with the new tendencies did not render him insensible to the value of less revolutionary developments of art. He had great interest and respect to spare for Brahms' music, and encouraged its cultivation by Brendel's society (Allgemeiner Deutscher Musikverein), on the committee of which he was very active.[39] There can be little doubt that the performance of the Rhapsody at Jena in March was the outcome of a friendly chat between Madame Viardot and himself and of their mutual sympathetic admiration of Brahms' art, which was shared by Dr. Ernst Naumann, an old personal acquaintance of the composer. Since the performance of the German Requiem in 1869 already chronicled, up to the present day, Brahms' music has been well represented in the programmes of the Jena societies under Naumann's direction.

The Rhapsody was given on March 19 under Grimm at Münster, and a little later at Capellmeister Hegar's benefit concert at Zürich. It became a favourite work with Frau Joachim, who sang the solo times innumerable with extraordinary power and sympathy and invariable success.

Brahms' Rhapsody, Op. 53, is composed to a fragment—set also by J. F. Reichhardt (1752-1814)—from Goethe's 'Harzreise im Winter,' which has for its subject the poet's reflections on a visit paid by him to a young hypochondriac whose melancholy had, as he feared, been confirmed by the influence of his own 'Werther's Sorrows.' Goethe's efforts to raise the youth from his state of mental depression had no immediate visible result, though he ultimately recovered from his malady, and the three verses selected from the poem for musical composition conclude with a prayer to the Father of love on his behalf. Such a text was eminently suited for musical expression by a composer who, intensely realizing the problems of life, shaped his course by faith in the power of love; and the Rhapsody furnishes another striking illustration of the strength of imagination which enabled Brahms so to absorb himself in his text as to be able to present it in musical sound—to capable listeners—with a strength and reality usually associated only with impressions of sight. Let anyone who is familiar with the composition read through Goethe's poem from beginning to end, and note the accession of force with which the verses set to music by Brahms come home to him. He will be reminded of an object illuminated by sunlight that stands near others placed in shadow.

The first of the three sections of the single movement that constitutes the Rhapsody, an impressive orchestral picture upon which the independent recitative of the solo voice enters, may be accepted as the reflection of the poet's intense realization of the unhappy youth's condition. Its tones convey a penetrating impression of rich warmth and pity lying behind the deepest gloom. The feeling of the second section is no less concentrated, though it is expressed with more calm:

'Ah! how comfort his sorrows
Who in balsam found poison?
Who from the fulness of love
Hath drunk but the hate of men?
Once despised, now a despiser,
Secretly he consumeth
All his own best worth
In fruitless self-seeking.'

The noble declamatory passages of the voice are supported by an accompaniment that becomes agitated or intensely still in accord with the course of the poet's self-questionings, which reach their only possible and beautiful resolution in the third section:

'If thy Psalt'ry containeth,
Father of love, one tone
That can reach his ear,
Oh, refresh his heart!
Open his obscurèd sight
To the thousand sources
Near to the thirsty one
In the desert.'

Here, by a fine inspiration, the chorus of men's voices enters for the first time *pianissimo*, supporting the solo voice in fervent supplication.

Words and music are fitly associated throughout the movement, which is a treasure amongst works of art, and it is impossible to say that either of its parts is superior to the others, though the divine outpouring of love and pity in the last section often seems to appeal, especially, to the hearer listening for the first time to the composition. This, however, is really due to its position, which contains and brings to an issue the effect of what precedes it. The work has long since been generally recognised as one of the finest of Brahms' shorter compositions, and continues to be more in demand every year, though it had no great immediate success.

'I send you my Rhapsody,' Brahms wrote to Dietrich in February, 1870, a week or two after its publication; 'the music-directors are not exactly enthusiastic about the opus, but it may, perhaps, be a satisfaction to you that I do not always go in frivolous 3/4 time!'

It sprang from the composer's very soul.

'He once told me he loved it so,' says Dietrich, 'that he placed it under his pillow at night in order to have it near him.'

The Studies without opus number, Nos. 1 and 2, after Chopin and Weber, were published in 1869 by Senff; and the first two books of Hungarian Dances by Simrock, in the duet form for Pianoforte in which they obtained enormous popularity. It was not until 1872 that they were issued in the arrangement as solos, in which, as we know, they had formed part of Brahms' répertoire during some years of his virtuoso career.[40] Dunkl, a publisher of Budapest, used to relate in after-years that Brahms, on the occasion of one of his early appearances in that city, called on him and offered a selection of six of the Dances for an absurdly small sum. Dunkl said he would give his answer after hearing them in the evening. They had no success and the publisher refused them, a proceeding which he afterwards found considerable reason to regret.

The stirring events of the year 1870, the series of triumphs won by German arms, and the federation of the various independent States under the headship of Prussia which was to lead to the extraordinary development of German political power and industrial progress that has been witnessed by the present generation, were followed by our composer with a mixture of ardent emotions, in which that of swelling patriotic pride gained the predominance as each day brought news of fresh victories won by the soldiers of the Fatherland. His vehement exultation at the results of the war found embodiment in a great 'Song of Triumph' for chorus and orchestra, with which he was occupied in 1871, and the first chorus, completed early in the year, and sent at once to Reinthaler, was performed from the manuscript in Bremen Cathedral on Good Friday, April 7, under the composer's direction, at a concert given by the Singakademie in memory of those who had fallen in the war.[41] There is no need to dilate on the feelings which dominated Brahms during the writing of this extraordinary work. They blaze out of it with an intensity and an endurance of passion that well fit it to occupy its own peculiar place amongst the great events that startled Europe at the opening of the seventies. It commemorates heroic deeds in truly heroic strains. By his choice of a text the composer at once raised the scope of his work to a level above that of an ordinary *Te Deum* for victory in war; and the words selected by him from Revelation xix., which admit, throughout each portion of the composition, of an application to the overpowering occurrences of the time, were precisely those for whose setting he alone of modern composers—we may even say of all composers who have succeeded the two giants of the eighteenth century—was, by his temperament, genius, and attainments, pre-eminently fitted.

The Triumphlied consists of three great movements for double chorus and orchestra, the third of which contains a few passages for baritone solo.

'*Alleluia; salvation and glory and honour and power unto the Lord our God: For true and righteous are his judgments.*'

The solemnly jubilant orchestral prelude, the entry of the full double chorus with loud and sustained Alleluias, lead to the principal theme of the first movement, already suggested in the prelude, and derived—though this is hardly appreciable by the unpractised ear of a general audience—from the Prussian national air, which is identical with England's 'God save the King.' This theme or some portion of it almost invariably accompanies the phrase, '*Salvation, honour*, etc., *unto the Lord*,' which, with its surrounding Alleluias, forms the text of the first portion of the movement, constructed entirely from diatonic harmonies. The words '*For righteous and true are his judgments*' are set to the broad themes of the middle portion, to which some heightened effect is imparted by very sparing use of the more familiar chromatic chords. The third section is a varied repetition of the first with a coda. The movement is sustained at the white heat of jubilation until the beginning of the close, when a few tranquil bars, in the course of which the voices die away to rest, and the instruments are subdued to a *pianissimo* that becomes ever softer, prepare for the glorious outburst with which the chorus terminates. The second movement has three varying sections:

'*Praise our God, all ye his servants, and ye that fear him, great and small.*

'*Alleluia, for the Almighty God hath entered into his kingdom.*

'*Let us be glad and rejoice and give honour to him.*'

The first section opens with pure melodious beauty and lofty serenity, and displays in its course numerous points of imitation, direct and by inversion, which are easily discoverable by the student. It is succeeded by a blast of trumpets, an outburst of Alleluias, and the announcement of the Lord's reign by the voices of the two choirs which enter successively on a sounding tonic pedal; the basses imitating the basses, then the tenors the tenors, and so on, at half a bar's distance. This proclamation section is appropriately concise and of superb grandeur. We hear in it 'as it were the voice of a multitude, and as the voice of many waters, and as the voice of mighty thunderings'; whilst the third section, partly woven, by various kinds of imitation, from the phrases of 'Nun danket Alle Gott,' which is sounded prominently by the flutes and trumpets, is animated by a singularly naïve spirit of light-hearted happiness and rejoicing.

'*And I saw heaven opened, and behold a white horse: and he that sat upon him was called Faithful and True, and in righteousness he doth judge and make war.*

'*And he treadeth, the winepress of the fierceness and wrath of Almighty God.*

'*And he hath on his vesture and on his thigh a name called a King of Kings and a Lord of Lords. Alleluia. Amen.*'

Subdued awe; firm, proud confidence in a mighty, beneficent ruler; a flash of fierce remembrance of injury—all are rendered with a power, a vividness, a picturesque strength, that are not transcended, even if they are equalled, by anything ever composed in the domain of choral music for the church or the concert-room; and the greatness and glory of 'a King of Kings and a Lord of Lords' are celebrated in the long final portion of this gorgeous third movement with dazzling brilliancy of effect, sustained and augmented up to the very end.

The first chorus, performed before the audience of two thousand people assembled in Bremen Cathedral on the evening of Good Friday, 1871, reached its effect to a very considerable extent.

'It has a broad and, as it were, popular character, is conceived simply and wrought with sincerity,' writes the correspondent of the *Allgemeine Deutsche Musikzeitung*.'

The *Bremen Courier* says:

'One again recognises the titanic capacity of the composer. The work is a vocal joy-symphony, of imposing power and exalted feeling. Praise is due to all concerned in the performance for they have facilitated the understanding of the composer to a large portion of the audience.'

The Dietrichs came from Oldenburg to hear the new work. Circumstances prevented the attendance of Frau Schumann and Joachim. Neither artist had returned from what had at this period become an annual visit of each to England, which, in Frau Schumann's case, generally extended over at least two months, and in Joachim's occupied the six weeks of Lent.

Pending Frau Schumann's return, Brahms remained among his friends in the north, and played his D minor Concerto at the Bremen orchestral subscription concert of April 25 with great success, giving pieces by Bach, Scarlatti, and Schumann in the second part. Frau Schumann was back in Lichtenthal early in May, and Brahms settled into his usual lodgings there a few days before her arrival. The present writer had the happiness of immediately following her, and the reader interested to learn particulars of the summer life of quiet work and simple pleasures that followed is referred to the Recollections placed at the beginning of our first volume. The details there given are too slight and too personal to be appropriate in the body of the present narrative, though they may be found to have a value of their own for those interested in whatever throws additional light on the true, lovable nature of Brahms.

It was about this time that our composer's art began to make perceptible progress in London. No immediate result was perceptible from the performance of the B flat Sextet led by Joachim at a Monday Popular concert of 1867, but from the beginning of the seventies we find Brahms' name appearing with some regularity in London programmes. No opportunity was lost by Frau Schumann, Joachim, or Stockhausen for making propaganda for their friend's music in private artistic circles. The performance of the Requiem at Sir Henry Thompson's house in the summer of 1871, under Stockhausen, has already been noted. Of minor incidents of the time in this connection, the singing of two duets from Op. 28 by Madame Viardot-Garcia and Stockhausen at a party given by the lady in London on June 10 may be selected for mention.[42]

In the same year the call of Bernhard Scholz to Breslau added another to the list of towns, now to increase rapidly, year by year, in which Brahms' art came to be cultivated with particular vigour. Scholz, who had held successive appointments in Hanover and Berlin, had been on terms of familiar acquaintance with the composer from an early period of both their careers. He now found himself in a position, as conductor of the Breslau orchestral subscription concerts, freely to gratify his admiration of the master's art. From this time not only were Brahms' new orchestral works given, with few exceptions as they appeared, at the Breslau subscription concerts, but any existing deficiencies in the Brahms education of the musical public were supplied by performances of the two Serenades and the Pianoforte Concerto. The composer himself played the last-named work at

Breslau in 1874 and 1876, when the orchestra was of course conducted by Scholz. No less attention was devoted to the chamber music. At the concerts of the resident string quartet-party arranged by Concertmeister Richard Himmelstoss, at which Scholz or Julius Buths often assisted as pianist, the two Sextets, the Quartets and Quintet, and later works in their turn, were frequently heard, and to the successful results of these efforts, to the warm response they elicited from the musical circles of Breslau, we owe the composition of a genial and now favourite work of our master, the Academic Festival Overture, the appearance of which will be noted in its place.

Amongst the friends who visited Lichtenthal during the summer of 1871 were Allgeyer, Levi, and Stockhausen, and on September 8 the 'Song of Destiny,' completed in May, was rehearsed at Carlsruhe.

'Hyperion's Schicksalslied,' by Friedrich Hölderlin (1770-1834), sets forth the serene, passionless, unchanging existence of the celestials, surrounded by the clear light of eternity; and its contrast, the ever-shifting, suffering life of humanity, wrapped in the darkness of inscrutable mystery. The poem is entirely fatalistic, containing no comment on what it depicts.

'Ye wander above in light
On tender soil, blessed immortals!
Glistening divine breezes
Touch you gently,
As the fingers of the artist
Sacred strings.

'Calm as the sleeping child
Breathe the celestials;
Chastely guarded
In modest bud,
Their spirits bloom eternally,
And their blissful eyes
Gaze in quiet, eternal stillness.

'But to us it is given
On no spot to rest;
Suffering men
Vanish, blindly fall
From hour to hour,
As water thrown
From rock to rock,
Year-long down into uncertainty.'

In Brahms' setting we have yet another fine choral work, characteristic from every point of view, musical, æsthetic, and psychological—one, moreover, which is of quite peculiar interest and value, since it contains an express confession of that creed of love to which the present writer has several times referred as being traceable throughout the composer's life and works. The contrasted pictures of celestial and human existence are set with the vivid force which we have noticed in our brief studies of preceding works, the pathos and tragedy surrounding the lot of mankind being treated with the deep, passionate feeling which is invariably displayed by the composer when he is occupied with this or kindred subjects. Brahms' 'Song of Destiny' does not, however, terminate with Hölderlin's, nor could it have done so. Another passion lived stronger within him than that with which he contemplated the phenomena of human suffering, uncertainty, and death; and he has known how to supplement his text with a short, but most exquisitely conceived, orchestral postlude, which, whilst it rounds the work musically into a whole, brings to the despairing soul a message of consolation, hope, faith, courage, such as it is within the peculiar province of music to convey, and which has the more power over the heart since it cannot be translated into articulate words.

That Brahms actually had some such intention in adding the postlude is in the personal knowledge of the present writer. He regarded it as not merely accessory, but as being, in a sense, the most important part of his composition. In rehearsing the work, it was over this portion that he lingered with peculiar care; and when conducting its performance he obtained from the postlude some of his rarest and most exquisite effects of ethereal tenderness.

The work was performed for the first time from the manuscript on October 18, 1871, under the composer's direction, at a concert of the Carlsruhe Philharmonic Society. The overture and garden-scene from Schumann's 'Faust' headed, and the conclusion of the second part—both under Levi's direction—closed the programme, which further included two of Schubert's songs. Fräulein Johanna Schwarz and Stockhausen were the soloists of the occasion.

The impression made by the new work upon the audience of Carlsruhe was profound, and the composer returned to Vienna gratified and pleased by an immediate success which the experiences of his career had by no means led him to regard as a foregone conclusion.

The Schicksalslied was published by Simrock in December, and was performed early in 1872 in Bremen, Breslau, Frankfurt, and Vienna.

The only other original publications of 1871, the two books of Songs, Op. 57 and 58, were issued by Rieter-Biedermann.[43] All the texts of Op. 57 are original poems or imitations (Nos. 2, 3, 7) by G. F. Daumer, whose texts are amongst the most passionate of those set by Brahms. The composer seems to have imagined a portrait of the poet more or less in correspondence with his verses, and Claus Groth tells an amusing story of the shock sustained by Brahms on taking the opportunity of a visit to Munich to call on Daumer.

'I loaded myself with all the books of my songs that contain something of his. I found him at last, in an out-of-the-way house, in an out-of-the-way street, and was shown to equally retired apartments. There in a quiet room I found my poet. Ah, he was a little dried-up old man! After my sincerely respectful address, on presenting my music, the old gentleman replied with an embarrassed word of thanks and I soon perceived that he knew nothing either of me or my compositions, or anything at all of music. And when I pointed to his ardent, passionate verses, he signed me, with a tender wave of the hand, to a little old mother almost more withered than himself, saying, "Ah, I have only loved the one, my wife!"'

The opening of the year 1872 marks the beginning of a new period, not in the artistic, but in the private life of Brahms. It found him installed in the historic rooms in the third story of No. 4, Carlsgasse, Vienna, which were to remain to the end of his life the nearest approach to an establishment of his own to which he committed himself. He had lodged in Novaragasse, Singerstrasse, Poststrasse 6, Wohlzeile 23, Ungargasse 2, had stayed with his friends the Fabers—had, in fact, since his first visit to Vienna, changed his residence at least with each new season. When he took possession of his rooms in Carlsgasse 4 on December 27, 1871, he had moved for the last time. Here he lived for a little more than a quarter of a century, here he died. He continued as he began, a lodger in furnished apartments, renting his Carlsgasse rooms in the first instance from a Frau Vogel, who, with her husband and family, occupied the rest of the dwelling. Brahms' accommodation consisted of three small rooms communicating one with the other. The middle and largest contained his grand piano and writing-table, a small square-shaped instrument to which a tradition was attached, and a table and chairs arranged, German fashion, in front of a sofa. Here he received his visitors. In a smaller room were his bookshelves and a high desk for standing to write. There were cupboards for his music, which in time overflowed into the rooms as he required more space for his collections of original manuscripts, engravings, photographs, etc. A few engravings adorned the walls, and his little bust of Beethoven reminded him pleasantly of the old home in the Fuhlentwiethe. Frau Vogel was responsible only for his mending, for the cleaning and dusting of his rooms, and for opening the house-door to visitors. He took his early dinner at a restaurant—the 'Kronprinz,' the 'Goldspinnerin,' the 'Zur schönen

Laterne,' and, for about the last fourteen years of his life, at the 'Zum rothen Igel,' in the Wildpret Markt—and read the newspapers afterwards over a cup of black coffee at one of the coffee-houses, in his latter years generally the Café Stadtpark. He supped either at home, with a book for company—when his fare usually consisted of bread-and-butter and sausage, with a glass of beer or light wine—or again at a restaurant, when, as at dinner, he liked to be joined by his intimates. Needless to say, the private hospitality of friends was abundantly at his command whenever he chose to avail himself of it.

The second performance of the Song of Destiny—the first since publication—took place at the Gesellschaft concert of January 21, under the direction of Anton Rubinstein, who held the post of 'artistic director' of the society during the season 1870-71, succeeding Herbeck on his appointment as capellmeister of the imperial opera.

The gratification which must have been felt by the composer at the exceptional impression created by his work on his Austrian public was to be clouded a few days later by news of his father's grave illness. Jakob had been ailing for a year past, and had been obliged to resign his post at the Philharmonic, together with smaller engagements, and accustom himself to the sight of his beloved double-bass standing mute in a corner of his parlour. Johannes, perceiving that advancing years were beginning to tell on his father, had prescribed a change of residence from the fourth story of 1, Anscharplatz to a first-floor flat in the same street, but the failure of strength had not been recognised as serious. Jakob did not complain of any particular symptoms, and it was only on the occasion of his fetching the doctor to his stepson Fritz Schnack, who had been brought home ill from St. Petersburg, that he bethought himself to ask advice on his own account, when his alarming condition became immediately apparent to the physician. Johannes, who was immediately sent for, was on the spot without delay, and spent the next fortnight at the bedside of the stricken man, whom he watched with tenderest care and tried to cheer with loving encouragement. But the end was near. Jakob was in the grip of a fatal malady which had ravaged his constitution continuously during the past twelve months, though his sufferings were neither acute nor prolonged. He died on February 11, in his sixty-sixth year, from cancer of the liver, in the presence of his wife and two sons, and an estrangement of some duration between Johannes and the less energetic Fritz—returned from two years' absence in Venezuela—was healed at his death-bed. The son's grief, as may be expected from all that we have related of his clinging family affection, was profound. His consolation was found in endeavours for the protection and comfort of the woman who had brought contentment to the closing years of Jakob's life, and he stayed on with Frau Caroline after the funeral, helping her to make necessary arrangements and to look through his father's little possessions. The old indentures of apprenticeship, the document of citizenship, memorials of Jakob's early struggles and modest personal successes, passed into the composer's keeping. A small portrait in oils, of little value as a picture, but bearing evidence of having been a good likeness of Jakob in his early manhood, was left with the widow. 'Mother,' said Johannes excitedly the day before his departure from Hamburg, turning suddenly to Frau Caroline after standing for some minutes in silence before the painting, 'as long as you live, this of course is yours, but promise that at your death it shall come to me in Vienna!' The promise, readily given, was destined to remain unfulfilled. Frau Caroline, her stepson's senior by more than six years, was to outlive him.

Brahms' care for his father's widow did not cease with his return to his occupations in Vienna. When Fritz Schnack was convalescent, and the year sufficiently advanced for change of air to be desirable, he was sent with his mother to Pinneberg, a pleasant country town of Holstein in great repute with the citizens of Hamburg on account of its health-giving climate. The visit proved so beneficial that Johannes decided to settle his stepbrother there permanently to carry on the business of a watch and clock maker, which he had hitherto followed in St. Petersburg. He established him in a pleasant shop, providing him with all the requisites for a new start, and wished to guarantee a comfortable home for Frau Caroline as mistress of her son's modest household; but the bright, energetic widow did not like the idea of relinquishing her own activity. It was settled, therefore, that she should return to Hamburg and to her business of taking boarders in the first-floor flat in the Anscharplatz, on the condition, rigorously extorted by Johannes, that she was to draw upon him in all cases of need for herself or her son. Brahms was wont to complain to his stepmother in after-years that she did not sufficiently fulfil her part of the bargain, to scold her because she did not ask for money, and to propose and insist on holiday journeys for herself and Fritz; and from the day of his father's death to that of his own the kind, capable housewife continued to be the representative to the great tone-poet of the simple, restful tie of family affection to which he clung from beginning to end of his career.

Elise Brahms was supported by her brother until her marriage, some time later than our present date, with a watchmaker named Grund, a widower with a family, and was the recipient of his generosity until her death in 1892. Fritz, 'the wrong Brahms,' as he was sometimes called, by way of distinguishing him from Johannes, gained a good position in Hamburg as a private teacher of the pianoforte, and was for some years on the staff of visiting teachers at Fräulein Homann's ladies' school at Hamm—an establishment which enjoyed distinguished English as well as German patronage. He had only so far followed in his brother's footsteps as to have been the pupil successively of Cossel and Marxsen, and to have made a few public appearances in Hamburg as pianist in his own Trio concerts. His talents might have carried him farther if he had been more active and ambitious. 'Is this your pianoforte-teacher's pace?' demanded Johannes sharply on one of his visits to Hamburg, as he was striding along the street in front of his brother, who could not or would not keep up with him. Fritz was a favourite with his friends; he possessed his share of the family humour, and was never known to brag. 'How is your great brother?' an acquaintance asked him one day. 'What do you mean?' retorted Fritz, who was tall and thin; 'I am bigger than he is!' He died unmarried in Hamburg in 1886, at the age of fifty-one.

Preliminary arrangements were made in good time for the performance of the completed Triumphlied at the Rhine Festival of 1872, held in Düsseldorf; but as the date drew near the committee strangely refused to invite the composer to conduct his work, and Brahms therefore withheld the manuscript. It was performed for the first time on June 5 at a farewell concert arranged by the Grand-Ducal Orchestra and the Philharmonic Society of Carlsruhe jointly, for their departing conductor Hermann Levi, who had been called to the post of court capellmeister at Munich, which he held with brilliant success until failing health compelled his retirement in 1896. Both Frau Schumann and Stockhausen contributed to the programme of the concert, Stockhausen, as a matter of course, singing the short solo of the Triumphlied. The performance seems to have been a fine one, though the chorus at command only numbered 150 members. An enthusiastic account of the work sent from Carlsruhe to the *Allgemeine Musikzeitung* by Franz Gehring concludes:

'We Germans may feel proud that such an artist has been inspired by the impression of the most momentous events to which our history can point, to the composition of such a triumph-song. To the year 1870 attaches, not only the renown of our arms, but a new epoch of our musical art.... It is based upon the modern development of long familiar forms and modes of expression. That this development has shown itself to be true and healthy (who had not foreseen it in Brahms' German Requiem!) is the merit of the German master Brahms, the greatest of the present day!'

Comparatively few musicians will be found in these days to deny that Gehring's words were justified by the development of Brahms' own career, though it cannot be concealed that a new epoch such as that to which the reviewer looked forward seems to have closed for the present with the master's death.

Contrary to Brahms' established custom, he accepted a concert-engagement in the course of the summer, and appeared with immense success at the Baden-Baden Kursaal subscription concert of August 29 as composer, conductor, and pianist, with his own A major Serenade and Schumann's Pianoforte Concerto. Amongst the visitors to Lichtenthal in the course of the season was Reinthaler, who had been present at the performance of the Triumphlied at Carlsruhe, and returned later to spend a short holiday near his friends.

With the beginning of autumn, 1872, a period of ten years had elapsed since Brahms' first visit to Vienna, and it will help the reader to obtain a clear view of the development of his career as a composer if we pause for a moment at this point, to consider what had been its special features during the decade in the course of which he had gradually come to regard Vienna as his home. We shall find that it had been entirely logical and continuous, and singularly independent of those influences of his changed environment to which imaginary effects on his art and temperament have not seldom been attributed.

We observe, in the first place, that only one solo has been added to the long list of important works for the pianoforte, accompanied and unaccompanied, which Brahms carried with him to Vienna in 1862, and of this one it must be said that the Paganini studies in two books, immensely brilliant and ingenious though they be, cannot be seriously regarded from the musical standpoint of the Handel or other preceding sets of variations, but must be accepted more or less as diversions of the composer's leisure hours. Several of the variations are little more than transcriptions for the piano of some of those written by Paganini on the same theme for the violin.

In the domain of chamber music, where, so far as it is yet possible to anticipate the verdict of posterity, Brahms' place will be found amongst the greatest composers of all periods, we find that his first series of masterpieces for pianoforte and strings has been brought to a close with the addition of two works—the Horn Trio performed in the autumn of 1865, and the Sonata in E minor for pianoforte and violoncello, whilst by the side of the String Sextet in B flat has been placed another in G major, not indeed transcending, but different from, and in every way worthy of, its companion. With the enumeration of these published works must be associated the mention of two others of peculiar interest in our survey because they mark a fresh stage of Brahms' matured development. The two String Quartets in C minor and A minor were kept in the composer's desk for some years before they were finally completed. The significance of their appearance, which we shall have to note in 1873, as landmarks in Brahms' career, is best illustrated by the remembrance that twenty years had elapsed since the fastidious self-criticism of the young musician of twenty had caused the withdrawal of a string quartet from the list of works proposed by Schumann for the consideration of the publishers.

Brahms' fertility as a song-writer for a single voice was constant, though it matured and varied in its manifestations with the onward progress of his life. We have already referred to some of the phases of its long middle period. The decade we are considering witnessed the publication of eight books of miscellaneous songs and three books of the Magelone Romances.

In the Liebeslieder, waltzes for pianoforte duet and vocal quartet, we have the riper artistic fruition of the mood which produced the vocal quartets, Op. 31, 'Alternative Dance Song,' 'Raillery,' and 'The Walk to the Beloved,' composed at Detmold; and to the same early period the Waltzes for pianoforte duet dedicated to Hanslick primarily belong.

The splendid achievement, however, which pre-eminently distinguishes this portion of Brahms' career is to be found in another domain: that in which we may now, in 1872, contemplate the literal fulfilment of Schumann's much discussed prophecy; that in which 'the masses of chorus and orchestra *have* lent him their powers.' The composer has most truly 'sunk his magic staff and revealed to us wondrous glimpses of the spirit world.' The period which produced the German Requiem, the Song of Destiny, and the Song of Triumph (1866-1871) could hardly be surpassed in the brilliancy of its own special branch of achievement, and with the completion of the last of these works the growth of Brahms' powers upon this particular line of development had reached its summit. The choral works in which the master hand of the great composer was to be again revealed, whilst they afford additional opportunities of enjoyment to the lovers of his art, could not, from the nature of those that had preceded them, increase the lustre of his fame.

Of works for orchestra alone the two Serenades published in 1860 are still the only examples. As we have seen,[44] Brahms, in the summer of 1862, showed Dietrich the first movement of the C minor Symphony, 'which appeared, greatly altered, much later on,'[45] but since then the composer's invariable answer to his friend's inquiries had been that the time for a symphony had not yet arrived. The ten years we are considering are, in fact, characteristic of the composer as well by their silence as by their song. We cannot doubt that just as his choral works were the ultimate outcome of a long period of retirement and study, of which we have traced the early as well as the late results, so the period of his symphonic achievement was being gradually prepared for by special work as fundamental and unwearied. Of this we shall very soon have to note the perfected first-fruits on the appearance of a short orchestral composition, now amongst the most familiar and valued of the treasures with which Brahms has enriched the musical world.

CHAPTER XVI
1872-1876

Publication of the 'Triumphlied,' with a dedication to the German Emperor William I.—Brahms conducts the 'Gesellschaft concerts'—Schumann Festival at Bonn—Professor and Frau Engelmann—String Quartets—First performances—Anselm Feuerbach in Vienna—Variations for Orchestra—First performances—'Triumphlied' at Cologne, Basle, and Zürich—Resignation of appointment as 'artistic director' to the Gesellschaft—Third Pianoforte Quartet.

Brahms returned to Vienna for the concert-season of 1872-73 with a new and absorbing interest before him. He had accepted the appointment of 'artistic director' to the Gesellschaft der Musikfreunde, thereby undertaking the duties of conductor, not only of the society's concerts, but of the bi-weekly practices of its choral society. The usual scheme of the Gesellschaft concert-season, extending from about the middle of November to April, comprised four regular, and two extra, concerts with orchestra and chorus, one at least of which was devoted to an oratorio or other great choral work.

'Brahms will now conduct the Gesellschaft concerts,' writes Billroth on October 25; 'he is preparing Handel's *Te Deum* and "Saul," two Bach cantatas, his "Triumphlied," etc. At present he is all enthusiasm over the direction of the choral society, and enraptured with the voices and the musical talent of the choir. Should the results be favourable, he will, I think, persevere; a failure might suffice to discourage him so much as to deprive him of all inclination for the work....'

The season opened on November 10 with the following programme:

1. G. F. Handel:	*Te Deum* for the Dettingen celebration of victory, 1743.
2. W. A. Mozart:	Aria for Soprano, with obl. accompaniment for pianoforte and orchestra (Frau Wilt).
3. (*a*) J. Eccard: (*b*) H. Isaak:	'Ueber's Gebirg Maria geht.' 'Inspruk ich muss dich lassen.' Choruses *a capella*.
4. F. Schubert:	Symphony in C major (arranged for Orchestra from the Pianoforte Duet, Op. 140, by J. Joachim).

This selection hardly invited an enthusiastic demonstration from a mixed audience, but the performances were well received, and the occasion resulted in a substantial artistic success for Brahms, and in the removal of the doubt which had been entertained, even in some friendly quarters, as to his fitness for his new duties. The inclusion of the so-called symphony by Schubert was mentioned with disapproval by some of the papers, though the masterly instrumentation of Joachim's arrangement—made, we may add, at Schumann's suggestion—was duly acknowledged.

The second concert, the first 'extra' of the season, was in every respect brilliant. It included the second performance of the complete Triumphlied, published shortly before by Simrock with Brahms' dedication to His Majesty the Emperor William I. The original title inscribed on the manuscript of the work—'Song of Triumph on the Victory of German Arms'—was shortened on publication to the simple 'Song of Triumph.' The programme of December 6 was as follows:

1. Handel:	Concerto for Organ and Orchestra.
2. Mozart:	Offertorium for double Chorus, Orchestra, and Organ.
3. Gluck:	Aria from the opera 'Alcestis' (Frau Joachim).
4. J. S. Bach:	Prelude and Fugue in E flat for Organ.
5. J. Brahms:	Song of Triumph for Solo, eight-part Chorus, Orchestra, and Organ (solo, Dr. Krauss).

The performances of the great organ-player S. de Lange, invited from Rotterdam for the occasion, on the society's new instrument, which had been inaugurated at the previous concert by Bibl; the singing of Gluck's aria by Frau Joachim; the rendering of two choral works, both new to the audience, the productions of two masters each representative of his day, with the art history of a century lying between them, combined to make a programme of peculiar and varied interest. The Offertorium, an unpublished work composed by Mozart in his twenty-first year, was written for double chorus and organ, to which the composer afterwards added two violins. Brahms now availed himself for the support of his voices of the entire string band, and the performance of the beautiful and unfamiliar work made a great impression. It was published almost immediately by J. P. Gotthard of Vienna. The most important event of the concert was, of course, the first performance in Vienna of the performer's Song of Triumph.

'A truly magnificent work, which produced a profound and enduring impression,' says Schelle; 'the German victories have been the occasion of its composition.... Both as regards its form and its treatment of masses, this work bears the stamp of a masterpiece. The performances were excellent. The society's concerts could certainly be in no better hands.'

The Triumphlied was given a week later, December 14, in Munich, under Franz Wüllner, and was again reviewed at length in the *Allgemeine Zeitung* of the 25th in a highly interesting article by Franz Pyllemann.

'The orchestra develops truly royal splendour.... What wealth of tone-combination, what intoxicating charm of colouring, strike the ear of the listener! The knowledge shown in the use and application of the most appropriate and noble means of expression, as offered by the various instruments, must be noted with deep admiration. Brahms' mastery in the handling of chorus has long been common knowledge. He makes great demands on his singers, and does not readily restrict the development of an artistic idea on account either of their convenience or their uncertainty. But, how his choral movements sound! In this respect, the master stands nearer to the heroes of choral composition, and especially Handel, than any other modern musician. He has studied their works; he has most intimately fused their, for our time, almost enigmatical technique with the many resources of modern art; so that we might often suppose ourselves to be listening, as regards his thematic work, the polyphonic construction of his parts, to a masterpiece of the eighteenth century, whilst the character of the themes, the quality of the harmonies, the condition of the form, on the whole and in detail, are entirely modern, are quite specifically "Brahms."'

The work was given at the Gewandhaus Concerts, Leipzig, on February 27, 1873.

The effect of the second 'regular' Gesellschaft concert of the season, on January 5, 1873, was marred by a series of misfortunes. Three works were announced for performance:

1. Hiller: Concert Overture in D major.

2. Schumann: 'Des Sängers Fluch.'

3. Mendelssohn: 'Die Walpurgis Nacht.'

Hiller, who happened to be staying in Vienna, had promised to conduct his overture to 'Demetrius,' the most successful of his four works in this form, but, owing to an accident to the music, it was necessary to substitute another, which proved ineffective. The drummer was attacked by sudden illness on the day of the concert, and the substitute provided proved unequal to the emergency; Hiller was obliged to rap for silence immediately after beginning the performance of his work, and to recommence. A similar mishap attended the course of the 'Sängers Fluch,' under Brahms' direction, in consequence of a misunderstanding between the solo vocalists and the harpists. Mendelssohn's work alone went without a blemish.

A very great success was obtained at the next concert, on February 28, the second 'extra' of the season, with Handel's oratorio 'Saul,' given for the first time in Vienna. The great work was received with enthusiasm, and the performance pronounced perfect both by public and press.

This was followed, at the next 'regular' concert on March 23, by a varied programme:

1. Bach: Easter Cantata, 'Christ lag in Todesbanden.'

2. Haydn: Symphony in C major.

3. German Folk-songs for unaccompanied mixed Chorus:

(*a*) 'In stiller Nacht.'
(*b*) 'Dort in den Weiden steht ein Haus.'

4. Schubert: 'Ellen's zweites Gesang' (arranged for Soprano solo, women's Chorus, and Instruments by Brahms).

5. Beethoven: Chorus from 'Die Weihe des Hauses,' for Soprano solo, Chorus, and Orchestra.

The attitude of the audience during the early part of this concert was somewhat doubtful, the opening cantata being followed with earnestness, but with scanty demonstrations of approval. At the entry of the chorale at the close of the work, however, an electric feeling passed through the packed hall as at the release from strained attention, and the applause which followed was loud and resounding.

'It is hardly possible to bestow enough praise upon the performance of the cantata,' says Schelle (the *Presse*); 'the choral society and their conductor Brahms acquitted themselves most splendidly of their task, and warm acknowledgment is also due to Herr Organist Bibl.'

Similar praise is given to the performance of the other numbers of the programme, special mention being made of the folk-songs, one of which had to be repeated.

'In a word,' concludes the critic, 'the satisfaction caused us by the beautifully arranged concert must, we think, have been equalled by that felt by Brahms at its success.'

Billroth gives an interesting account, in a letter dated March 29, of the energy and success of Brahms' work in this new field of labour.

'Brahms is extremely active as a conductor; he has achieved incomparably fine performances, and receives the fullest recognition from all who take art earnestly. His "Triumphlied," given with organ and an immense chorus, produced a marvellous effect here; great masses are required for its performance, it is monumental music....

'At the last concert Brahms ventured upon one of the most difficult of Bach's cantatas, composed to Luther's text, "Christ lay in bonds of death," which had never before been performed. The Viennese accepted this with amiability from such a favourite as Brahms. Two unaccompanied folk-songs which came next ("In stiller Nacht" and "Der schönste Bursch am ganzen Rhein") awakened such a storm of applause, however, that one almost felt afraid the house would fall in. The old King of Hanover was almost beside himself with musical intoxication. One becomes quite drunk with the beautiful quality of sound produced by this choir, whose increase and decrease (*f.* and *p.*) are carried on like those of one voice....'

Sufficient detail has now been given of the Gesellschaft concert-season of 1872-73 to show the wisdom of the committee in their choice of a new 'artistic director,' and it only remains to mention the advertised 'last' concert of April 6. Two works were brought to a hearing:

1. Bach: Cantata, 'Liebster Gott, wann werd' ich sterben.'

2. Cherubini: Requiem in C minor.

The success of the performances may be inferred from the fact that the programme was repeated two days later at an additional concert hastily arranged to fulfil the general demand for an encore.

Brahms was singularly unfortunate this year in his efforts to secure a quiet retreat for the pursuit of his usual summer avocations. Flying, after two days' residence in lodgings in Gratwein, Styria, from the attentions of some 'æsthetic ladies' who began to threaten his peace, he took refuge in the attic of the 'Seerose,' an inn in the Bavarian village of Tutzing, on Lake Starnberg, to receive, the very night of his arrival, a formal written invitation to make one, during his stay, of a light-hearted fellowship of youthful authors, painters, and musicians who held their meetings in the house. An early hour of the morning witnessed his second abrupt departure, the only answer vouchsafed to the missive being its torn fragments scattered on the floor of his room. He took refuge this time with Levi at Munich, and made his headquarters at his friend's house during the early part of the summer, seeing much also of Allgeyer, who had been invited to settle professionally in the Bavarian capital shortly after Levi's departure from Carlsruhe. Later on Brahms attended the Schumann

Festival at Bonn (August 17-19), arranged, by Joachim's suggestion, for the purpose of assisting a fund for the erection of a memorial to Schumann in the city where the master had passed the two last sad years of his life, and where a Beethoven monument had been unveiled in 1871. There were orchestral concerts on the 17th and 18th, both conducted by Joachim, excepting in the case of one work (Wasielewsky), and a matinée of chamber music on the 19th, the programmes, in which Frau Schumann, Frau Joachim, Stockhausen, and others took part, being entirely selected from Schumann's works. The festival closed with a social function, an excursion by steamer to Rolandseck. The presence at Bonn of each member of the remarkable quartet of great musicians, whom we have seen closely bound together by ties of artistic and personal friendship through nearly twenty years, was made the more interesting by the addition of Ferdinand Hiller, the intimate ally of all four. Many other old friends were there, of whom Freiherr von Meysenbug, as reviving Detmold memories, should be particularly mentioned. Brahms made some new acquaintances also, notably Professor Engelmann and his gifted wife, known in the musical world for a few seasons as the pianist Fräulein Emma Brandes, who retired from a public career on her early marriage.

Brahms, though taking no active part in the concerts, was not at all averse to contributing to the private artistic pleasures of the week. The most memorable of these was the first introduction to a few of his friends of the Variations on a theme by Haydn, which he played with Frau Schumann in the version of the work for two pianofortes. Another day he turned into a pianoforte warehouse in the course of a walk with Wasielewsky, and sitting down before one of the instruments extemporized one waltz after another.

After leaving Bonn he paid his annual visit to Lichtenthal, where Frau Schumann and her daughters also stayed for a few weeks, though it was no longer their place of residence. They moved this year to Berlin, and in future only visited Baden-Baden for occasional change. Brahms sometimes met his old friends there in the summer until the year 1878, when Frau Schumann accepted an appointment at the Conservatoire of Music founded by Dr. Hoch at Frankfurt. She then sold her house at Lichtenthal, and Brahms' subsequent association with the neighbourhood was limited to rare visits of a few days. Frau Schumann continued to live at Frankfurt from this time, though she resigned her duties at the conservatoire some years before her death.

Meanwhile Brahms spent several weeks of this and succeeding summers at his old lodgings, and one day in August of this year he played the finally completed String Quartets in C minor and A minor, and the 'Rain-songs' to Frau Schumann. She had heard the C minor Quartet, as the reader may remember, in the summer of 1866. The composer played both works to Dr. Hermann Deiters when he was staying at Bonn in 1868.

Claus Groth's poem 'Rain-song' and the shorter one 'Echo,' which form the texts of Nos. 3 and 4 of Brahms' Op. 59, were particular favourites of our master. He composed the 'Nachklang,' of which he chose the title, twice. The published version is the second of the two. Musical readers will remember that melody and accompaniment are used again in the duet Sonata in G major.

Both String Quartets were performed privately in Berlin by Joachim and his colleagues. They were played for the first time in public; that in A minor in Berlin at the Joachim Quartet concert of October 18 from the manuscript; that in C minor at the Hellmesberger concert of December 11 in Vienna from the printed copies.

BRAHMS AT THE AGE OF 40.

The appearance of these two works as Op. 51, Nos. 1 and 2, forms, as we have said, another and important landmark in the development of Brahms' career. The String Quartet holds a position of peculiar significance in the art of music, and a composer, by selecting this form for the exercise of his powers, exposes them to the most unfailing test to which his calibre as a musician can possibly be submitted. He must possess not only fertility in the production of purely musical concentrated ideas, and ideas capable of development; the power to develop them, which means many things, and the capacity for shaping them into clear structure; but he must be able to express them with the most bare and simple musical means, with four strings. From the rapid effects of strong and strongly contrasted sensation producible by the pianoforte, or the varied tone-colour of the orchestra, he is precluded. With his four strings he can interest, delight, touch, but hardly astonish his hearers. The String Quartet is absolute music in its purest form, and but few works in this domain can survive their birth unless they be destined to attain a long life. The means are perfect for the end, but this is difficult of achievement; only the quartet of a master has much chance of being heard after its first few performances. It will be evident to the reader that Brahms was fitted by many essential characteristics of his genius for success in this branch of art, though it cannot cause surprise that one of his great qualities, the power of waiting for results, should have strengthened his fastidiousness in accepting as final the fruits of his studies in a form which had been brought to ideal perfection by Haydn and Beethoven, each in their day. On the great musicianship manifest in Brahms' quartets, on his mastery over his means, his power of completely balancing his four parts, of making each a separate individuality whilst all blend harmoniously as equal constituents of an organic whole, it is only necessary to insist here in so far as these qualities are elements in another feature which pre-eminently marks our master's chamber music for strings: the extraordinary beauty of its structure. Throughout the three quartets and two quintets for strings composed by Brahms there is not only no mere passage writing, but it would be difficult to point to a single note that could be called superfluous. Each seems to have been placed with loving care by the master hand of the great musical architect, the artist builder, as an essential part of the whole large design. When we examine the thoughts themselves and their development we find that we are, as in all Brahms' works, in the presence of a powerful and fascinating individuality. Ideas and treatment are the master's own, not easy at once to understand, but offering almost inexhaustible opportunity for discovery and enjoyment to listeners willing to earn such rewards. The two quartets, Op. 51, are more or less severally representative of contrasted sides of Brahms' individuality. The first, in C minor, is generally characterized by fire and impetuosity, exquisitely relieved by the tender romance of the second movement; No. 2, in A minor, is conceived in a softer vein. The last movement of this work contains a beautiful example of the characteristic Brahms coda; the augmented vigour of the climax is preceded by a period of tranquillity that seems to place the listener in an atmosphere of mystic exaltation, to afford him 'glimpses of a spirit world' from which the previous thoughts of the movement flow towards him in transfigured tones. Lovers of the master's music will recall a similar feature in other works. In the opening theme of the first movement, which is suggestive of Joachim's early device F.A.E.—

[Listen]

we may, perhaps, perceive a passing reference to the remembrance of his friend which must certainly have been present to Brahms' mind as he planned these works. Instances of the composer's mastery of the art of modulation, of his boldness and facility in going to, and returning from unexpected and distant keys, may be found in the two quartets as in the majority of his instrumental compositions. They were dedicated by Brahms to 'his friend Dr. Theodor Billroth of Vienna,' and were published in the autumn by Simrock.

Amongst those who had looked forward with particular expectancy to the opening of the great World Exhibition that was held in Vienna in the autumn of 1873 was the painter Anselm Feuerbach. He had, the previous year, accepted the offer of an appointment as director of the historical class about to be formed in the Imperial Academy of Plastic Arts of that city, but had begged for a year's leave of absence in Rome before entering on his new duties, in order that he might finish two great pictures, 'The Battle of the Amazons' and 'The Second Symposium,' the exhibition of which he conceived likely to establish his fame and to secure him an authoritative position on taking up his residence in Austria. The nearly finished pictures were sent to Vienna in March or April, and Feuerbach followed them in May, 1873, but it turned out that they could not be hung in the Exhibition gallery on account of their great size. The painter determined, therefore, to exhibit them one after the other in the 'Künstler-Haus,' and, in order to secure the advantage of association in the mind of the public with so favourite a celebrity of Vienna as Brahms had at this time become, he requested the master to sit to him on his return in October in order that his portrait might be exhibited with the other pictures.

Feuerbach was a small man of ultra-refined appearance and manners, and a countenance of rather melancholy expression that had evidently been of striking beauty in his youth. He was accustomed to be made much of by ladies, was extremely sensitive and self-centred, and inordinately vain, and had confidently persuaded himself that his pictures were to achieve an instant and overwhelming success.

'My pictures are splendid and all but finished,' he wrote to his mother on October 2; 'why should I feel a moment's anxiety since I have eminent power in my hands; genius and position.... The Symposium also is quite exquisite, I may say so now as I have seen the Vatican.'[46]

Brahms, who had, as we have seen, a long-standing acquaintance with Feuerbach and sincerely admired his powers, mounted the many flights of stairs leading to the artist's temporary studio more than once. His attention was particularly called to the 'Battle of the Amazons,' on which, as it was to be exhibited first, Feuerbach was busy with the finishing touches. He mentioned it several times in a reserved manner to Groth, who was in Vienna for the Exhibition, saying he was anxious to have his opinion of it, and persuaded him to pay a visit to the studio one day to be presented to Feuerbach. Groth, however, on coming away, found that he was unable, as Brahms had been, to express himself warmly about the great painting, and merely agreed with our master in 'not understanding' it. Brahms, intimately acquainted with the artist circles of Vienna, evidently could not shake off his apprehension as to the result of the exhibition, and took an opportunity of speaking a word of warning to Feuerbach, advising him to be cautious, and to introduce himself to his new public with a smaller work. The integrity of the composer's ideas of friendship and the misunderstanding of his motives which was its frequent result, as well as the general soundness of his judgment in matters on which he ventured to give advice, are well illustrated by the affair. His words produced an immediate effect very different from that intended by him. The wound they inflicted on the irritable susceptibility of the painter was so painful as to deprive him of the power of concentrating his mind upon the 'Amazons' for several subsequent days, and he found it impossible to go on with Brahms' portrait.

'Another evening spoilt by Brahms,' he wrote on November 3; and again: 'I was not for a second angry with Brahms, but I have put his canvas aside for the present.' It was never taken up again.

The pictures were duly exhibited in turn, and it may be said that the final breakdown of Feuerbach's never robust constitution was the ultimate result. Not criticism only or even chiefly, but torrents of contempt, derision, insult were poured upon his work.

'A storm broke over my head by which I could at least reassure myself as to the importance of my pictures. I could not sit down to table without finding jests, raillery, caricature—unfortunately always bad—beside my plate, and the story of my discomfiture was related in the house from roof to cellar. I was told that everyone, from the professor to the porter's boy, was laughing at my bad picture.'

'Almost the entire press, independent and mercenary alike, was arrayed against Feuerbach,' says Allgeyer.

His pupils, however, offered him the mute sympathy and support of punctual attendance and respectful attention at class, and the Minister remained loyal to him. He retained his appointment till the close of 1876, though ill-health prevented him from performing his duties during the last half-year. He died at Nürnburg in 1880. His friendship with our master did not terminate with the incident of the pictures.

'Brahms has lent me his fur-coat for my journey,' he wrote in February, 1875, on the eve of his departure for Rome.

The 'Battle of the Amazons' was presented by the artist's mother to the city of Nürnburg in the year 1889, and hangs there in the picture gallery of the Town Hall. Many of the studies for the 'Amazons' and the 'Symposium' were purchased by King Ludwig II. of Bavaria, and presented by him to the Royal Pinakothek at Munich.

Of the many letters of congratulation received by Allgeyer after the appearance of his 'Life of Feuerbach' in 1894, one of those most highly prized by him came from Brahms.

Brahms paid one visit to the great Exhibition in the company of Groth and other friends, though the noise and bustle of such a scene were by no means to his taste. He was more anxious that his friend should see and hear what was really characteristic of Vienna. 'You must go to the Volksgarten on Friday evening when Johann Strauss will conduct his waltzes. *There* is a master; such a master of the orchestra that one never loses a single tone of whatever instrument!'

Having promised to arrange a meeting between Frau Dustmann of the imperial opera and Groth, Brahms came to the poet's hotel one morning, and entering the room where he was lying in bed with a bad feverish cold, exclaimed delightedly: 'Come to me this evening, the Dustmann will sing to you.' 'But you see I am ill,' returned Groth testily. 'You will be astonished,' continued Brahms, whose boast it was that he had never in his life been really ill, '*there* is a singer, *there* is an artist; *she* will please you!' 'Ah, my dear fellow, I really cannot come,' pleaded the other, 'Johann has just put a cold compress on, I am so miserable!' 'She is very seldom free just now; she cannot come another day.' 'Surely you see how miserable I am. How I should like to come, but I cannot,' persisted Groth. Then Brahms turned to go. 'You are a Philistine!' he declared angrily as he left the room.[47]

The ante-Christmas season of 1873, signalized on its immediate opening by the performance of the String Quartet in A minor at Berlin, already referred to, was further rendered distinctive in Brahms' career by the first performance from the manuscript of the Variations for Orchestra on a theme by Haydn, which took place at the Vienna Philharmonic of

November 2 under Dessoff's direction. The masterly and attractive work consists, as most amateurs are aware, of eight variations and a finale on the 'Chorale St. Antoni.' The composer adheres almost entirely to Haydn's harmonies in the giving out of the theme. The variations are constructed on the principle often observable in his works in this form; they constitute, as it were, a series of little movements each woven more or less appreciably from the matter of the chorale, but each with a character of its own and complete in itself, while the entire composition is gathered together and rounded into a whole by the finale. Brahms' vivid and original imagination of tone-effect is very clearly discernible throughout the work, and is especially illustrated in it by his original and effective employment of the double bassoon.

The variations were received by the crowded audience, and reviewed by the press, with warm welcome and with grateful appreciation of their beauty and perfection, if with some trace of disappointment that he who 'held the sceptre' in the domain of music for the chamber and the concert-room, and must of all living musicians be pre-eminently qualified for the composition of a symphony, should be the very man to refrain from writing one. Brahms, however, was well aware of the gigantic difficulty of the task that lay before him in the writing of a symphony that should successfully encounter that ordeal of comparison with the greatest works of its class which had become inevitable by the fact of his acknowledged supremacy in other forms. The ultimate cause of his delay and the pledge of his future victory are alike to be found in the nature of his artistic convictions, which, holding him loyal to the traditions of the past masters of instrumental music, made it impossible to him to seek novelty by compromising with modern methods. Brahms elected to wait until, with the gradual ripening of his powers to full maturity, he should feel, not only that he had something of his own to say in the highest domain of pure music, but that he had mastered the power of expressing it in a manner true to himself. Had he never felt assured on these two points it is certain that no symphony of his would ever have been made public, no matter to what sum of months the hours might amount which he had devoted to the study and practice of writing for the orchestra. Having now given a sign of his whereabouts he again drew a veil over the course of his artistic development, and, appearing before the public during the next three years only on ground which he had already made his own, revealed no more upward stages of his achievement until he at length stood victoriously before the world on its summit.

The variations were performed for the second time on December 10 under Levi in Munich.

The Gesellschaft season opened under Brahms' direction on November 9, with Beethoven's Overture, Op. 115, and Handel's 'Alexander's Feast.' A varied programme was given at the second concert of December 7:

1. Schubert:	Overture to Fierrebras.
2. Schubert:	Aria for Tenor (written in 1821 for introduction into Herold's Opera 'Zauberglöcken' at the Kärnthnerthor Theater, Vienna; unpublished). Herr Gustav Walter.
3. Volkmann:	Concertstück for Pianoforte and Orchestra. Pianoforte, Herr Smetansky.
4. (*a*) Joh. Rud. Ahle (1662) (*b*) J. S. Bach	} Unaccompanied Choruses.
5. Bach:	Cantata, 'Nun ist das Heil,' for double Chorus, Orchestra and Organ.
6. Jac. Gallus:	Unaccompanied Chorus, 'Ecce Quomodo.'
7. Beethoven:	Choral Fantasia for Pianoforte (Smetansky), Orchestra, and Chorus.

The publications of the year, all issued in the autumn, were, in addition to the String Quartets, the version for two Pianofortes of the Haydn Variations (Op. 56*b*), by Simrock, and a set of eight Songs (Op. 59), by Rieter-Biedermann. Of these, four are set to texts by Claus Groth, which include 'Rain-songs' and the lovely 'Dein blaues Auge hält so still.' The Variations for Orchestra were published by Simrock in 1874.

Brahms was at this time quite immersed in his various kinds of work.

'I am so enormously occupied that I see my best friends only very rarely and by accident,' he wrote in December to the present author.

It had now become his custom to decline invitations for the Christmas festival, and to spend it, partly at the open-air Christmas market, where he made himself happy by purchasing gifts for the poor children whom he found crowding round the tempting wares, and partly at home, where he would look in for half an hour at the family party gathered in front of his landlady's Christmas-tree; no doubt contributing his share to the surprises of Christmas Eve, the 'sacred evening' when, throughout the length and breadth of Germany and Austria, innumerable trees are lighted up at about the same hour, and the great exchange takes place of presents to which, in many cases, the preparation and savings of a year have been consecrated. A New Year's present of a special kind received by Brahms this winter was the Maximilian Order for Art and Science conferred on him by King Ludwig II. of Bavaria.

The year 1874 was unusually full of movement and varied excitement for our composer. From January onwards he was besieged with invitations, many of which he accepted, to conduct his works at concerts and festivals in North Germany, the Rhine, Switzerland, and was obliged to reply in the negative to Dietrich's request, received in the beginning of spring, that he would include Oldenburg in his arrangements.

'DEAR FRIEND,

'I am more than sorry, but you are too late! I have already promised so much, and shall not be coming to your neighbourhood!

'If you had written earlier I could have arranged with Hanover, Bremen, etc., for, *seriously*, I should be too glad to go to you again....'

The third Gesellschaft concert of the season (1873-74) took place on January 25. That the performances under Brahms would be above criticism had become by this time almost a foregone conclusion, and, beyond recording the great success achieved by Goldmark's 'Hymn of Spring,' it is only necessary to give the programme of the occasion:

1. Rheinberger:	Prelude to the Opera 'The Seven Ravens.'
2. Goldmark:	'Frühlings Hymne' (May musings, from the Swedish of Geijer), for Contralto solo, Chorus, and Orchestra. (First performance, under the composer's direction.)
3. Mozart:	'Davidde Penitente,' Cantata for Soli, Chorus, and Orchestra.

A few days later Brahms left Vienna to fulfil a group of engagements in Leipzig, a circumstance which in itself affords some indication of the rapid strides by which his career had lately been advancing towards the full sunshine of success that was to flood the latter portion of his path through life.

The relations between Brahms and the city which owed its brilliant reputation as a musical centre to Mendelssohn's influence had been at no time really sympathetic. The attitude of expectant toleration that had been more or less adopted towards him by both its extreme parties after his first visit in 1853 had resulted on the one hand from Schumann's essay, and on the other, from the confidence felt by the Weimarites and expressed by Liszt that his 'new paths' must eventually bring him into close touch with themselves. Gradually, however, it, became clear how mistaken was the belief that the young musician would drift towards acceptance of the extreme new tendencies, whilst the originality of his musical thoughts and of his manner of expressing them was abhorrent to the inflexible conservatism that had come to represent the traditions of the Gewandhaus. If, moreover, there is every reason to surmise that Mendelssohn himself had no hearty appreciation of Schumann's genius, it is equally probable that neither Rietz, who conducted the Gewandhaus concerts from 1848 to 1860, nor Reinecke, who succeeded him, was in very warm sympathy with that of Brahms, and the predilections of the public followed those of their accredited guides.

Brahms' works were, it is true, generally given at the orchestral or chamber concerts of the Gewandhaus soon after publication, but, excepting the Triumphlied, with its special appeal to the patriotic sentiment of the great German people, they met with but scanty response from an audience little accustomed to the exertion of trying to follow the expression of a new and original artistic individuality. That Reinecke was by no means an ideal conductor of them naturally resulted from the fact that by training, by conviction, and by practice, he was attached to a rigidly formal school of modern musical thought, and it can surprise no one that he should have been unable entirely to realize the deeper and richer utterances of Schumann's young prophet. Brahms' chamber music fared differently in the hands of David, who was almost alone amongst the authorities of the Gewandhaus in his sympathy for the composer's genius. To these considerations it must be added that not only the pianist, but the composer Rubinstein, had, as we indicated in an early chapter, an enthusiastic following amongst the typical Leipzig public who were disposed to resent any claim to recognition that might threaten to rival that of their favourite.

In spite, however, of the fact that Brahms was no party man, in Leipzig, as in almost every other city where his music was heard, it struck a root, imperceptible at first, but growing deeper and stronger and more extended with every year that went by. The attention bestowed on it by Brendel's society has been frequently referred to in these pages; it was cultivated, also, by Riedel's celebrated choir. A more representative illustration, however, of a certain mysterious power inherent in Brahms' works of finding their way sooner or later, and not seldom it is sooner, to the heart, in spite of their intellectuality, their difficulty, their reserve, is furnished by the case of two sisters, daughters of the head of one of the great bookselling houses of

Leipzig. The Fräulein Weigand did not live in a musical 'set,' nor were they personally acquainted with Brahms or his friends, but not long after their first casual introduction to his music in the middle of the sixties, when they were young girls, the appearance of each of his new works had come to be an event in their lives. 'You from Leipzig!' exclaimed Hermann Levi, with whom the sisters had a passing acquaintance in the summer of 1871. It was not until three months before the composer's death that these ladies had any personal communication with him. Then, hearing of his hopeless illness, they resolved to address him for the first and last time, and in January, 1897, they wrote to him telling how they had always loved his music and followed his career. No one who really knew him will doubt the pleasure that the letter gave to the dying master. In answer he sent his photograph with his autograph, 'Johannes Brahms,' and the inscription, 'To the two sisters as a little token of heart-felt thanks for their so kind account.'

Of the professional critics of Leipzig, Bernsdorf of the Signale remained to the last irreconcilable to Brahms' art; but, on the other hand, Dörffel of the *Leipziger Nachrichten* watched the appearance of his works with profound interest and reviewed them with extreme sympathy and acumen. There was during the sixties no influential 'Brahms' community in musical Leipzig, no active 'Brahms' propaganda in the houses of wealthy amateurs. Such occasional admirers as the composer may have had in this circle were to be met in the drawing-room of the lady introduced to the reader in an early chapter as Hedwig Salamon, since married to the composer Franz von Holstein. At the beginning of the seventies, however, a few well-known residents were to be found who had a strong bond of union in their common sympathy with Brahms' genius. Of these, in addition to the von Holsteins, may be particularly mentioned Philipp Spitta, now remembered in all parts of the musical world as the author of the standard Bach Biography, Alfred Volkland, Herr Astor, of the firm of Rieter-Biedermann, and later on its head, and the distinguished composer Heinrich von Herzogenberg, who settled in Leipzig in 1872 on his marriage with Elisabeth von Stockhausen. This lady, endowed in an extraordinary degree with beauty, goodness, intellectual and artistic gifts, domestic qualities, and any other imaginable graces and perfections, soon came to be numbered with her husband amongst the ardent devotees of Brahms' art. It will be convenient to mention here also that Theodor Kirchner settled in Leipzig in 1875, the year in which Spitta accepted a call to Berlin.

All these circumstances put together seem to explain the master's visit to Leipzig, where he had made no public appearance since the Gewandhaus concert of November 26, 1860, when he and Joachim had conducted each other's Hungarian Concerto and Serenade in A major without success.

Brahms was now to conduct a performance of 'Rinaldo' at a concert of the University Choral Society at the Gewandhaus on February 3, and the Haydn Variations, three Hungarian Dances, and the 'Rhapsody' (solo, Frau Joachim) at the Gewandhaus subscription concert of February 5. His presence in Leipzig was further welcomed by the performance of the G minor Pianoforte Quartet at the Gewandhaus chamber concert of February 1, and by the performance of a Brahms programme by the *Allgemeiner Musikverein* on January 30. On January 17 one of the string quartets had been performed at the Gewandhaus concert by David and his party.

The moment when Brahms stepped on to the Gewandhaus platform, the acknowledged representative, in at least two domains of musical art, of the greatest masters who had preceded him, must have been one of quiet satisfaction to himself if he cast a thought backward to the evening, more than thirteen years ago, when he had last appeared in the same hall, and, not for the first time, unsuccessfully sought the suffrages of the same public. Even now, however, though he was received with the respect due to a musician of his great standing, he was not to taste the enjoyment of feeling that he had aroused the enthusiasm, hardly that he had awakened the sympathy, of his audience. The Gewandhaus public, rarely demonstrative, preserved its special attitude of coldness and reserve towards him, and though he may have enjoyed the society of his personal friends, he was probably glad to find himself back again in the genial atmosphere of his surroundings in Vienna, where, in spite of the survival of a hostile attitude in certain organs of the press, his ground had become practically his own.

The Haydn Variations were performed in February or March at Breslau (twice), Aachen and Münster, under the respective conductors of the subscription concerts, and on March 13 the composer assisted, but with little success, in the performance of a Brahms programme at an Academy concert, Munich, under Levi, conducting the new work, and playing the solo of the D minor Concerto. In spite of Levi's continued efforts the musical circles of Munich remained indifferent to the master's music. The Haydn Variations were heard for the first time in London at the Philharmonic concert of May 24, 1875, under W. G. Cusins.

The programmes performed at the two 'extra' concerts of the Vienna Gesellschaft were: On March 2—

1. Schubert: *Kyrie* and *Credo* from the Mass in B flat.
(Unpublished; first performance.)

2. Schumann: Music to 'Manfred.'

On March 31—Handel's 'Solomon.'

'We can only thank the conductor for bringing this work forward; the performance was ideal,' says one of the critics in his notice of the oratorio.

The last concert of the season, on April 19, presented a varied programme:

1. Haydn: Symphony in E flat major.

2. A. Dietrich: Concerto for Violin (Violin, Herr Lauterbach).

3. J. Brahms: Schicksalslied.

4. J. Rietz: Arioso for Violin with organ accompaniment.

5. J. S. Bach: Pastorale for Orchestra from the Christmas Oratorio.

6. Handel: Last Chorus from the first part of 'Solomon.'

Brahms' leisure was considerably curtailed this summer. Of the numerous engagements fulfilled by him after the close of the Vienna concert-season three may be particularly mentioned. He conducted the Triumphlied at the first concert of the Rhine Festival (Cologne, May 24-27), at the Jubilee anniversary concert of the Basle Choral Society, and at a concert of the Zürich Music Festival (July), and on each occasion the great song was received with acclamation. With this work we may, perhaps, especially associate the honour of the Prussian Ordre pour le Mérite which was conferred later on the composer by the Emperor William I. He was elected an honorary member of the Royal Academy of Arts, Berlin, in the course of the summer.

'Brahms is becoming so popular,' writes Billroth on June 2, 'and is everywhere made so much of, that he could easily become a rich man with his composition if he could take it lightly. Fortunately this is not the case.'

The Triumphlied was performed in the German imperial capital on December 17, 1874, under Stockhausen. It was given under Levi at the great Bismarck Festival in Munich, and was heard in London at a concert given in St. James's Hall by George Henschel, December 2, 1880, for the benefit of the Victoria Hospital for Children, Chelsea.

The magnificent work is now but seldom performed: partly, no doubt, because it was composed to celebrate a particular series of events in history, partly because of the difficulty of securing the large chorus necessary for its due effect, partly, perhaps, on account of the demands it makes on the attention of the listener. Whatever be the cause, the fact itself is to be deeply regretted. The work has sometimes been criticised as wanting in contrast of mood. Undoubtedly it is, from beginning to end, a song of passionate exultation which scarcely makes pause from the first note to the last, and the listener requires time and repeated hearings to become familiarized with its brilliancy before he can follow it with pleasure; but it is full of varied features of interest to lay hearers, and especially to those who will devote a little time to its study before listening to its performance. To the musician it appeals as a marvel of polyphonic art, though it contains no elaborated features of harmonic or contrapuntal learning that might have been prejudicial to its character as a national strain. It is literally 'a sound of many voices saying Alleluia.'

The master lodged this summer near Nidelbad, above Rüschlikon on Lake Zürich. Amongst the friends and acquaintances old and new with whom he had intercourse were Bargheer, Hegar, G. Eberhard, Gottfried Keller, Bernhard Hopfer, Professor and Frau Engelmann from Utrecht, and J. V. Widmann. Brahms made Widmann's acquaintance at this time at the house of Hermann Götz, and seems to have been immediately attracted by him; partly, perhaps, because the younger man had the courage of his opinions, and ventured to oppose him in argument. The acquaintance, cemented during the three days of the Zürich Festival, grew into an intimate and lasting friendship, to which the musical world is indebted for Widmann's well-known and delightful 'Recollections,' already several times referred to in these pages.

Hegar mentions[48] that the works which occupied Brahms during his stay at Rüschlikon were the second set of Liebeslieder, the book of songs, Lieder and Gesänge, Op. 63, and the Vocal Quartets, Op. 64. It was at this time, also, that he finally completed the Pianoforte Quartet in C minor. The songs and quartets were published in the autumn by Peters; the four Duets for Soprano and Contralto, Op. 61, and the seven Songs for mixed Chorus, *a capella*, Op. 62, were issued about the same time by Simrock. The Neue Liebeslieder and the C minor Quartet for Pianoforte and Strings did not appear till 1875.

From this time onward Brahms' copyrights were acquired, as each new work was completed, by Simrock of Berlin, with only four exceptions—Nänie, Op. 82; six Vocal Quartets, Op. 112; thirteen Canons, Op. 113, which were bought by Peters of Leipzig; and a Prelude and Fugue for Organ, published in 1881 as a supplement to the *Musikalisches Wochenblatt* without opus number. In future, therefore, we shall mention the publication, but not the publisher, of the works. Those compositions which were originally acquired from the composer by Breitkopf and Härtel were resold by this firm to Simrock later on, and appear, therefore, in the complete published catalogue of Brahms' works as Simrock's publications.

The third and, as it turned out, the last season of Brahms' work as artistic director of the Gesellschaft der Musikfreunde opened in due course, and at the two ante-Christmas concerts of the season 1874-75 the following programmes were performed: On November 8—

1. Rubinstein: Overture to the Opera 'Dimitri Donskoi.'

2. Beethoven: Pianoforte Concerto in E flat. (Pianoforte, Herr Brahms.)

3. Brahms: Songs for mixed Chorus, *a capella*, Op. 62—
(*a*) Waldesnacht.
(*b*) 'Dein Herzlein mild.'
(*c*) Von alten Liebesliedern.'

4. Berlioz: 'Harold in Italy.' Symphony in four parts.

On December 6—Beethoven's Missa Solemnis in D major.

Neither concert seems to have reached the usual high-water mark of success. Of the first programme the items most heartily appreciated were the three choral part-songs, which, attractive in themselves and sung to perfection, were applauded to the echo. Of doubtful wisdom was the selection of the pianist of the occasion. Brahms, who probably yielded to the persuasion of his committee, and was, perhaps, guided in his choice of a concerto by the circumstance of having played Beethoven in E flat in the spring at Bremen, had, as we have seen, given up regular pianoforte practice for some years, and it was inevitable that his performance should be affected by this fact. Berlioz's symphony, which may have owed its place in the programme to our master's broad view of his duties as the artistic director of an important society, was not performed with any great aplomb or heard with particular favour, though extra time and particular pains had been spent on its rehearsal.

Beethoven's great Mass, given on December 6, was followed with strained attention that was rewarded by a good, though, if Brahms' supporters in the press are to be trusted, not a perfect, performance.

'How different are these days from those of the forties,' remarks one of the critics, 'when many a music lover would rise and leave the room before the commencement of a work by Beethoven.'

The String Quartet in A minor was performed for the first time in Vienna at Hellmesberger's concert of December 3, when the andante and scherzo met with considerable appreciation.

'I have heard the string quartets several times this winter,' writes Billroth in January, 1875. When we played them in Carlsruhe as pianoforte duets, we took all the tempi much too fast. Brahms desires very moderate *tempi* throughout, as otherwise, owing to the frequent harmonic changes, the music cannot become clear.... Beethoven, Schumann, Wagner, Brahms, in their riper works of the last period, all have a preference for the andante *tempo*.

'If you should infer from all I have said that I am much with Brahms, you would be mightily mistaken. I have only seen him twice during the whole winter.... We correspond, however; he is pleased when I write to him about his things.'

The composer was plunged in his own special work, and would allow neither private nor public calls to occupy his attention, though he made an exception in favour of Bernhard Scholz's invitation to pay an artistic visit to Breslau at the close of the year. His doings during the next few months afford but little material to chronicle, and we have to record only the last four Gesellschaft programmes given under his direction, and to lay special stress upon the extraordinary scene of enthusiasm that followed the performance of the German Requiem on February 28, 1875. The rendering of the work on this occasion was one of those, rarely occurring, which seem to hold the audience spellbound by a magnetic sympathy with the music. It brought with it in some mysterious way the sudden flash of revelation. The whole audience, as it were, knew Brahms that day, and most of what was left to be conquered, that was worth conquering, in the musical opinion of Vienna was finally captured. The phenomenal demonstration, joined in by musicians of all schools, Wagnerians not excepted, that occurred on the termination of the great work, noteworthy from its contrast with that earlier one of 1867 which followed the performance of the first three choruses, was the more striking since Wagner had conducted some excerpts from the 'Ring' in the same hall a few days previously, and had been the recipient of a similar ovation.

January 10, 1875:

1. Mendelssohn:	Overture to the Opera 'Camacho's Marriage.'
2. Joachim:	Hungarian Concerto. (Violin, Herr Joachim.)
3. Brahms:	Rhapsody. (Solo, Frau Joachim.)
4. Schumann:	Fantasia for Violin and Orchestra. (Herr Joachim.)
5. J. S. Bach:	Whitsuntide Cantata, 'O ewiges Feuer,' for Soli, Chorus, Orchestra, and Organ.

February 28:

1. J. S. Bach:	Prelude for Organ in E flat, arranged for Orchestra by Bernhard Scholz.
2. Mozart:	Aria from 'Davidde penitente.'
3. Brahms:	A German Requiem.

Good Friday, March 23:

J. S. Bach:	Passion Music (St. Matthew).

April 18:

Max Bruch:	Odysseus.

At the close of the season Brahms laid down his conductor's bâton to make room for the return of Herbeck, whose former services, especially in the formation of an independent orchestra, had laid the society under a debt of gratitude, and who, unable to endure the annoyances incidental to his position as capellmeister of the opera, resigned the post. Brahms continued his association with the Gesellschaft as a member of the committee, taking great interest in its councils, and exercising influence on the concert-programmes and the appointment of professors to the conservatoire. Each year that went by added to the warmth of the esteem with which he was personally regarded and to the deference shown to his judgment by the members of the society, who were all proud of this link of association with him.

Writing in May to his stepmother from idyllic summer quarters, he says:

'DEAR MOTHER,

'I will let you know in haste, that I am living quite delightfully at Zigelhausen near Heidelberg. Thank you also for the socks you have again knitted for me.... I am not leaving Vienna, I have only given up my appointment. You do not know the circumstances, and it would be too prolix to tell you why. I am, however, remaining there—and gladly. Write to me if you want money now, or later when the holidays come off!...

'Affectionately Your JOHANNES.'

'I must tell you that people are very often surprised at my knitted socks, and that I am taken such good care of!'[49]

'Brahms has had very interesting programmes. Unfortunately we have lost him and Dessoff (Philharmonic) as conductors. Both have been pushed out, and both pushed out by Herbeck,' writes Billroth in the month of June.

Brahms invited Dietrich to visit him at Zigelhausen.

'I saw his new works, but cannot now be quite sure which they were,' says Dietrich in his 'Recollections.'

We may confidently conjecture that chief amongst them must have been the first symphony, upon the completion of which Brahms was at this time concentrating his attention, and it is probable that he also showed the sketches of the second symphony to his old friend.

It was this year that Brahms consented to become a member for the music section of a commission for the awarding of certain gratuities granted annually by the Austrian Government to poor artists of talent who have produced promising works. Three members appointed by the Minister of Education for each of three sections—poetry, music, and the plastic arts—examine the applications and work sent, and judge between them. The fund was established in 1863, and the original adjudicators in the music section were Hanslick, Herbeck, and Essen. Brahms now replaced Essen, and a little later Goldmark succeeded Herbeck. The compositions were sent in the first place to Hanslick, who generally made a selection from them for Brahms' inspection, keeping back such as did not fulfil the required conditions or were hopelessly bad. In the *Neue Freie Presse* of June 29, 1897, Hanslick made public a few of the communications he had received from Brahms on these occasions, the first of which, dated September, 1875, was as follows:

'DEAR FRIEND,

'Parcels such as your last are generally so thorny that some kind preliminary guidance like yours is most welcome and necessary as a help in finding one's way through. This time, however, things are not so bad, and seem to me fairly simple. Dvořák and Reinhold thoroughly deserve your proposal by their performances. In Lachner's case (blind) well-justified sympathy counts for something. M. certainly merits some help meanwhile. I mean he ought to win the money more decidedly next year. N. N. alone appears to me so undeserving of the gratuity that it might be given uselessly in his case. Just look again at his small and great sins. They are the most unmusical in the packet. Alas, if he should progress further! At all events he should desire and use the money for instruction and not for a libretto!'

The Quartet in C minor for pianoforte and strings, published in the autumn, was produced at Hellmesberger's concert of November 18 by Brahms, Hellmesberger, Bachrich, and Popper, and was played in Hamburg on January 3, 1876, by Levin, Böie, Schmall, and Lee.

This composition must, as the reader is aware,[50] be referred to more than one period of Brahms' activity, and it can hardly be accepted as a representative work of either. Standing about midway, as to date of publication, between his two great series of masterpieces for pianoforte and strings, if it is to be classed amongst either, it must indubitably be reckoned with that of the sixties. Internal no less than external evidence, however, leaves little doubt that it points back to a still earlier date. The master of the seventies has so far succeeded in remodelling the work of early youth as to have given to the world in the quartet an interesting, and, on the whole, a clear, presentment of many noble musical thoughts, but it can hardly be said that he has effected its transformation into a homogeneous or apparently spontaneous work of art. Kalbeck mentions that a memorandum of Brahms assigns the date 1873-74 to the third and fourth movements. This, however, may probably refer only to their final completion. The second movement (the scherzo), which undoubtedly belongs to the period of the pianoforte sonata numbered as Op. 1, is consistently characteristic of the composer at that date. The first and third movements suggest a transition period. The character of the ideas of the opening allegro with its impressive, deeply serious, first subject, and of the andante with its sustained melodious phrases, seems to give promise of the power which, manifested in a different mood, was reached in the earlier-published companion works. Of the finale it must be said that its themes are lacking in interest and developed mechanically. It may be surmised that the composer's pruning-knife was freely used in the course of his successive revisions of the work, and perhaps not only for the purpose of shortening it, but also for that of thinning out the score. From the circumstance that this is neither so luxuriant in detail nor so thickly instrumented as those of the other two pianoforte quartets, the C minor has, perhaps, the one advantage amongst the three of being the most readily appreciable at first hearing. It must, however, as the author conceives, be rated, as a completed work of art, decidedly below its glorious companions.

The relative popularity attained by the three pianoforte quartets in England may be fairly estimated by comparing the numbers of their respective performances at the Popular Concerts, London. The A major, introduced in January, 1872, was given ten times up to October, 1900, inclusive. The G minor, first performed in January, 1874, was given twenty-six times up to March, 1900. The C minor, first played in November, 1876, was not heard again until December, 1893.

CHAPTER XVII
1876-1878

Tour in Holland—Third String Quartet—C minor Symphony—First performances—Varying impressions created by the work in Vienna and Leipzig—Brahms and Widmann at Mannheim—Second Symphony—Vienna and Leipzig differ as to its merits.

A journey to Holland early in 1876 brought unmixed gratification to the master. He conducted the Haydn Variations, and played the D minor Concerto at Utrecht on January 22 before an audience which received him with warm greeting, and gave every possible evidence of appreciation of his works. Immense applause followed each movement of the concerto, and at its close, when enthusiasm was at its height, two youthful ladies advanced to the platform, each bearing a cushion on which a wreath was placed, one decorated with ribbons of the Austrian colours (black and yellow), the other with those of Holland (red, white, and blue), which they smilingly presented to the composer. Brahms, not always inclined to receive tributes of the kind with urbanity, entered thoroughly into the happy spirit of this occasion, and showed plainly by his manner of accepting the compliment his pleasure at the charming way in which it had been offered. He was the guest during his several days' stay at Utrecht of Professor and Frau Engelmann, in whose house he at once became at home, dividing his time between walking, talking, playing with the children, making music with his hostess, seeing friends, and was in genial mood throughout the visit. It may be remarked *en passant* that Brahms in a companionable frame of mind was not accustomed to let his friends off easily. His constitution was so robust, his spirit so active, his interests so numerous, that he liked, and expected others to like, to sit up talking with vivacity until the small hours of the morning, and would rise after about five hours' rest as unwearied and energetic as though he had had what would be for most people a normal amount of repose. It was a matter of course wherever he stayed that the means for making a cup of coffee should be left every night at his disposal for the next morning, and he generally returned from an early walk at about the hour when the household was beginning to stir.

After leaving Holland the master took part as conductor and pianist in concerts at Münster, where he directed the Triumphlied, Mannheim and Wiesbaden, playing the D minor Concerto on each occasion. He was, of course, the guest at Münster of Grimm and his wife. At Mannheim he stayed with his friend the well-known capellmeister Ernst Frank, who in the course of his career was associated as conductor with the musical life of

Würzburg, Vienna, Mannheim, and Hanover. The Wiesbaden concert is still vividly remembered by the present Landgraf of Hesse, who, then a young lad, heard Brahms for the first time on the occasion, and received an impression which laid the foundation of his enduring enthusiasm for the master's art.

Staying in the summer at Sassnitz in the Isle of Rügen, Brahms there completed his third String Quartet in B flat major, and announced the work in September to Professor Engelmann, to whom it is dedicated. It was played in Berlin before a private audience towards the end of October by the Joachim Quartet party, and by the same artists for the first time in public at their concert of October 30 in the hall of the Singakademie, on both occasions from the manuscript. The first concert performance after publication was that of the Hellmesberger party on November 30 in Vienna.

The general remarks offered in the preceding chapter on Brahms' chamber music for strings are to be applied to the Quartet in B flat major. Of its particular characteristics we may note the joyousness of the first movement, and the weird fantastic pathos of the third, in which a special relation is maintained between the viola and first violin. In the theme—of distinguished simplicity—and variations, with which the work closes, we have a concise but beautiful example of the composer's facility in this form.

The String Quartet in B flat was the first of the three composed by Brahms to be heard at the Popular Concerts, London. It was played on Monday, February 19, and Saturday, March 3, 1877, by Joachim, Ries, Straus, and Piatti. The A minor was performed on Monday, October 31, 1881, by Straus, Ries, Zerbini, and Piatti, and the C minor on Monday, December 7, 1855, by Madame Norman-Néruda, Ries, Straus, and Franz Néruda. These (Op. 51, Nos. 1 and 2) were not immediately repeated.

The great event of the year 1876 in the career of Brahms was the appearance of the long looked for symphony. As in the case of the Schicksalslied and the completed Triumphlied, the composer chose to produce his work for the first time at Carlsruhe, preferring, maybe, to test it for his own satisfaction in the comparative privacy of a small audience before submitting it to the searching ordeal of performance in either of the great musical centres of the Continent. The musical life of Carlsruhe had suffered sadly by the departure of Levi in 1872, and it was not until the appointment of Dessoff to the post of court capellmeister, on his resignation of his duties in Vienna in 1875, that the city began to regain some of its former artistic prestige. The performance on November 4, 1876, from the manuscript, of Brahms' first Symphony by the grand ducal orchestra under Dessoff, in the composer's presence, was a musical event that revived the recollections of a brilliant past, and added a new and abiding distinction to the artistic traditions of the small capital.

The work was heard a few days later in Mannheim, and on the 15th of the month in Munich; on both occasions under the composer's direction. Four other performances from the manuscript quickly followed—in Vienna (Gesellschaft), December 17, in Leipzig, January 18, and Breslau, January 23, 1877, in each case under the composer, and in Cambridge, March 8, 1877, under Joachim's direction.

The Symphony in C minor, whose appearance marks the period of Brahms' achievement in the highest domain of absolute music, and the last that remained to him for conquest, is in the first place remarkable from the fact that it cannot properly be ranged beside the works in the same form produced by either of the two masters who were, chronologically speaking, his immediate predecessors. By its accomplishment, no less than by its aim, it must be regarded as the immediate successor to the symphonies of Beethoven in the same sense as these were the direct descendants of the symphonies of Mozart and Haydn, and it establishes Brahms' right to be accepted in its own domain as the heir, *par excellence*, of one and all of these masters. This alone were much. Still more important, however, is the fact that our composer has known how to graft upon the symphony form inherited from Beethoven, Mozart, and Haydn, the giant stock of Bach's learning and resource, studied and absorbed by him until they had become a part of his own artistic individuality, in such a manner as to revivify it root and branch, and make it a supple instrument in his hand, not for the mechanical imitation of what had been done before him, but for the 'highest ideal musical expression of his own time.'[51] Few who listen with quickened ears to an adequate performance of the C minor Symphony can be in doubt that whilst in outward form and manner of construction it may be regarded as at once the epitome and the latest result of the past history of classical instrumental art, it is in spirit representative of its own time and even anticipatory of the future; that it not only reflects the soul of the musician, poet, and philosopher, but is suggestive of the higher vision of the prophet. It is this fact, for those who accept it as a fact, that constitutes the highest significance of Brahms' first symphony, and lends a real meaning to Bülow's well-known apophthegm of 'the three B's': Bach, Beethoven, and Brahms.

The shrill, clashing dissonances of the first introduction at once place the listener in the atmosphere of stern grandeur, passion, mystery, that surround, not this or that human life, but existence itself, in its apprehension by human intelligence; and the allegro to which it leads seems to the present writer to present as near an analogy as art can show to the processes of nature, built up as it is—first and second subjects and their treatment—from a few notes; from what one of the Vienna critics called 'mere twigs of thematic material'; from germs which are produced and reproduced, are transformed and reformed, and developed into a great organic whole instinct with noble, living melody. The solemnly fervent andante sostenuto, the graceful, innocent allegretto with its sufficiently contrasted trio, afford the mind the refreshment of change of tone after the stormy splendour of the first movement; but the note of tragedy is resumed with the first sounds of the wonderful adagio that precedes, and essentially contains, the allegro of the fourth movement. Here, for some twenty-eight bars, the tension of feeling increases till destiny itself seems to be held in suspense; then, with the resolution of a chromatic chord, the horn sounds the unexpected major third of the key in a six-four of the tonic triad, and, continuing its strange, passionate cry, gradually disperses the mists of doubt and apprehension that have held the hearer as in a thrall, and carries him forward to the sublimity of joy that dwells in the final allegro.

'The last movement of your C minor Symphony,' wrote Billroth to Brahms in 1890, fourteen years after its first performance, 'has again lately excited me fearfully. Of what avail is the perfect, clear beauty of the principal subject in its thematically complete form? The horn returns at length with its romantic, impassioned cry as in the introduction, and all palpitates with longing, rapture and supersensuous exaltation and bliss.'

These words were not written by a fantastic dreamer, but by one of the most renowned scientific and practical surgeons and busiest men of his time, and in using them he did not employ a mere rhetorical phrase. The quality of imagination which speaks through Brahms' first symphony is akin to that of the early Sonata in F minor, though it is expressed in the later work with the help of more than twenty years additional study and experience. It is that of a seer of visions, and seems to culminate, in the passage to which Billroth alluded, in an ecstasy of wonder and joy. Brahms undoubtedly rose to the full height of his great powers in this first symphony, which remains unsurpassed in workmanship and sustained loftiness of idea, as well as in regard to the range of emotion to which it appeals.

It goes without saying that the supposed merits and demerits of the work became the subject of heated argument between the partisans and antagonists of the composer's art, the particulars of which would scarcely prove interesting to readers of the present day. In giving some account of the first impressions made by the symphony, we shall quote from those notices only which, whilst they are in themselves not without value, appear to have been written in a candid spirit, and do not offensively betray the influence of party bias. The reputation attaching to Hanslick's name, and the moderation of his style, seem to make it necessary to include something from his report, though he was avowedly a stanch admirer of Brahms' music, and had little liking for that of the New-German school. To balance this, we shall give a few sentences from the *Wiener Zeitung*, a journal to which, as the reader may remember, no suspicion can attach of handling our master's works with an excess of cordiality. It is necessary to explain, for the benefit of such readers as are not familiar with Brahms' large works, that the references to Beethoven's ninth symphony occurring in some of the press notices are occasioned by what has sometimes been described as Brahms' intentional allusion, in the principal theme of his finale, to Beethoven's setting of Schiller's 'Ode to Joy' in the last movement of the great 'ninth.' The so-called allusion consists, not so much in a similarity of melody in Brahms' theme to that of Beethoven, as in its being written in the same hymn-form and harmonized as plainly as possible. There is no doubt whatever that everyone who listens to Brahms' first symphony thinks immediately, on the entrance of the final allegro, of Beethoven's ninth. The association passes with the conclusion of the subject; Brahms' movement develops on its own lines, which do not resemble those of Beethoven.

'In this work,' says Hanslick (*Neue Freie Presse*), 'Brahms' close affinity with Beethoven must become clear to every musician who has not already perceived it. The new symphony displays an energy of will, a logic of musical thought, a greatness of structural power and a mastery of technique such as are possessed by no other living composer. It would be a sorry mistake to attempt to criticize a work so serious and difficult of comprehension immediately after hearing it for the first time. Various listeners may have found the music more or less clear, more or less sympathetic; the one thing that we may speak of as a simple fact, accepted alike by friend and foe, is that no composer has yet approached so nearly to the great works of Beethoven as Brahms in the finale of the C minor Symphony.'

'... Brahms was an important personality, one to be treated most seriously before he wrote the symphony,' we read in the *Wiener Zeitung*; 'to our thinking his position remains just as it was. The strong moral earnestness, the depth and purity of his conception of the world and of life, and the intellectuality, which have always obtained for the esteem of the noble-minded and withheld from him the favour of the masses, are to be found again in this work. None the less, however, are the shadows there which but too easily accompany such lights; the want of inspiriting fancy, the absence of sensuous charm, and a sullen asceticism almost amounting to insipidity. His musical language has lost nothing of its mysterious reticence, of its close conciseness, of the elevation that on the whole distinguishes it, nor has it gained in facility, clearness, or comprehensibility.... So there is nothing that can be admired without reserve, until with sure step, with strong, proud gait that reminds one of the majesty of Beethoven, the finale strides out. After a bar or two of deeply sorrowful complaint, it braces itself to a turbulent pizzicato of the strings, as a man who would get rid of pain by nerving himself to action.... With the entry of the chorale, the hearer experiences a sensation of brightness as at the rising of the sun after a night of sorrow. The last mists disappear as before the breaking light, and the movement closes in strong, healthy gladness.... Here the arts of music and poetry mingle indissolubly, and the musical, cannot be separated from the poetic, impression. Here is a truly great artistic achievement, the value of which is but slightly prejudiced by the consideration that the "joy" theme has an unmistakable resemblance as of son to father to that of the "ninth" symphony. This movement is worthy of the man who composed the German Requiem.'

Dörffel, of the *Leipziger Nachrichten*, wrote:

'The interest of all present was centred on the new symphony, which, on the whole, justified the great expectations with which it had been awaited. Its effect on the audience was the most intense that has been produced by any new symphony within our remembrance. Schumann in his time did not attain such.... The composition is to be viewed and measured from the standpoint of Beethoven's ninth, and of Schumann's second, symphony. The aim of the three works is the same. To reach it, Brahms, well-equipped and daring spirit as he is, goes his own way. He is great in attack as his two predecessors, and has the same wide vision over the domain of spiritual-human existence.... As regards uninterrupted energy of creative power, we would give the palm to the first movement. The second, with its fervour and longing, accords with it. To the third we should gladly have listened longer. It supplied a counterpoise of sentiment to what had gone before which had not been maintained long enough when the movement closed. Of the finale we would almost venture to surmise that it gave the composer the most trouble. Here he relinquishes his independence, and flies to Beethoven in order to get new force for his climax. We do not regard the resort to Beethoven as accidental, but believe the composer to have been well aware of it. He came, however, to one over whom he could not prevail.

'A long pause followed the symphony; one, however, that was not long enough in some measure to quiet the exaltation of mind produced by the work. The songs and variations which followed, and which we should have welcomed at another time, were almost tiresome to us. Let the symphony be repeated soon, and, if possible, without other music.'[52]

Louis Ehlert says of the symphony:

'Brahms has a wide-reaching and speculative brain, and is a mixture of the musician of the good old times who heard many voices sounding together within him, whose very cradle cover was embroidered with a contrapuntal pentagram, and of the man of the present day with his variously cultured intellect.... What distinguishes his music from that of all his contemporaries is the mysterious apparition within it of another world—its gentle, pathetic tapping at the heart.

'The first movement of the symphony is, perhaps, the most artistically important of the work.... An inexorable causality proceeds from bar to bar, stayed by no illusion, and softened only by the distant light of a few solitary stars. In the introduction and finale the enigmatical sphinx seems to call to us, "That which ascends from me, mounting upwards to battle and to life, sinks back again within me. Of all life I, the eternal riddle, am the beginning and the end."'

It will be evident from what has been said that whatever the impression to be derived from familiar acquaintance with the symphony, immediate enthusiasm could hardly have been anticipated from any large general public—least of all by Brahms himself; but the presence at most of these first performances of devotees specially qualified for apprehending something of the significance of the work generally secured for it more than a mere *succès d'estime*. The listeners of Munich were the least appreciative. Those of Carlsruhe, Mannheim and Breslau were friendly. At Vienna certain favoured friends were privileged to listen to a private performance of the symphony by Brahms and Ignaz Brüll, in the composer's arrangement as a pianoforte duet, at the pianoforte house of his friend Herr Hoffabrikant Friedrich Ehrbar, and went to the concert, therefore, with minds partially prepared for what they were to hear. At Leipzig a note of enthusiasm was perceptible at the crowded public rehearsal which preceded the Gewandhaus concert, owing partly to the fact that Brahms' Leipzig adherents had been strongly reinforced by the advent of friends from outside, some of whom added warmth and prestige to the occasion by their mere presence. The feeling for our master's art which, as we have seen, had been slowly growing amongst a number of Leipzig residents who belonged to no musical 'set,' will have been expressed with added zest and enjoyment when it was found that Frau Schumann and Joachim and Stockhausen had come to hear the symphony, whilst to the support of the von Herzogenbergs, von Holsteins, Theodor Kirchner, and other resident or lately resident friends, was added that of the Grimms from Münster, Dr. Hermann Deiters from Bonn, Professor and Frau Engelmann from Utrecht, Simrock from Berlin, and many other distinguished guests. Enthusiasm is contagious, and already at the rehearsal a success was ensured for the work, though perhaps it was not very warmly helped by the official patrons of the Gewandhaus.

'A regular Brahms party meeting had been organized,' says Bernsdorf in the *Signale*, now as ever inveterate in his own party bias, in which a fairly strong contingent from outside was associated with the resident admirers and champions of the composer. It is therefore a matter of course that the consumption of enthusiasm was enormous, and that the success of the symphony was one exceptional in the annals of the Gewandhaus.'

A large party of friends assembled at supper at the Hôtel Hauffe after the concert. Brahms' health was proposed in genial fashion by Stockhausen. 'Hab' ich tausendmal geschworen,'[53] he suddenly sang out, starting to his feet and raising his glass. Needless to say that the toast, which was the more effective from the sense of victory filling the minds of those who had assisted at the evening's triumph, was honoured with the utmost enthusiasm.

The performance of the symphony by the Cambridge University Musical Society was given under special circumstances. Early in the year the university offered the master an honorary degree, acceptance of which would have involved him in a visit to England, since, by one of the university statutes, its degrees may not be conferred *in absentia*. Brahms was not asked to write a new work for the occasion, a request he would properly have resented, but was merely invited to visit Cambridge for the purpose of receiving the degree, and was so far gratified by the compliment as to hesitate about his answer. Perhaps his mere reluctance to decline the invitation in spite of his dread of English customs and his ignorance of the language, may be accepted as stronger testimony of appreciation than might have been implied in the effusive acceptance of many another man. It may be doubted whether he would in any case have prevailed upon himself to undertake the journey; an indiscreet advertisement, however, inserted in *The Times* by the Crystal Palace directors, who had heard a rumour of his possible visit, that if he should come he would be asked to conduct one of their Saturday concerts, immediately decided him to decline the University's proffered honour. He acknowledged the invitation by entrusting the MS. score and parts of the symphony to the care of Joachim, who was about starting on his yearly visit to England, for performance at Cambridge.

The programme of March 8 was as follows:

PART I.

W. G. Bennett: Overture, 'The Wood Nymph.'

Beethoven: Concerto for Violin and Orchestra.

Violin, Dr. Joachim.

Brahms: A Song of Destiny.

Bach: Violin Solos, Dr. Joachim.

Joachim: Elegiac Overture (in memory of H. Kleist).

PART II.

Brahms: Symphony in C minor.

The Symphony and the Elegiac Overture, the latter composed by Joachim in acknowledgment of the honorary degree offered him by the University and conferred in the afternoon of March 8, were given under his direction; the remainder of the programme was under that of the society's conductor, C. Villiers Stanford.

The concert attracted a great audience, which included prominent musicians from various parts of the United Kingdom. The impression created by the symphony was profound, and, following that of the German Requiem and of the great chamber music compositions and songs which had now for some years been finding their way to the hearts of music lovers in this country, formed, as Stanford says, 'an imperishable keystone to Brahms' fame amongst Britons.'[54] The new work was performed in London a few weeks later at the Philharmonic concert of April 16, under W. G. Cusins.

Probably Brahms' Vienna friends and admirers little dreamed how near they had been at this time to losing their favourite. The position of municipal music-director at Düsseldorf was pressed on his acceptance in the autumn of 1876, and he was sufficiently tempted by it to be characteristically unable to decide on a negative answer. He was, indeed, so long in coming to a final resolution, that the Düsseldorf authorities had every reason to feel persuaded they had secured him for the opening of the year 1877. At the last moment he wrote: 'I cannot make up my mind to it.' This seems to have been the last occasion on which he entertained the idea of binding himself to the performance of fixed duties, though it has been surmised that he might have consented at a somewhat later period to associate himself with a high class for composition at the conservatoire of the Vienna 'Gesellschaft,' if he had been approached by the principal, Josef Hellmesberger, on the subject of forming one.

Certain incidents belonging to the autumn of 1877, related by Widmann in his Brahms' 'Recollections,' show that at this time, when the master had successfully proved his powers in every form of composition for the concert-room, the old desire to try his hand at writing for the stage revived within him. Brahms and Widmann met at Mannheim, and were present at the production, on September 30, of Götz's unfinished opera, 'Francesca di Rimini,' under Frank. In the course of a long *tête-à-tête*, held on their return to their hotel after the performance, Brahms clearly explained his views on the subject of opera texts, 'letting it be seen,' says Widmann, 'that any resolution he might have formed against composing an opera might give way were he to find himself in possession of a libretto really to his liking.'

The convictions professed on this occasion by the composer may be traced to an attitude of mind similar to that to which we referred on recording his conversation with Bulthaupt. Strange as it may appear, they have a fundamental kinship with those which led Wagner to embark on his career as a musico-dramatic reformer, though the methods proposed by Brahms were not only much more drastic than those pursued by Wagner, but ran, as Widmann has observed, directly in the opposite direction from that taken by the development of modern art as represented by this master.

'The composition of music to the entire drama seemed to Brahms unnecessary and even mischievous. Only the culminating points and those parts of the action should be set for which music would be an inherently suitable medium of expression. The librettist would thus gain space and freedom for the dramatic development of his subject, whilst the composer would be at liberty to devote himself solely to the purposes of his art which would be best served if he were able to concentrate his energies on a definite situation such as a jubilant *ensemble*.'

From this it would appear that the incongruity essential to the very existence of what is generally understood as Opera, as distinct from the early German Singspiel, was so strongly felt by Brahms as to seem to him incompatible with dramatic truth, and to be absolutely prohibitive in his own case of the dramatic exercise of his art. The matter is, however, susceptible of another explanation.

It is clear that Brahms, when contemplating the composition of an opera, was bound by the necessities of his position to seek the attainment of dramatic truth in a direction other than that in which Wagner had led the way with such triumphant result. Every circumstance in the careers of the two men, and not least the representative position achieved by each in his own sphere, precluded the possibility that Brahms should run the risk of appearing to seek to emulate Wagner on his own ground, though it would be difficult to believe that he at no time cast longing thoughts towards the logical, consistent, rich means of artistic effect offered by the Melos.[55] No one can doubt that if he had been in a position, and had chosen, to use it, he would have employed it in his own way and for his own original purposes and effects. The skill with which he might have handled it in opera is to some small extent indicated in the Rhapsody (Goethe's 'Harzreise'), where the method of the two first sections is very much that of the Melos, whilst the prayer, affording an opportunity 'inherently suitable for musical expression,' reverts to the rhythmical melody of musical tradition. That Brahms had a respect almost amounting to veneration for Wagner's powers is matter of common knowledge. Though he was never present at a Bayreuth performance, he had studied Wagner's scores exhaustively, and, in the sense of his intimate acquaintance with them, was accustomed to call himself the 'best of all Wagnerians.' An anecdote related by Richard Heuberger,[56] to whom the master gave informal instruction in composition for a time from early in 1878, is highly illustrative in this connection. Heuberger says:

'... Continuing his corrections, Brahms did not confine himself to remarks on the composition itself, but considered the handwriting also worthy of his notice. He pointed out that I had not placed crotchet under crotchet, and that this impaired the legibility of the manuscript; he advised me to be particular to slur the groups of notes with exactness.... "Look here," he said, fetching from the next room Wagner's autograph score of "Tannhäuser," which he opened at the long B major movement of the second act; "Wagner has taken pains to place each of the five sharps exactly in its place on *every* line of *every* page, and in spite of all this precision the writing is easy and flowing. If *such* a man can write so neatly, you must do so too." He turned over the entire movement and pointed reproachfully to almost every sharp. I felt continually smaller, especially as Brahms talked himself into a kind of didactic wrathfulness. I was struck completely dumb, however, when, on my remarking that Wagner must be held chiefly responsible for the confusion prevailing in the heads of us young people, Brahms cried as though he had been stung, "*Nonsense*; the *misunderstood* Wagner has done it. Those understand *nothing* of the real Wagner who are led astray by him. Wagner's is one of the clearest heads that ever existed in the world!"'

That Brahms was aware that the resolution to compose an opera would place him in a net of difficulties that might practically be summed up in the one word 'Wagner' is no mere conjecture. Fräulein Anna Ettlinger, an intimate friend of Levi and Allgeyer, who knew Brahms well both at Carlsruhe and Munich, relates in an article on Levi, that Brahms answered a question put to him in Munich in the course of the seventies, as to why he had written no opera by saying, 'Beside Wagner it is impossible.' It may fairly be concluded that Brahms, in the late seventies, merely 'coquetted,' as Widmann expresses it, with the idea of composing for the stage, though no doubt with considerable regret.[57]

It cannot be said that the subjects he proposed to Widmann appear happy, but his suggestions must not be taken too seriously.

'He recommended to me Gozzi's magical farces and fabled comedies, especially "King Stag" and "The Ravens." He was also interested in "The Open Secret," and preferred Gozzi's lighter arrangement of the piece to Calderon's more formal original.... After reading "King Stag" carefully through several times, I was not only seized with a certain hopelessness as to whether I could ever succeed in making a rational, poetical opera text out of this mad farce, but disturbed by the anxiety as to whether, even if it were successfully adapted, it could really interest a modern theatre-going public.... I found myself continually thinking that such an opera, even though Brahms had composed for it the most beautiful, glorious music, as would undoubtedly have been the case, could not be regarded as essentially anything else than a sort of second "Zauberflöte," and thus as a retrogression in the development of operatic art.'[58]

Nothing, in short, resulted from the talk between Brahms and Widmann, and the suitable libretto was, as we know, never found. This is, perhaps, little to be regretted. Not, indeed, because the composer lacked the dramatic instinct necessary for the successful composition of opera. No one who has heard him quote a few lines from a classical play can doubt that he possessed this qualification in an eminent degree, and his sensitiveness to dramatic effect was matter for frequent comment by those who accompanied him to the theatre. It is, however, difficult to imagine that Brahms could have been content to compose music to a purely comic text, or, indeed, to one that did not contain elements of deep pathos; whilst a quasi-comic opera, in which allegory lay hidden, must almost certainly have been found, as Widmann perceived, unsuitable to modern taste. On the other hand, Brahms' constitutional shyness and reticence, fostered through long years of varied experience until they became invincible, must, we believe, have proved obstacles to the successful completion of a serious opera in any practicable meaning of the word, even if they had allowed him to attempt one. They are more or less traceable in the libretto difficulty; in his suggestion of 'King Stag,' which he recommended especially on account of its fun, 'accompanied throughout by the most pathetic earnestness'; in other words, because the earnestness is covered by the fun. It is difficult to imagine the man who habitually veiled the tenderness of his nature behind a playful saying or an abrupt manner, who did not allow himself to inquire about the possibilities of passionate feeling that might lie dormant within him, coming out of his reserve to use the strong play of emotion as the immediate and capital medium for his effects. The energy of feeling, the deeply pathetic beauty which vitalize the master's purely instrumental music, are surrounded and protected by an intellectual atmosphere which, on a first hearing of his larger works, sometimes seems to amount to austerity, and to repel rather than attract. His love-songs—those of them which are not folk-songs—are for the most part dreamings of an ideal, and not the ideal of a man who could lay his heart bare on the theatre boards. Not wholly fanciful is the association in which Brahms, in a letter to Widmann, jokingly placed his two life renunciations, of the composition of an opera and of marriage. The extracts from favourite authors entered by Johannes during the early fifties in the little manuscript books described by Kalbeck, the passages found in 'The young Kreisler's treasure-chest, March, 1854,' remain significant not only of the young musician of twenty, but also of the master of forty, fifty, sixty years, and the quotation from Friedrich v. Sallet might probably stand as the true history of Brahms' inner life.

'One generally finds the highest degree of what is called *openness* in the most frivolous and thoughtless persons; of that which is called *reserve*, in the deepest, richest and truest minds. And, indeed, I am glad to be communicative, and like a full, free flow of conversation during the clinking of cups; whatever noble thought may have occurred to me should not have been gained for myself, but, if possible, for the world. Nevertheless, there is in the mind a holy of holies. I would not bring that forth which shines brightly there, hidden away in the inmost recess, to glimmer vainly and childishly in the universal light of day. Let it remain there in sacred night. I dare not even tell it in barren words to my friend, however noble, not even to my beloved (if I had one). To what purpose? I might use one single misleading expression, the other might misunderstand one single expression, and my divine image, reflected from a concave mirror, become a distortion, common or trivial, or even deformed and ridiculous.... To analyze and describe the sacred within us is a shameless desecration. If the other has a spiritual eye that is worthy to perceive, he may quietly await one of those blissful moments when the curtain of mists breaks and a swift, comprehensive glance into the sanctuary of the temple is allowed to the worthy one, and in such moments is celebrated the high festival of friendship as of love. For myself, I dare reveal nothing of it in words save in poetry. There I may do so, for it happens in some divine way that is incomprehensible to me....'[59]

We have henceforth, therefore, only to observe the unwearied energy with which Brahms, during the succeeding years, added one work after another to the list of his compositions in each and every branch of serious music for the chamber and the concert-room: songs, vocal duets, choral works and instrumental solos accompanied and unaccompanied, concerted music for solo instruments, symphonies. The publications of the year 1877 were the Symphony and the four sets of Songs, Op. 69, 70, 71, 72, twenty-four songs in all, some of the texts of which are by Carl Candidus, Carl Lemke, Gottfried Keller, etc., and others imitations of folk-songs of various nationalities. Dr. Deiters says of them in his 'Johannes Brahms':

'As it seems to us, the composer identifies himself here more and more closely with classical form and achieves ever purer refinement of his material. Turn where one will (we mention for instance "Des Liebsten Schwur" from Op. 69) there can be no hesitation in counting these songs with the best to be found of their kind. Again we are constantly reminded of Franz Schubert, whose wealth of melody is revived, whilst in conciseness of construction, in conscious mastery of form, he is here greatly surpassed.'

Heuberger gives a pleasant glimpse of Brahms co-operating in a festival performance arranged for December, 1877, by the Academic Choral Society of Vienna in honour of its distinguished honorary member, Billroth. Invited by Heuberger, Dr. Eyrich's successor as conductor of the society, to take part in the proceedings, the master at once promised to conduct two of his choruses, 'Ich schnell mein Horn' and 'Lied vom Herrn von Falkenstein,' as arranged for the occasion for men's voices by Heuberger, and, on his appearance at the last rehearsal to go through the well-prepared compositions, was greeted with a hurricane of welcome by the over two hundred students who formed the choir. At the festival performance next day

'Brahms joined in the students' songs as lustily as his rough, broken voice would permit. He had, as he told me, a very good soprano voice as a boy, but had spoilt it by singing too much during its mutation period.'

Of another occasion, a party at Billroth's house, when choruses by Brahms and Goldmark were to be performed, Heuberger relates:

'By Brahms' suggestion I directed the preliminary practices which took place at the houses of some of his friends, the Osers and others. The day before the party Brahms and Goldmark came to the last rehearsal. The so-reputed cross-grained Brahms now conducted his "Marienlieder" and other works without much alteration of the nuances that I had practised. Goldmark, on the contrary, who was as much liked in private life as he was dreaded at rehearsal, studied indefatigably on and on.'[60]

The publication of Brahms' first Symphony in C minor was almost immediately followed by the appearance of a second one in D major, completed during the summer months of 1877 at the beloved Lichtenthal. It was, like the earlier work, played by Brahms and Brüll before an invited circle at Ehrbar's as a pianoforte duet (composer's arrangement) a few days before the date, December 11, first announced for its performance at a Vienna Philharmonic concert. Cause arose at the last moment for the postponement of this event, and the work was given for the first time in public at the succeeding Philharmonic concert of December 30, under Hans Richter's direction. The second performance, conducted by Brahms, took place at the Leipzig Gewandhaus on January 10, 1878.

The early fortunes of this second symphony were singularly various, and contrasted strangely with those of its predecessor. In Vienna, where the first had been received with reserve, the second achieved an instant, almost popular, success. It was warmly received by the audience, and was discussed by nearly all sections of the press in terms of cordial approval. It was of a 'more attractive character,' more 'understandable' than its predecessor. It was to be preferred, too, inasmuch as the composer had not this time 'entered the lists with Beethoven.' The third movement was especially praised for its 'original melody and rhythms.' The work might be appropriately termed the 'Vienna Symphony,' reflecting as it did 'the fresh, healthy life only to be found in beautiful Vienna.' In Leipzig, on the other hand, the work was little better than a failure. The impression of the preceding year was felt in the general applause, emphasized by a thrice-repeated flourish of trumpets and drums, which greeted the composer's entrance, and the audience maintained an attitude of polite cordiality throughout the performance of the symphony, courteously applauding between the movements and recalling the master at the end; but the enthusiasm of personal friends was not this time able to kindle any corresponding warmth in the bulk of the audience, or even to cover the general consciousness of the fact. The most favourable of the press notices damned the work with faint praise, and Dörffel, whom we quote here and elsewhere because he alone of the professional Leipzig critics of the seventies seems to have been imbued with a sense of Brahms' artistic greatness, showed himself quite angry from disappointment.

'The Viennese,' he wrote, 'are much more easily satisfied than we. We make quite different demands on Brahms, and require from him music which is something more than "pretty" and "very pretty" when he comes before us as a symphonist. Not that we do not wish to hear him in his complaisant moods, not that we disdain to accept from him pictures of real life, but we desire always to contemplate his genius, whether he displays it in a manner of his own, or depends on that of Beethoven. We have not discovered genius in the new symphony and should hardly have guessed it to be the work of Brahms had it been performed anonymously. We should have recognised the great mastery of form, the extremely skilful handling of the material, the conspicuous power of construction in short, which it displays, but should not have described it as pre-eminently distinguished by inventive power. We should have pronounced the work to be one worthy of respect, but not counting for much in the domain of symphony. Perhaps we may be mistaken; if so, the error should be pardonable, arising as it does from the great expectations which our reverence for the composer induced us to form.'

Possibly Dörffel's expectations had been founded too definitely upon his admiration of the first symphony, which may have caused him to take for granted that he would find in the second a reiteration of the exalted moods of its predecessor. The two works should not, however, be weighed in the balance one against the other, but should be considered side by side for the reason that they are not only different, but, as it were, supplementary. The first partakes of the nature of an epic in so far as it is conceived on a grand scale and is dominated throughout three of its four movements by a passionate intensity of feeling which is occupied only with the sublimities, whether of pain or of joy, and which, even after the pain has been conquered, seems to touch the joy theme itself with the pathos of a past tragedy. The second symphony is an idyll that is chiefly animated by the spirit of pure happiness and gently tender grace. A second symphony quickly following the first, which had shown any attempt to emulate that great work on its own ground, must of necessity have been doomed to result in artistic failure. The second symphony which the master actually wrote was one which, whilst it probably satisfied a need of his mind for the refreshment of change, was the appropriate sequel to its predecessor both in regard to its calm serenity of mood and to the clear melody of the thematic material in which the mood is so perfectly expressed. Those who are inexorable in their demands for 'originality' may, however, be referred to the 'adagio non troppo,' which, with its melodious phrases and its beautiful tone effects, its varied rhythms and its mysterious intention, offers opportunity for the energetic attention even of the accustomed listener, and is the one movement of the work which can hardly be at once followed with entire pleasure by the less initiated.

Meanwhile the first symphony was quickly making its way through Europe. It was given with enormous success on November 11, 1877, at a concert of the Royal Academy of Arts, Berlin, by the orchestra of the music school under Joachim, and was very inadequately performed on the 16th of the same month at a Hamburg Philharmonic concert under von Bernuth. By the strongly-expressed desire of many musicians of the city, the composer was invited to conduct a repetition performance at the Philharmonic concert of January 18, 1878, when the work achieved considerable success. It was heard the same month in Bremen and Utrecht under Brahms, in Münster (J. O. Grimm), Dresden (F. Wüllner), and in February for the second time in Breslau (Scholz), and made its way in the course of a few seasons to Basle, Zürich, Rotterdam, Amsterdam, the Hague, Edinburgh, Glasgow, and New York.

Brahms now, at the age of forty-four, was, indeed, in the enjoyment of almost unclouded recognition and success, which could be but little affected by the lack of enthusiasm of this or that audience. His position had become the more firmly established from the circumstance that very few of his works had taken the public by storm. The majority of them had grown almost imperceptibly into general acceptance by sheer force of their intrinsic value, of which but a modicum is to be found on the surface. It is certainly the case that at the outset of his modest entry on a public career he had gained with a single stroke, once and for always, the enthusiastic suffrage of some of the princes of his art; but the voice of Schumann, potent as it was, could be and had been only of avail to procure him a hearing—appreciation was, by the nature of things, beyond its control; and though Frau Schumann and Joachim and Stockhausen untiringly used the influence of their position as best beloved among the foremost favourites of the public to make a way for his music, even they could not immediately secure for it enthusiasm. This it had gradually to gain by the independent means of its indwelling virtue, the insistency of its appeal, not to the outward seeming, but to the very heart of things.

A noteworthy addition was made in the course of the year 1877 to the ranks of Brahms' most stanch and influential supporters in the person of Hans von Bülow. Remark has already been made on the change observable in the early seventies in the attitude of this gifted, witty, whimsical, uncompromising, true-hearted musician towards Brahms' art. The publication of the first symphony completed his conversion, and he soon afterwards began an active propaganda on the master's behalf, to which, carried on as it was with characteristic vehemence and eccentricity, and started at the very moment when the great composer was achieving the highest summit of fame, an entirely fictitious importance has sometimes been ascribed in regard to its effect upon the outward development of Brahms' career. That von Bülow during the last ten or twelve years of his public activity partially devoted his energies to the task of forcing the master's works upon certain more or less indifferent audiences, whom he harangued and lectured concerning their lack of interest, had no bearing on the facts that Brahms' place amongst the immortals had been assured, by practically general consent, with the first few performances of the German Requiem, and that by the beginning of the eighties acceptance of his art had become world-wide. Bülow's new partisanship, destined to bring in its train distinguished friendships that were truly prized and reciprocated by the master, was touching from its sincerity, but is not of essential importance to Brahms' biographer. It is, however, pleasant to be able to add to the extracts already quoted from Bülow's writings three which, dated October and November, 1877, mark the beginning of a new epoch in his own career, and in that of Brahms the commencement of an agreeable and valued personal intimacy. The paragraphs are to be taken merely as illustrations of Bülow's changed sentiments, and not as necessarily expressing the personal views of the present writer.

'Only since my acquaintance with the "*tenth*" symphony, alias the *first* symphony of Johannes Brahms, that is since six weeks, have I become so inaccessible and hard towards Bruch pieces and the like. I do not call it the "*tenth*" in the sense of its relation to the "*ninth*"....'

'I believe it is not without the intelligence of chance that Bach, Beethoven, and Brahms are in alliteration.'

'The imagination of Bach seems, in his clavier works, to be dominated by the organ, that of Beethoven by the orchestra, that of Brahms by both.'

CHAPTER XVIII
1878-1881

Hamburg Philharmonic Jubilee Festival—Violin Concerto: first performance by Joachim—Pianoforte Pieces, Op. 76—Sonata for Pianoforte and Violin—First performances—Brahms at Crefeld—Rhapsodies for Pianoforte—Heuberger's studies with Brahms—Second Schumann Festival at Bonn—The two Overtures—Breslau honorary degree.

With the rapidly-increasing appreciation of Brahms' art observable during the second half of the seventies throughout the entire musical world, the condition of his private circumstances changed rapidly also. At the time he completed the second symphony it was very far removed from that of twelve years back, when he had been obliged, by lack of ready cash, to purchase the music-paper required for the manuscript of the Requiem in small instalments. He never deviated from the simple manner of daily life agreeable to him by nature and habit, but we find that in the early spring of 1878 he added to the short list of his personal pleasures one that became to him a source of unfailing delight, that of a journey to Italy. On this his first visit, made in April, in Billroth's company, he stayed in Rome, Naples, and Sicily, and returned subjugated once and for all by the witcheries of the South. Neither of his Italian tours was associated with a musical purpose; they were undertaken solely for the refreshment of body and mind by a holiday ramble amidst beauties of nature and art, to which his temperament made him peculiarly sensitive, and amongst a people whose *naturel* was congenial to him.

'I often think of our journey,' writes Billroth on May 7; 'that you were so charmed with everything doubles my pleasure.'

The new symphony was included in the Rhine Festival, held this year at Düsseldorf under Joachim and Tausch. Amongst Joachim's duties was that of conducting the performance of his friend's work, concerning which we read in a contemporary journal:

'The performance of Brahms' second symphony under Joachim was a feast such as we have seldom heard. The audience was jubilant after each movement, and would not be satisfied till the third was repeated.'

And again in a final summary:

'The most brilliant event of the festival was the performance of Brahms' symphony.'

The composer spent the summer at Pörtschach on Lake Wörther in Carinthia, a spot where, as he writes to Hanslick, 'so many melodies fly about one must be careful not to tread on them.' In the same letter[61] he talks playfully to his old friend, who, remaining a bachelor till past fifty, had lately surprised his acquaintances by marrying a lady many years his junior, of his intention to compose a new symphony for the winter, 'that shall sound so gay and charming you will think I have written it expressly for you, or rather for your young wife.'

This idea, probably not seriously entertained, was put aside, but the reflection of the composer's happy mood is to be found in several of the pianoforte pieces written by him at this time—notably in No. 2 of Op. 76—and in the last movement of the great violin concerto he was composing for Joachim.

An event was to take place in the last week of September which no doubt possessed a peculiar interest for Brahms, though it was not of an unmixed character: the celebration of the fiftieth anniversary of the Philharmonic Society of his native city of Hamburg, which had been founded in 1828 by a few music-lovers, with W. Grund, a composer and teacher of the city, as its conductor. The festival was to last five days, and to include three great orchestral concerts in the Saagebiel Hall and an excursion up the Elbe to Blankenese. Four symphonies were to be performed: Haydn in G minor, Beethoven's 'Eroica,' Schumann in C major, Brahms in D major. Frau Schumann was to play Mozart's Pianoforte Concerto in D minor; Joachim to perform with Concertmeister Bargheer, Spohr's Duo Concertante for two violins in B minor. A great assemblage of musicians was expected, and Brahms had been invited, but at the beginning of September no one in Hamburg knew whether or not he intended to be present, and the directors of the festival, finding themselves very near a predicament, resolved to appeal to Hanslick, who had received and accepted an invitation, to procure his answer for them. The letter which Hanslick immediately wrote to Pörtschach elicited from Brahms the following reply:

'PÖRTSCHACH, *Sept., 1878.*

'You have once already publicly preached to me the doctrine of decorum; I do not wish this to occur, from no fault of mine, a second time, and tell you, therefore, that it will be the Hamburgers' concern if I do not appear at their festival. I have no opportunity for showing politeness and gratitude; on the contrary, some rudeness would be in place if I had time and inclination to lose my temper over the matter. I do not wish to disturb yours by detailed communication and will therefore only say that in spite of inquiry, not a word has been said about honorarium or any sort of remuneration. I, poor composer, am appraised at doubtful value and lose all right to sit at the festival table, next to your wife, let us say. I therefore beg this time for indulgence for my anyway impaired reputation as a polite man. As regards the symphony, indeed, I do not beg for indulgence, but I fear that unless its direction be offered to Joachim as I wish, there will be a miserable performance. Now, the dinners are good in Hamburg, the symphony is of a favourable length—you can dream whilst it is going on that you are in Vienna! I am thinking of going to Vienna very soon....'[62]

This dubious epistle need not be taken too seriously, true though it is that the composer rightly made it a point throughout his career that his work should be paid for, and, so to speak, at full market value. The tone adopted by him on this occasion must be partly referred to the remembrance of the old sore, which, perhaps, never quite healed—to the mortification which had on two occasions cut deep into the heart of the loyal Hamburger when his fellow-citizens offered to a stranger the opportunity he would have welcomed to settle in their midst. It is not wonderful that the invitation to attend, and presumably to take part in, the Jubilee Festival of the society of which, had he so chosen, he ought since many years to have been the artistic chief should have revived past memories in the mind of the renowned master whose mere presence could now invest the occasion with a peculiar significance. All's well that ends well, however. How Brahms settled the matter with the committee must be left to conjecture, but it is certain that he astonished friends and acquaintance by coming to Hamburg with a long flowing beard grown during the summer, which changed the character of his face almost beyond recognition. It was, as we know, his second experiment of the kind, and the beard, which he from this time permanently retained, certainly added to the grandeur of his head, though some of his old friends may occasionally have looked back with regret to the days when the firm, purposeful mouth contributed its share to the expression of his countenance.

Nothing was ultimately wanting that could contribute to the success of the Hamburg celebration. The first concert, on September 25, was devoted to three of the musical giants—Bach, Handel, Beethoven; that of the 26th to Haydn, Mozart, Cherubini, Schumann, and, in memory of the society's first conductor, W. Grund. The morning of the 27th was given up to rehearsal—especially of Brahms' new symphony, under the composer's direction; the afternoon, to the excursion and banquet. Almost everyone had come from everywhere. Besides those who were taking part in the concerts there were Hiller, Gernsheim, Gade, Reinecke, Reinthaler, Grimm, Flotow, Theodor Kirchner, Verhülst (from the Hague), Hanslick, Claus Groth, not to mention Grädener, of early days, and a host of old Hamburg friends. Our master was in genial mood, and chatted gaily with acquaintances old and new during the run down the river, but a sign showed that his thoughts were with the past. Claus Groth, who was placed at the banquet next to Brahms, relates that the proposer of the composer's health referred in his speech to the old proverb of the prophet's unworthiness in his own country, and pointed out its inapplicability in the case of the day's ceremony, 'when the society unites with me in praise and love of our Johannes Brahms.'

'Brahms turned to me,' continues Groth, 'and whispered in a deep and serious tone, "This of my case! Twice was the vacant conductor's post of the Philharmonic Society given to a stranger whilst I was passed over. If it had been offered me at the right time I should have become a methodical citizen, and could have married and become like other men. Now I am a vagabond!"'

That Brahms would under any circumstances have summoned up sufficient courage to commit himself to the irretrievable step of matrimony we may be permitted to doubt. That one obstacle which prevented him was his own fear of the interruption that such a change might cause to his own almost too orderly and methodical habits is fairly certain.

The boat started from Blankenese on its return journey to St. Pauli's landing-bridge, Hamburg, at 9.30 p.m., and at the moment of its departure three rockets were sent up from deck and three shots fired from shore, by arrangement with the inhabitants of the numerous villas that line the bank of the Elbe, as a signal for the illumination of houses and gardens, which accordingly gave graceful testimony to the returning musicians of the widespread interest felt in the occasion.[63]

The third and concluding concert of the festival took place on the evening of Sunday, September 29, with performances of Weber's 'Oberon' overture, Songs by Schubert, Spohr's Concertante for two violins, Brahms' second Symphony, under his own direction, and Mendelssohn's 'Walpurgis Nacht.'

'The delight of the public at Brahms' symphony was most enthusiastically expressed,' says Hanslick. 'Brahms, who was received with orchestra flourish and laurel wreath, himself conducted, and Joachim played first violin in the orchestra. At the close of the symphony the ladies of the chorus and in the first rows of the audience threw their flowers to Brahms, who stood there, in the words of his own cradle-song, "covered with roses."'

Ludwig Meinardus, of the *Hamburger Correspondenten*, after giving a detailed and most appreciative account of the several movements of the work, continues:

'Brahms himself conducted his symphony, which is sealed with the stamp of immortality, in his native city before an audience of thousands raised to festival pitch, in which mingled a large number of musical authorities from outside. The enthusiasm was increased by this circumstance, and by the simplicity and quiet energy with which Brahms handled the bâton. It prepared for him an ovation as he ascended the conductor's desk in the shape of a big laurel wreath, a flourish, and a stormy welcome from those upon and in front of the platform; it broke out after each of the four movements, and increased at the close of the third to a *da capo* demand to which the conductor and composer only at length and with the reluctance of modesty resolved to yield; it was expressed finally, at the close of the work, by persistent recalls and by a rain of flowers which poured from all sides upon the admired and revered composer.'

The last few words seem to remind us of the early sixties, and to bring us once more face to face with the Halliers, Völckers, Wagners, Fräulein Laura Garbe, and other former members of the ladies' choir, many of whom were still resident in Hamburg, and, having retained their old affectionate admiration of their young musician without a jot of abatement as they watched his course during the passing years, now brought affection, admiration, and sympathetic triumph dressed in graceful guise to throw at the feet of the famous master. Marxsen, prevented by considerations of health from joining the excursion down the river, was present at the concert, beaming with joy; Böie, too, associated with early performances of the B flat Sextet and the G minor Pianoforte Quartet, was there, whilst the presence of Christian Otterer, who had played viola as an old friend at the subscription concert given by the youthful Hannes at the 'Old Raven,' carried the associations of the evening back almost to the year of the composer's birth. Two names which we should gladly have included are missing from the list of our old acquaintances. None would have more heartily rejoiced in the events of the evening than Friedrich Willibald Cossel, now some thirteen summers passed away; and what may not be imagined of Jakob Brahms' exultant pride had six more years of life been spared him! We may picture the pursed-up lips, the gratified expression of the eyes, the playful assumption of dignity towards his own particular chums, the tears of joy with which he would have answered Joachim's cordial hand-grasp, the shy, gratified whisper to Carl Bade, 'Ik segge nix' (I shall not speak), when some distinguished musician or charming lady had desired to be introduced to him as the father of his son. Frau Cossel was present with her talented daughter Marie (Frau Dr. Janssen), and the old family ties so treasured by our master were represented by Elise and Fritz, and by kind Frau Caroline with her son Fritz Schnack, who entertained an almost adoring affection for his stepbrother. Frau Caroline was invariably present at any concert in Hamburg in which Johannes took part, by the composer's express desire. Elise begged her brother after the concert for the wreaths that had been presented to him.

'So you want to brag with them?' said he; 'come to me early to-morrow morning; we will go together and lay them on father's grave.'

It may be added here, for the sake of completeness, that some time later, on von Bernuth's contemplated resignation, a representative of the Philharmonic Society called on Groth to ask his opinion as to the probability of Brahms' acceptance of an offer of the conductorship. He pointed out that the then committee could not justly be blamed for the mistakes of their predecessors, which they were anxious to repair as far as might now be possible, and Groth, after discussing the matter in detail, consented to lay it informally before Brahms. We cannot wonder that no answer was received to his communication; it must seem obvious to most minds that the master could neither accept nor decline an offer which had not been made. Had the committee decided to risk the slight mortification of a refusal from Brahms by writing a definite proposal to him, it is certain that he would have replied to it, though it seems unlikely that he would have uprooted himself from the city where he had formed intimate friendships now that one of the principal attractions which Hamburg had possessed for him—the presence of his parents—had ceased to exist.

The publications of the year include, besides the Symphony in D major, a set of 'Ballads and Romances' for two voices, dedicated to Julius Allgeyer, the first of which has the Scotch ballad 'Edward' for its text.

Of other early performances of the second symphony we may mention those of October 22 in Breslau, under the composer, and of November 23 in Münster, under Grimm. Such a furore was created in Münster that the work was repeated by general desire at the concert of December 21.

At the Vienna Gesellschaft concert of December 8, No. 1 of the two Motets, Op. 74, for unaccompanied chorus was sung, under the direction of Edward Kremser, from the manuscript parts. All four movements, the first and last in four, the second and third in six, parts, made a deep impression, and in spite of the serious character of the work it was followed by long-continued applause. The texts have the characteristics usually preferred by Brahms for his sacred compositions, and, taken together, are expressive of courageous, trustful resignation in the face of mystery. The music, exquisitely suited to the words, furnishes another example of deeply serious feeling clothed in the beautiful forms of early contrapuntal art.

Great interest was aroused in the musical circles of many lands by the announcement that Joachim would play a violin concerto by Brahms at the Leipzig Gewandhaus concert of January 1, 1879. Such an event was bound to raise a particular question, connected not only with Brahms' musical career, but with the history of musical art. Many concertos for violin solo with orchestral accompaniment had been produced since the days of Viotti, through those of Mozart and Spohr, down to the publication in 1877 of Max Bruch's second in D minor, and, of the most favoured, few had retained more than an occasional place in concert-programmes. Two only had survived the test of time as the pre-eminent masterpieces of their class; those of Beethoven and Mendelssohn. If no work of the kind could be placed exactly with Beethoven's Violin Concerto, yet, even as compared with this supreme achievement, no thought of inferiority could be applied to that of Mendelssohn, which immediately on its production took the place it had ever since held as one of two *chefs-d'œuvre*. The question which now naturally suggested itself was whether Brahms' new work would take its place as a third by the side of its two greatest predecessors. It was the more interesting because, though the composer was not now breaking essentially new ground, yet his one previous concerto had been composed for the pianoforte, and whilst two decades had elapsed since its completion in final form (Detmold, autumn of 1858), and first public performances (Hanover and Leipzig, January, 1859), it bore distinct traces of a still earlier period, with which we now know it to have been associated. The experience of a life, therefore, may almost be said to have intervened between the two works.

Turning to our old friend Dörffel, already doubly proved impartial, for his immediate impressions of the Gewandhaus concert of January 1, we find his report very interesting reading.

'No less a task,' he says, 'confronted Brahms, if his salutation to his friend were to be one suitable to Joachim's eminence, than the production of a work that should reach the two greatest, Beethoven and Mendelssohn. We confess to having awaited the solution with some heart palpitation, though we firmly maintained our standard. But what joy we experienced! Brahms has brought such a third work to the partnership. The originality of the spirit which inspires the whole, the firm organic structure in which it is displayed, the warmth which streams from it, animating the work with joy and light—it cannot be otherwise—the concerto must be the fruit of the composer's latest and, as we believe, happiest experiences.

'The first movement is broad, with sharply defined contrasts through which, however, the serious-soft mood is preserved; the second is short, very thoughtful and fervent; the last, very spirited and attractive. There is, however, a quite unusual handling of the instrument, and again, a breath in the orchestra, which make us look forward with delight to the study of the score; we have seldom been so enthralled by the composer's genius. But Joachim played, also, with a love and devotion which brought home to us in every bar the direct or indirect share he has had in the work. As to the reception, the first movement was too new to be distinctly appreciated by the audience, the second made considerable way, the last aroused great enthusiasm.'

Bernsdorf was less unsympathetic than usual. He considered the concerto 'one of the clearest and most spontaneous of the composer's works.' Both Joachim and Brahms, who conducted the orchestra, had to respond to numerous recalls.

Joachim, to whom the concerto is dedicated, brought the manuscript with him to England, and performed it at the Crystal Palace Saturday concert of February 22 (August Manns), at the Philharmonic concerts of March 6 and 20 (W. G. Cusins), at some of his appearances in the north of Britain, and, a little later, at a concert of the Royal Academy of Arts, Berlin, when the accompaniment was played by his school orchestra. Published in the course of the year, it has ever since held a conspicuous place in his répertoire. The violinists Brodsky and, a little later, Frau Roeger-Soldat were amongst those who associated their names in a special manner with the early life of the work, which has recently been frequently performed with immense success by Fritz Kreisler.

If the mood of this great concerto has, as Dr. Deiters remarks, something in common with that of the second symphony, the sentiment is maintained at a loftier height than that of the earlier composition, the limpid grace of which has an immediate fascination for a general audience. The concerto requires time for full appreciation, and though, by general consent of the initiated, it undoubtedly occupies a position on the plane assigned to it by Dörffel, it would be too much to assert that it has as yet entirely conquered the heart of the great public. It is gradually making its way, however, to what will probably become unreserved popularity.

The year 1879 is of particular interest in our narrative, not only in relation to the Violin Concerto, but also because it included the publication of two books of Pianoforte Pieces, Op. 76, the several numbers of which are entitled 'Intermezzo' or 'Capriccio'; and the first performance from the manuscript of a Sonata for pianoforte and violin. We have traced the remarkable continuity of Brahms' development as a composer during the first ten years of his connection with Vienna, in its relation to the period which directly preceded his earliest visit to the city. The period dating back from 1862 to 1852 is not so unbroken. Quite another sequel than the actual one might have been anticipated from the fact that of the first ten of the composer's published works six had been pianoforte solos, five of them in other than variation form. We have watched his progress from one stepping-stone of excellence to another in this form, from the early beauties of the examples contained in the Sonatas, Op. 1 and Op. 2, through the astonishing technical advance displayed in Op. 9, up to a masterpiece, the

Handel Variations and Fugue, Op. 24, and have still had to add one more work to the list, the Paganini Variations, with imposing characteristics of its own; but we have not had to record the appearance of a single unaccompanied pianoforte solo in any other form in the course of the twenty-five years which succeeded the completion of the Ballades, Op. 10, in 1854 (published in 1856). Only now when the narrative has been brought to the point appropriate for the contemplation of these facts is it possible to point out the true significance to our master's career of the four years of study passed in complete retirement by the composer, as distinct from the pianist, Brahms, that followed the close of 1854. On his reappearance in 1859 and 1860 with a number of new works, not only had his technique been reformed, and transfigured, but the tendency of his career changed. The fascination exercised over his mind by the pure style of part-writing practised by the best masters of the early Italian schools, and the extent of resource he had acquired by constant assimilation of the treasure of Bach's learning, had given him an irresistible bent towards the composition of works that led up to the Requiem and Triumphlied on the one hand, and the String Quartets and Symphonies on the other; and the same influences would naturally dispose him towards the writing of chamber music for pianoforte and strings rather than for pianoforte alone. It is well known that his innate fastidiousness in regard to his own work was augmented in the case of his first symphony by his never-ceasing consciousness of Beethoven's overwhelming achievements in this domain; and his abstention, after his earliest period, from the publication of a pianoforte sonata may have been partially due to a similar, and perhaps even stronger, feeling that Beethoven's sonatas cannot be succeeded. It is, however, difficult to believe that Brahms' would not have persevered and conquered—conquered in the sense of producing something appropriate to his time—in the one case as in the other if he had felt a real impulse to do so, and it may possibly be true that his genius was better suited for the forms in which he worked than for those which he avoided.

The two books of Pianoforte Pieces, which, with the two Motets, Op. 74, dedicated to Philipp Spitta, the Violin Concerto, and the three Pianoforte Studies after Bach without opus number, formed the publications of the year 1879, contain, in all, eight numbers. Some of them, written with simplicity of style and pervaded by a spirit of dreamy content or graceful happiness, have become familiar to music-lovers; others present difficulties both to listener and performer which have hindered their popularity. Several contain interesting examples of the composer's facility in the art of rhythmic and contrapuntal device.

The Sonata for pianoforte and violin in G major, performed from the manuscript by Brahms and Hellmesberger at the Quartet concert of

November 20, is a pearl of pure and delicate imagination. The vivacity of the first movement is painted in pale moonbeam tints, and must, as one fancies, vanish before the first warm ray of sunshine. There is more substantiality about the gentle melancholy of the adagio, though this movement, again, is haunted by a strain of mystery. The last movement, written in rondo form, has for its first subject that of the beautiful 'Rain-Song' already alluded to, and is a very dream of wistful charm. Brahms' very original treatment of the pianoforte arpeggio, which is one of the distinctive features of his style of writing for the instrument, is well illustrated in the first movement of this work, in which the arpeggio is raised from the mere position of a brilliant passage to that of an essential part of the entire conception. A particularly clear light is thrown also upon the composer's relation to Bach by the study of the sonata, the methods of which are inherited from those of the early giant-musician, as exemplified in his sonatas for clavier and violin; and whilst Bach's methods flow as easily within the forms of the Austrian masters as though they had always been an inseparable part of them, the association is animated by the distinctive individuality of our Brahms. Not, however, as it impressed itself upon us in his first great series of works for pianoforte and strings. The spirit of the Sonata in G is essentially that of the master's later period of maturity. In it we feel that he has not only his powers, but his emotions, well in hand, and has reached a period of life when he can afford to look back calmly to the conflicts of the past. This no mere fancy; we find as we proceed in the study of Brahms' art, not that the nature of the man changed as he grew older, but that, whilst the sunshine of complete recognition which brightened his later path through life is felt in the clear spirit of some of his works, the reserve which characterizes others is now dictated by the complete self-mastery which it had been one of the efforts of his life to attain, and which lends them a singular and pathetic charm as of consciously half-revealed power and beauty.

The Sonata in G major is the fourth composed by Brahms for pianoforte and violin. The first, belonging to his first period, had, as we know, been mysteriously lost on the eve of publication. The second and third were rejected after completion by the composer's relentless self-criticism, and the manuscripts destroyed by his own hand. The publication of this one, known as the first, took place quite at the beginning of the year 1880, and the work was played with immense success by Brahms and Joachim during a short concert-tour they made together in the Austrian provinces during the last week of January and the first of February. In the course of his visit Joachim performed the Violin Concerto at one of three orchestral concerts given by him in the large hall of the Vienna 'Gesellschaft,' with the result to be expected from the association of two names so dear to the Austrian public.

The sonata was performed for the first time in England at the Monday Popular concert of February 2 by von Bülow and Madame Norman-Néruda, and at the Wednesday Popular concert, Cambridge, on the 25th of the same month by C. Villiers Stanford and Richard Gompertz. One of the earliest performances in Germany was that by Scholz and Himmelstoss at Breslau on February 24.

Brahms' first appearance at Crefeld on January 20 must be particularly recorded for two reasons: in the first place because it introduces us to a group of friends, his pleasant associations with whom are commemorated in the dedication of one of his later works. A considerable amount of music was performed during this first visit, and more on subsequent ones, in the informal, sociable way Brahms liked, at the houses of Herr and Frau Rudolph von der Leyen, with whom he always stayed, and of their relatives, Herr and Frau Alwyn von Beckerath. Herr von Beckerath, a good amateur performer, played viola in the resident string quartet led by Professor Richard Barth, a former pupil of Joachim, an old acquaintance of Brahms, and well known later on as von Bernuth's successor at Hamburg, who was always present with his colleagues at these private gatherings; and the enjoyment of the circle was enhanced during Brahms' later visits to Crefeld by the singing, to the master's accompaniment, of Fräulein Antonia Kufferath. This lady (now Mrs. Edward Speyer) has interesting recollections connected with the Crefeld visits. Amongst them is that of Brahms, who when once a composition was published allowed it to pass from his mind, sometimes almost completely, coming unawares upon a difficult passage in the accompaniment of one of his songs, and having an instant's struggle with it. At the end he turned to Fräulein Kufferath, saying, 'That is really difficult to read at sight!'

The musical event which gives particular distinction to the Crefeld concert of 1880, the programme of which included Brahms' second Symphony, 'Harzreise' Rhapsody and Triumphlied, was the performance by the composer of two new solos for the pianoforte, the Rhapsodies in B minor and G minor, generally accepted as the finest of Brahms' shorter works for the instrument. The second one especially, marked 'molto passionato ma non troppo allegro,' is an inspiration from beginning to end, and though not long, its length is sufficient to balance its grandeur of idea and to give the effect of completeness to its performance. Billroth, to whom Brahms, always needing sympathy, confided the manuscripts on their completion in the early summer of 1879, returned them with the words:

'The second piece has quite fascinated me. In both pieces there is more of the young, heaven-storming Johannes than in the other late works of the mature man.'

The Sonata in G, Op. 78, the Rhapsodies, Op. 79, and the third and fourth books of Hungarian Dances for Pianoforte Duet, without opus number, were the publications of 1880.

It may have been noticed by the reader that, in our record of the early performances of Brahms' works during the closing seventies, no mention has been made of Munich. The reason is not far to seek, and is such as might almost have been anticipated. The time arrived when the paths of Brahms and Levi separated, and its occurrence may be definitely dated in November, 1876, when our master visited Munich to conduct his first symphony, and stood there for the last time on a concert platform.

The attraction felt by Levi towards Wagner's art and personality had grown continually stronger since his preparation of the 'Meistersinger' for performance at Carlsruhe in 1869 and the establishment of personal relations between himself and Wagner to which it led; and his enthusiasm for the man and his works received extraordinary stimulus from the first performances of the 'Nibelungen Ring,' at which he was present, in the temporary theatre at Bayreuth in August, 1876. The impulsive expression to Brahms of his boundless admiration, carried beyond the point which should have been prescribed by tact, seems to have convinced our master that future relations between himself and Levi would be embarrassing to both; and though he received his friend's outpourings without visible sign, he took the wise and friendly course of abstaining from further visits to Munich. Enough, it is hoped, has been related in these pages of Brahms' appreciation of Wagner's powers to exclude the suspicion that he was actuated by petty feeling in taking this line. Levi's want of self-restraint was in one sense an acknowledgment of the master's artistic generosity; but compliments of this kind should not be carried to extremes, and Brahms' courage in adhering to a course certain to expose him to misunderstanding saved Levi as well as himself from the danger of the false position which must inevitably have threatened their future intercourse. The wreath which Brahms sent to Bayreuth on Wagner's death in February, 1883, was not the sign of a mere decorous compliance with custom, but was a heart-felt tribute of recognition from the one great master to the other.

Brahms' separation from Levi necessarily involved a coolness between himself and Allgeyer, who was one of the closest intimates of the Levi circle, but this was only temporary, and was probably merely accepted by Brahms as one of the incidents of the situation. It was got over during a visit paid by Allgeyer to Vienna, and Brahms' pleasure at the renewal of personal relations between himself and his old friend may be read in the dedication of the 'Ballads and Romances' published in 1878, to which reference has already been made.

To Brahms' activity on the advisory committee for the granting of Government stipendiums to young artists, combined with the growing feeling of mental leisure which must have come to him at this period of his mature mastership, must be ascribed the willingness shown by him, from the middle of the seventies onward, to concern himself with the musical progress of certain young composers who were courageous enough to ask his opinion and advice, and in whose works he discerned talent. Mention has been made of his prompt and emphatic appreciation of Dvořák. Amongst other musicians of distinction who in their youth enjoyed the advantage of his interest and friendship are Drs. Richard Heuberger, Eusebius Mandycweski (now holding the important position of librarian to the Gesellschaft der Musikfreunde), von Rottenberg, and Jenner. We spoke in the last chapter of some of the incidents of the master's friendship for Heuberger, who says that Brahms' great talent for teaching became continually clearer to him. 'With gifted young people who had already passed through the school curriculum, he might have achieved great things.' His criticism was so ruthless and searching as to be at first profoundly discouraging, but he could praise warmly, too, and there was no mistaking the pleasure he felt in being able to do so. His remarks to Heuberger, chiefly called forth by points in the manuscripts—often songs—laid before him, and by suggested improvements, usually served to elucidate general principles. The close rhythmical association of music with words, the conditions indispensable to the admission of irregularity of bar rhythm, the construction of melody, are but a few of the important points that were handled in the brief, incisive, pregnant manner which illumined every subject that he touched upon.

'Do you think,' said he one day, taking exception to an expression inadvertently used by Heuberger apropos to the construction of his melody, 'that any one of my half-dozen passable songs "occurred" to me? I had to worry myself with them rarely! One must be able—don't take this literally—to *whistle* a song ... then it is good.'

'Those *must* have been eyes, but perhaps not so interesting to other people,' he said, pointing to the too drawn-out setting of the words 'I saw two eyes last Sunday morn,' in one of Heuberger's manuscripts, and he improvised the passage in the closer form which the composer has retained in his published song 'Bitt' ihn o Mutter.'

The committee formed in 1871 to consider a scheme for the erection of a monument to Schumann at Bonn had been so successful during the few years following the festival of 1873, in collecting funds for their object, that by the beginning of May, 1880, the memorial, designed and executed by the sculptor Donnhorf, had been placed over Schumann's grave in the Bonn cemetery, and nothing remained to be done save to unveil and deliver it over to the municipal authorities. These ceremonies were to be performed on the 2nd of the month, and to be followed by some festival concerts with programmes of the master's music.

Proceedings opened on the evening of May 1, when Frau Schumann, arrived with some of her family on a visit to her old friends the Kyllmanns, to whose house the reader was introduced in an earlier chapter, was greeted by a serenade, sung in the garden by the members of the Concordia and the Academic Vocal Union, which was followed by performances within doors of the 'Lotos Blume' and the 'Traumender See.' President Wrede then delivered an address, and on its conclusion introduced each member of the societies individually to Frau Schumann. With her permission, Herr Branscheidt sang two of Schumann's songs to the accompaniment of Concertmeister Lorscheidt, and after the great artist had acknowledged these compliments in a few suitable words, the vocalists returned to the garden to sing 'Thou in the wood hast wandered,' from Schumann's 'Pilgrimage of the Rose.' With this performance the programme of the evening terminated, and after Frau Schumann had again expressed her warm thanks the visitors withdrew.

The cemetery was crowded early the next day by friends desirous of witnessing the unveiling of the monument. Nearly twenty-four years had gone by since the simple funeral procession had followed Schumann's remains through the streets of Bonn; since a group of young musicians stood together at the open grave, supported by the sympathy of a concourse of friends and music-lovers, to take their last farewell of the illustrious dead. Now they were reassembled on the same spot to do honour to the beloved master's memory. Not one was missing. Brahms, Joachim, Dietrich, the three young chief mourners of the first occasion, stood together again as middle-aged men; Hiller the older friend, Grimm, and Bargiel, all were there, and Stockhausen, since many years one of the circle. The central figure in to-day's proceedings had been absent, prostrated with sorrow, from the funeral ceremony. Frau Schumann now stood with her daughters at the foot of the monument, her usual pathetic expression deepened by the rush of varied memories, but with controlled demeanour. Amongst those present in an official capacity were the mayor of Bonn, Herr Oberbürgermeister Doetsch; the sculptor, Professor Donnhorf, from Dresden; the president of the memorial committee, Professor Schaafhausen, and the members of the two choral societies with President Wrede.

The singing of the fine old chorale, 'Was Gott thut das ist wohlgethan' was the prelude to the address in which Geheimrath Schaafhausen gave the monument over to the city of Bonn. Whilst he was speaking the covering fell, and as he concluded many beautiful wreaths were laid on the grave to the accompaniment of a second chorale. An address of thanks was delivered on behalf of the city by Oberbürgermeister Doetsch, and the singing of a third chorale, with the placing of more wreaths, brought the formalities to a close. The following telegram was handed to the mayor in the course of the proceedings:

'The Society of Music-lovers and the Conservatoire of Vienna congratulate Bonn on the honour of having to-day erected the first memorial to Schumann as previously that to Beethoven.'

The programme of the orchestral concert which took place in the evening of May 2, beginning at six o'clock, included Schumann's E flat Symphony and Requiem for Mignon, conducted by Brahms; a poetic 'Prologue,' composed and recited by Herr Emil Ritterhaus of Barmen; the Manfred music conducted by Joachim, with Ernst von Possart, director of the court theatre of Munich, in the chief declamatory part; and as single exception in the list of Schumann's works, Brahms' Violin Concerto, conducted by the composer, and played by Joachim in so perfect and ideal a manner as to be, 'not merely interpretative, but absolutely creative.' A rain of bouquets followed its conclusion. Three works were given at the chamber music concert of the following morning: Schumann's String Quartet in A minor, led by Joachim; Spanisches Liederspiel; and Quartet for pianoforte and strings, of which Brahms and Joachim played the pianoforte and violin parts respectively.

To this year is to be referred the composition of the only two overtures published by Brahms. The 'Tragic,' the grave character of which may be inferred from its title, was performed for the first time in December at the fourth concert of the Vienna Philharmonic season. Dr. Deiters says of it:

'In this work we see a strong hero battling with an iron and relentless fate; passing hopes of victory cannot alter an impending destiny. We do not care to inquire whether the composer had a special tragedy in his mind, or if so, which one; those who remain musically unconvinced by the unsurpassably powerful theme, would not be assisted by a particular suggestion.'

The 'Academic Festival Overture' which we know, was the one out of three selected by the composer for preservation. It was composed in acknowledgment of the honorary doctor's degree offered to Brahms in 1880 by the university of Breslau, and was performed for the first time in that city on January 4, 1881, under his direction. The companion work, the Tragic Overture, and the second Symphony were included in the same programme. The newly-made Doctor of Philosophy was received with all the honour and enthusiasm befitting the occasion and his work, and was again stormily applauded on the 6th, when he performed Schumann's

Fantasia, Op. 17, his two Rhapsodies, and the pianoforte part of his Horn Trio, at a concert of chamber music.

In the Academic Overture the sociable spirit reappears which had prompted the boy of fourteen to compose an ABC part-song for his seniors, the village schoolmasters in and around Winsen. Now the renowned master of forty-seven seeks to identify himself with the youthful spirits of the university with which he has become associated, by taking, for principal themes of his overture, student melodies loved by him from their association with the early Göttingen years of happy companionship with Joachim, with Grimm, with von Meysenbug and others. Four of these, 'Wir hatten gebauet,' 'Hört ich sing' 'Was kommt dort,' and the 'Gaudeamus,' are introduced in the course of the movement, which is written in regular classical form, and the composer lingers with particular affection over the third one, the song that in student circles accompanies the merry 'Fox-ride,' which in the summer of 1853 carried Brahms so many leagues distant from the earlier stages of his life's journey. The favourite 'Gaudeamus igitur,' given with the full strength of the orchestra, brings the masterly and effective work to a brilliant conclusion. The two overtures, bearing to each other a relation analogous to that which exists between the first and second symphonies, furnish another instance of the composer's occasional habit of writing at once, or in quick succession, two works of the same form animated by contrasted subjective qualities. The 'Academic' has become very familiar to concert-goers, and has, so far, attained to more universal popularity than the impressive 'Tragic.'

Both works were performed from the manuscript, under the composer's direction, at the Leipzig Gewandhaus concert of January 13, but alike failed to make much impression. If, however, Brahms felt any disappointment at the persevering coldness evinced towards his art in the musical metropolis of North Germany, he must have derived some consolation from the success which attended the performances of the Academic Overture and other works conducted by him in Münster on January 22 and in Crefeld on the 25th, and by the warm welcome which awaited him in each of the Dutch cities—Amsterdam, the Hague, Haarlem—which he visited in the course of the same month. Holland, distinguished musically by its early appreciation of Schumann's art, was now repeating history by its enthusiastic acceptance of that of Brahms. In each town where he appeared he had opportunity to perceive how deeply his music had taken root in the country. Of his many distinguished Dutch friends may be mentioned the composer Verhulst, a man of eminent parts and attractive personality, who had enjoyed the friendship of Mendelssohn and of Schumann. Brahms did not this winter fulfil any public engagement at Utrecht, but he stayed there for a day or two as the Engelmanns' guest, and did his share of music-making in private. To one old habit he steadfastly adhered during the visit, though it had little to do with art. Every morning on returning from his early walk he made his way to the nursery, and after a game of romps carried one child or another on his shoulder down to breakfast. To say the truth, this was not an unmixed pleasure to the little ones, who were sometimes frightened at their elevation, for the master's gait was not of the smoothest. His persevering sociability, however, was generally rewarded in the end by the confidence of the little ones in which he felt such satisfaction.

It is interesting to find Liszt and Brahms crossing each other's paths again in the month of February, after a long interval of years that had been big with consequence, and not only to the younger musician; since the triumph of Wagner's art must for ever be associated with the name of its first generous protagonist. The two men were brought together by the occasion of a concert given in Budapest by Hans von Bülow, who, on arriving at the Hôtel Ungaria, found Brahms staying there, probably by preconcerted arrangement.

'Très cher unique,' writes Liszt to Bülow on February 13; 'I have taken a slight cold, and in order not to spoil the day and evening of to-morrow, must retire early to-night.

'Pray express my affectionate thanks to Brahms, and convey to him the invitation of Madame La Baronne Eötoos to luncheon to-morrow at 1 o'clock without ennui or vexation. Quite the contrary. I shall arrive at the Hôtel Ungaria at a quarter before one in order to conduct you to Her Excellency's house.'

It no doubt afforded genuine satisfaction to the warm-hearted von Bülow to place his two friends on a passing footing of sociability. He had already begun, in his new position as capellmeister to Duke George of Saxe-Meiningen, to which he had been appointed the previous year, to use the increased influence at his command in the interests of our master's art, and before the close of this his first season of activity in the Thuringian capital, Brahms' first and second symphonies and other works had been performed under Bülow's direction before a highly sympathetic audience at the concerts of the court orchestra.

The two Overtures, and 'Nänie,' to which we have yet to refer in detail, were published in the course of 1881.[64]

CHAPTER XIX
1881-1885

Second Pianoforte Concerto—First visit to the ducal castle of Meiningen—'Nänie'—Frau Henriette Feuerbach—Hans von Bülow in Leipzig—Brahms' friends in Vienna—Dr. and Frau Fellinger—Pianoforte Trio in C major—First String Quintet—The 'Parzenlied'—Third Symphony.

A holiday taken with Billroth in Sicily in the early spring was succeeded by Brahms' removal to summer quarters, chosen this year at Pressbaum, near Vienna. Here he was occupied with the composition of Schiller's 'Nänie,' to which Feuerbach's death had moved him, and of a second concerto for pianoforte and orchestra in B flat. The manuscripts of 'Nänie' and of portions of the concerto were soon lent to Billroth, the concerto movements being handed to him with the words, 'A few little pianoforte pieces.'

'It is always a delight to me,' writes Billroth, 'when Brahms, after paying me a short visit, during which we have talked of indifferent things, takes a roll out of his paletôt pocket and says casually "Look at that and write me what you think of it."'

The composer was pleasantly disturbed in August from his quietly busy life by a visit from Widmann, who was staying in Vienna, and who thus describes his meeting with the friend he had not met for three years:

'Walking through the garden, I came upon the master sitting reading at an open window on the ground floor of his idyllic dwelling, and at once instinctively felt that he had entered upon a period of his career when there could be no longer any thought of his commencing upon an entirely new domain of his art [opera]. It may sound absurd when I confess that the splendid, already slightly grizzled beard in which I saw him for the first time, and scarcely recognised him, seemed to me a symbol of the great composer's present personality, now entirely self-adequate and perfectly defined and assured within its own limits. I was so completely dumbfoundered, however, by the surprise of seeing this Jupiter head that a question burst from me as to the reason of the alteration. "One is taken for an actor or a priest if one is clean shaven," answered Brahms, complacently stroking the flowing beard. He now had a naïve satisfaction in his own appearance, and smilingly mentioned that his photograph with beard had been used in the Velhagen and Clasing school book edition to illustrate the Caucasian type.... The opera project was not mentioned....'[65]

Brahms accepted numerous invitations from Germany, Switzerland, and Holland to take part in performances of his new works. He had for some time relaxed his early caution, and was now generally ready to introduce his compositions to the public on their completion, though adhering to his old custom of retaining possession of the manuscript of an important work for his own benefit until after its first performances, when he allowed the business of engraving to proceed without delay.

The new Pianoforte Concerto was played by the composer in Stuttgart on November 22 (Court Capellmeister Seyfrix) first time; in Meiningen on the 27th; Zürich, Breslau, Vienna (Philharmonic), respectively December 6, 20, 26; Leipzig, Hamburg (Philharmonic), Berlin (Meiningen orchestra), Kiel, Bremen, Hamburg (Meiningen orchestra), Münster, Utrecht, in January, and Frankfurt in February, 1882. The work was received with immense enthusiasm throughout the tour, excepting at Leipzig, where it achieved only a *succès d'estime.*

During his visit to Meiningen, Brahms was the guest of the reigning Duke George and his consort, the Baroness von Heldburg. Three fine rooms *en suite* on the ground-floor of the castle were placed at his disposal, and in the most spacious of them, arranged as a music-room, one of the Duke's fine Bechstein pianofortes had been placed. The apartment, having direct access to the castle grounds, afforded the composer easy opportunity to indulge in his favourite recreation of walking.

Bülow had left nothing undone that could contribute éclat to his friend's first public appearance in Meiningen, which he heralded a few days beforehand by giving a performance of the German Requiem at an extra concert of the court orchestra. The concert-hall was completely filled on the evening of the 27th, and on the arrival of the Duke of Saxe-Meiningen and the Baroness von Heldburg, accompanied by Cardinal Prince Hohenlohe, the opening number of the Brahms programme, the Tragic Overture, was listened to by a breathlessly expectant audience. The first glimpse of the composer as he advanced to the platform to play the solo of the new Pianoforte Concerto in B flat caused an outburst of welcome which made it impossible for him to take his seat immediately, and the enthusiasm, growing with each movement, reached its climax at the end. 'Brahms and Bülow transported the audience to a state of exaltation,' wrote the critic next day. The Haydn Variations closed the first part of the concert; the second part, consisting of the C minor Symphony and the Academic Overture, was conducted by the composer. On its termination the Duke expressed his appreciation by decorating Brahms with the cross of his family order.

The visit to Meiningen marked the beginning of a cordial friendship between the art-loving prince and his consort on one hand and Brahms on the other, which brought many pleasant hours to the great musician. He always stayed at the castle when at Meiningen, where he was the centre of many private musical gatherings. Several times he was a guest at the castle of Altenstein, the Duke's country residence. Here, as at Meiningen, he was allowed perfect freedom of action, could work without fear of disturbance, take solitary walks in the neighbourhood, or saunter in the grounds in company, and was even permitted to retain his very unconventional style of dress during the day. In the evening he recognised the claims of ceremonial custom, and actually seemed to take a kind of pleasure in dressing for dinner and wearing his decorations. He did not abate one jot, however, of his usual independent expression of opinion, and would defend his own point of view with characteristic bluntness and tenacity no matter who might happen to differ from him. An instance of this trait, as well as of his singular political acumen, of interest at the present time, occurred at the beginning of the war between China and Japan. Brahms declared his belief, which was not shared by others present, in the ultimate success of Japan, and angrily anticipated the injustice by which the selfish interference of the Western Powers would deprive her of the fruits of victory. The Duke's answer, which reminded him that European interests were involved in the question, left him gruffly unconvinced, but the incident was allowed to pass.

It was not only by his illustrious host that the composer came to be loved. He made himself a favourite with everyone in the Duke's service with whom he came in contact; his visits to Meiningen and Altenstein Castles were regarded by the entire household as a distinction and pleasure, and the harmless jokes and playful sayings in which he continued to find a childlike satisfaction to the end of his life are remembered by these friends with affection and regret.

The concert at Zürich on December 6, the programme of which included the first performance of 'Nänie,' made an extraordinary impression, and was so brilliantly successful financially that, in the words of Steiner,

'the committee could not rest satisfied without giving visible and lasting expression to their feelings of gratitude and veneration towards the author of such glorious achievements.'

It took the form of a silver cup, designed for the occasion by Bosshard of Lucerne, and was forwarded to the master on its completion. Brahms wrote his thanks to Hegar in the following words:

'MOST ESTEEMED FRIEND,

'Your goblet has arrived, and the étui containing the musical silver angel glitters like an open altar shrine upon the piano. You cannot think how beautiful and kind it stands there, and with what pleasure I look at it!

'But now, please, use your best words to assure your esteemed fellow members of the great pleasure they have given me and how grateful I am for their kindness. You can easily supply details which I am shy of adding and which, if written, might sound trivial and vain. You, however, are aware that such a friendly token of appreciation and sympathy is a very serious matter....

'Now, with hearty greeting to you and yours,

'Yours most sincerely,

'J. BRAHMS.'[66]

In his setting of 'Nänie,' dedicated to Frau Henriette Feuerbach and performed from the manuscript at this concert, Brahms has conceived the calm fatalistic spirit of classical antiquity represented in Schiller's funeral dirge as perfectly as he has embodied in the music of the German Requiem the passionate intensity of the writers of the Old and New Testaments. A current of tender pathos glides evenly through the lament, which is somewhat strengthened during the passing image of Aphrodite bewailing the loss of her son, but not sufficiently to disturb the smooth onward flow of the passages proceeding continuously from beginning to end of the work. It seems to suggest the ancient Greek idea of death as the final decree of destiny, hardly to be dreaded, not to be questioned or resisted, immutable even in the presence of beauty, just as clearly as the powerful contrasts of the Requiem present the Biblical conception of death as an enemy to be opposed and finally destroyed in the victory of an all-conquering love.

Dr. Carl Neumann describes a visit paid by him to Frau Feuerbach when she was seventy-five years of age, at her house in Ansbach. He went through two rooms.

'In the first was a grand piano on which lay Brahms' "Nänie"; in the second, one might say, dwelt the departed. Tall green plants stood in the window recesses obscuring the light. What the mother had of her son's works hung on the walls. The coloured sketch of a "Descent of the Cross," a flower study belonging to the time when the frame of "Plato's Feast" was painted, a drawing of the standing Iphigenia looking towards the land of Greece—here was her altar....

'We left this room. She sat down to the piano, at first as if to rest; then asked if I knew Brahms' "Nänie," which, as an admirer of her son's art, he had dedicated to her. She gave me the music to follow and began to play it by heart....

'Suddenly I looked up.... The woman at the piano in the black dress, a black veil on her white hair, seemed changed. The tall figure, bent forward and lost in tones and memories; was it not the tragic muse herself and was she not sounding a song of fate?

'In the spring of 1886 she once again met Brahms and heard "Nänie" under Joachim.'[67]

The want of appreciation of the new concerto shown by the audience of the Leipzig Gewandhaus did not escape the notice of Hans von Bülow in his capacity as Brahms' champion, and he carried his band to Leipzig in the middle of March to give a series of three concerts, two of them respectively devoted to Beethoven and Brahms, and the other divided between Mendelssohn and Schumann. The Brahms programme included the C minor Symphony, Haydn Variations, and the D minor Concerto played by Bülow, the orchestra accompanying without a conductor. The applause which followed the movements of the symphony as the work proceeded was not hearty enough to satisfy the excitable capellmeister, who at the end of the third movement desired his orchestra to repeat it, and on the conclusion of the work turned round and addressed his audience. He had, he said, arranged the Brahms programme by express command of his Duke, who had desired that the Leipzig public should know how the symphony ought to be performed; and also to obtain satisfaction for the coldness manifested towards the composer on his appearance with the new concerto at the Gewandhaus on January 1. It need hardly be said that eccentric efforts such as this on the part of a musician for many years conspicuously identified with the New-German school could have no result one way or the other in directing the artistic leanings of the city.

Brahms' Pianoforte Concerto in B flat is of quite unusual dimensions, and differs not only from his first in D minor, but from almost every other preceding work of its kind, in containing four movements, the additional one of which, a long 'allegro appassionato,' succeeds immediately to the first allegro. Probably few hearers of the work would subscribe to the reason for this innovation given by the composer to his friend Billroth.

'When I asked him about it, he said that the opening movement appeared to him too simple; he required something strongly passionate before the equally simple andante.'

If anything of the usual meaning of the word 'simple' is to be attached to its use here—*i.e.*, something without complication and easy of comprehension—it must be said that the second movement of the concerto, in spite of its passionate character, is very much simpler than the first. Its plan, whilst containing points of originality, is perfectly symmetrical, and stands out in well-balanced proportions clearly evident to the imagination.

The first movement, on the other hand, is extraordinarily difficult to grasp as a whole, partly on account of its great length, but still more from the ambiguity of the rôle assigned to the solo instrument on its entry after the first orchestral 'tutti.' The principle to be traced in the first movements of the concertos of Mozart and Beethoven, by giving to the solo, on each entry, something of the character of a brilliant improvisation, supported by the band, on the material of a preceding 'tutti,' insures for it a clearly defined position, and, whilst preserving a due balance between the orchestra and the solo instrument, lends contrast to the movement as a whole. Brahms would almost seem, in the instance under consideration, to have deliberately degraded the pianoforte from its legitimate position as dominant factor in its own domain. True, it enters with eight bars' quasi-improvisatory restatement of the principal theme, but it sinks immediately afterwards to occupy the subordinate rôle of the answering voice in a kind of antiphonal duet with the orchestra, which it imitates almost servilely, fragment by fragment, during a lengthy succession of bars. This method of treatment robs the solo, not only of its effect, but almost of its very *raison d'être*, and, by blurring the outline of the movement, is probably chiefly answerable for the sense of fatigue, to which even Billroth confessed, that most people feel after listening to a performance of the entire work. This is not the place for a detailed discussion of the movement, which, with all its grandeur, scarcely realizes the great expectations warranted by its magnificent opening. A comparison of it with the first movement of Beethoven's Pianoforte Concerto in E flat will make the foregoing remarks clear, the more so as the ground-plan is much the same in the two compositions. The third and fourth movements of Brahms' concerto are as easy to follow as the second. The andante is fervent and melodious, and the finale offers to the ear a dainty feast of sound sparkling from beginning to end with graceful vivacity.

This concerto has, like its predecessor, sometimes been described as a symphony with pianoforte obligato. The comparison is in each case misleading. Both works are essentially based on the modern concerto form as established by Mozart.

The Concerto in B flat, published in 1882, was dedicated by Brahms to 'his dear friend and teacher Edward Marxsen.' It was performed—probably for the first time in England—by Charles Hallé at one of the famous Manchester concerts, and by Heinrich Barth at a Crystal Palace Saturday concert of November, 1884. The present author played it in London

December 13, 1888, at her matinée at Messrs. Broadwood's, and on February 14, 1891, at her private concert at the Royal Academy of Music, kindly accompanied in the composer's arrangement of the orchestral part for two pianofortes, on the first occasion by Mr. Otto Goldschmidt and Mr. Stephen Kemp, and on the second by Messrs. Stephen Kemp and Septimus Webbe. Frederic Lamond introduced it to the audience of the Philharmonic Society, St. James's Hall, on May 14, 1891. Since these dates the concerto has been frequently played in Great Britain by Leonard Borwick. Fräulein Marie Baumeyer of Vienna was the first lady to perform the immensely difficult work. She played it in Graz in 1883, and later, in the composer's presence, at one of her concerts in Vienna.

The other publications of 1882 were a book of Romances and Songs for one or for two voices, and two books of Songs for one voice. The two Overtures and 'Nänie' were issued in 1881.

Brahms passed a considerable part of the first quarter of 1882 in Hamburg, to the joy of his friends there. He had written in good time to Frau Caroline to bespeak his favourite 'corner room,' and made his headquarters from the beginning of January with his stepmother. He had accepted an invitation to conduct his Requiem at the annual Good Friday concert of sacred music at the Stadt Theater, and was occupied several weeks beforehand with preliminary study and rehearsals. The choir of 200 consisted of the members of the Bach Society and opera chorus combined. The performance, which took place on April 7, partook of the character of a solemn memorial service, and the audience properly abstained from applause, though the sixth number created an impression that would make itself audible. At the close of the concert the composer received a vote of cordial thanks tendered in the name of all present.

The master stayed, for the second time, at Ischl during the summer months. Billroth, who was in the neighbourhood, writes of him in August:

'I should like to enjoy myself in Italy from September 15 till October 1. Brahms wishes to accompany me.... He has been very busy lately. Three books of songs have been published. A string quintet and a trio are ready, both of them simpler, shorter, brighter than his earlier things; he strives consciously for shortness and simplicity. He lately sent me the manuscript of a true work of art, the "Parzenlied" [Song of the Fates] from Goethe's "Iphigenia." Very deep but simple.'

Brahms' Lodgings at Ischl.
By permission of Frau Maria Fellinger.

The journey to Italy duly took place, the proposed party of two being enlarged to one of four by the addition of Ignaz Brüll and Simrock. Original plans had to be modified on account of the exceptionally wet season, and the chief places visited were Vicenza, Padua, and Venice.

The personnel of Brahms' intimate friends in Vienna had remained on the whole much what it had become a very few years after his arrival in the Austrian capital. Of its closest circle the Fabers, Billroths, and Hanslicks, with whom must be associated Joachim's cousins, the various members of the Wittgenstein family—amongst them Frau Franz and Frau Dr. Oser—still formed the nucleus. An acquaintance with Herr Victor von Miller zu Aichholz and his wife had meanwhile ripened into warm friendship, and their house became one of those whose hospitality was most frequently and gladly accepted by the master. Amongst the musicians, Carl Ferdinand Pohl, author of the standard Life of Mozart, and, since 1866, archivar to the Gesellschaft, was one of his dearest friends. With the leading professors of the conservatoire his relations continued very cordial, and amongst the younger musicians to whom, in addition to his early allies, Goldmark, Gänsbacher and Epstein, he extended his friendly regard, may be mentioned Anton Door and Robert Fuchs. The feeling of warm friendship existing between Brahms and Johann Strauss has been commemorated in several well-known anecdotes. The autumn of 1881, however, brought to permanent residence in Vienna a family that before long made notable addition to the master's intimate circle. Special circumstances conduced to the speedy formation of a bond of friendship between Brahms and the new-comers, Dr. and Frau Fellinger. In the first place, they were friends of Frau Schumann and her daughters, and as such had an instant claim on his courtesy, which he acknowledged by calling on them as soon as possible after their arrival. In the second, his interest was awakened by the fact that Frau Dr. Fellinger was the daughter of Frau Professor Lang-Köstlin, the gifted Josephine Lang, whose attractive personality and talent for composition made a strong impression upon Mendelssohn when he was a youth of twenty-one and some six years the lady's senior. The story of Josephine, who at the age of twenty-six married Professor Köstlin of Tübingen, is given in Hiller's 'Tonleben,' and Mendelssohn's congratulations to her bridegroom-elect may be read in the second volume of the 'Letters.' The talent for art which had come to her as a family inheritance was transmitted to her daughter, though with a difference. Frau Dr. Fellinger's gifts have associated themselves especially with the plastic arts; in the first place with that of painting, but they have become well known in the musical world also by her busts and statuettes of Brahms, Billroth, and others belonging to their circle. Her photographs of our master are now familiar to most music-lovers. When it is added that Brahms found he could command in Dr. Fellinger's hospitable house, not only congenial intellectual sympathy, but the unceremonious intercourse with a simple, affectionate family circle in which he had through life found a pre-eminent source of happiness, it will easily be understood that he became a more and more frequent guest there, until, during the closing years of his life, it became for him almost a second home.

The master introduced two of his new works in the course of a few weeks' journey undertaken in the winter of 1882-83. According to Simrock's Thematic Catalogue, the Pianoforte Trio in C major, the String Quintet in F major, and the 'Parzenlied' constitute the publications of 1883. Early copies of the trio and quintet were sent out, however, and the works were publicly performed from them in December, 1882. An interesting entry in Frau Schumann's diary says:

'I had invited Koning and Müller to come and try Brahms' new trio with me on Thursday 21st [December]. Who should surprise us as we were playing it—he himself! He came from Strassburg and means to stay with us for Christmas. I played the trio first and he repeated it.'

Both works were performed on December 29 at a Museum chamber music concert—the Quintet by the Heermann-Müller party, the Trio by Brahms, Heermann, and Müller.

Amongst the early performances of the Trio were those on January 17 and 22 respectively in Berlin (Trio Concerts: Barth, de Ahna, Hausmann) and London (Monday Popular Concerts: Hallé, Madame Néruda, Piatti), and at Hellmesberger's in Vienna on March 15.

The work has not become one of the most generally familiar of the master's compositions, though it is not easy to say why. It contains no trace of the 'heaven-storming Johannes,' but, like many of the later compositions, it breathes, and especially the first movement, with a rich, mellow warmth suggestive of one to whom the experiences of life have brought a solution of their own to its problems, which has quieted, if it has not altogether satisfied, the aspirations and impulses of youth.

The Quintet in F for strings is, for the most part, bright, concise, and easy to follow. As one of its special features may be mentioned the combination of the usual two middle movements in the second. It was given in Hamburg on the 22nd and in Berlin on the 23rd of January, respectively by Bargheer and Joachim and their colleagues (it should be noted that Hausmann had at this time succeeded Müller as the violoncellist of the Joachim Quartet), at Hellmesberger's on February 15, and at the Monday Popular, London, of March 5.

Brahms conducted the first performance of the Parzenlied in Basle on December 8, 1882. Excellently sung by the members of the Basle Choral Society, the work met with extraordinary success, and was repeated after the New Year by general desire. Similar results followed its performance in other towns, of which Strassburg and Crefeld should be specially mentioned. The programme of the Crefeld concert included the fifth movement of the Requiem. 'What is your *tempo*?' Brahms inquired, on the morning of the rehearsal, of Fräulein Antonia Kufferath, who was to sing the solo. The lady, not taking the question seriously from the composer of the music, waived a reply. 'No, I mean it; you have to hold out the long notes. Well, we shall understand each other,' he added; 'sing only as you feel, and I will follow with the chorus.'

These are characteristic words, and valuable in more than one sense. To most of the few works to which the master has placed metronome indications—and the Requiem is amongst these—he added them by special request, and attached to them only a limited importance. An absolutely and uniformly 'correct' pace for a piece of genuine music does not exist. The pace must vary to some extent according to subtle conditions existent in the performer, and the instinct of a really musical executant or conductor will, as a rule, be a safer guide, within limits, than what can be at best but the mechanical markings even of the composer himself.

The Parzenlied, received with enthusiasm throughout Brahms' tour in Germany and Switzerland, was not equally successful in Vienna, where it was heard for the first time at the Gesellschaft concert of February 18 under Gericke. The austere simplicity of the music, which paces majestically onward with the concentrated, resigned calm of despair, adds extraordinary force to Goethe's poem, but does not appeal to every audience, and the work has never become a prime favourite in the Austrian Kaiserstadt. The song is set for six-part chorus with orchestra, in plainer harmonic masses and with less employment of imitative counterpoint than we usually find in the works of Brahms, who has accommodated his music here, as in 'Nänie,' to the classical spirit of the text. A singular deviation, however, which occurs in the course of the setting, from the uncompromising severity of the words, furnishes a remarkable illustration of the composer's unconquerable idealism. Comment was made in its place on the beautiful device by which he has sought to relieve the dark mood of Hölderlin's 'Song of Destiny'—the addition of an instrumental postlude which breathes forth a message of tender consolation that the poet could hardly have rendered in words. In Schiller's 'Nänie' the lament, with all its calm, gives expression to a sentiment of compassionate sorrow that is perfectly reproduced in the master's music. Goethe's Fates, however, in their measured recitation of the gods' relentless cruelty, would have seemed to offer no possible opportunity for even the inarticulate expression of ruth. Least of all, it might be imagined, could any concession to the demands of the human heart have been found in the penultimate stanza of their song:

'The rulers exclude from
Their favouring glances
Entire generations,
And heed not in children
The once so belovèd
And still speaking features
Of distant forefathers.'

Our Brahms, however, who, in spite of his increasing weight, his shaggy beard, his frequently rough manners, his unsatisfied affections, his impenetrable reserve, remained at fifty, in his heart of hearts, the very same being whom we have watched as the loving child of seven, the simple-minded boy of fourteen, the broken-hearted man of thirty, sobbing by the death-bed of his mother, cannot leave the dread gloom of his subject unrelieved by a single ray. He seems, in his setting of the last strophe but one, to concentrate attention on past kindness of the gods, and thus, perhaps, subtly to suggest a plea for present hope. How far the musician was justified in thus wandering from the obvious intention of his poet must be left to each hearer of the work to determine for himself. If it be the case, as has sometimes been suggested, that the variation was made by the composer in the musical interests of the piece as a work of art, it cannot be held to have fulfilled its purpose; for the striking inconsistency between words and music in the verse in question has a disturbing effect on the mind of the listener. We believe, however, that the true explanation of the master's procedure is more radical, and is to be found in the nature of the man in which that of the musician was grounded.

The Parzenlied was dedicated to 'His Highness George, Duke of Saxe-Meiningen,' and was included in a Brahms programme performed in Meiningen on April 2 to celebrate the Duke's birthday. The complete breakdown of Bülow's health necessitated his temporary retirement from his conductor's duties, which were divided on this occasion between Brahms and Court Capellmeister Franz Mannstädt, appointed to assist Bülow. Returning by a circuitous route to Vienna after a few days at the ducal castle, Brahms paid a short visit to Hamburg to take part in another Brahms programme arranged by the talented young conductor of the Cecilia Society, Julius Spengel. This was the first of several occasions on which the master gave testimony of his appreciation of Dr. Spengel's talents and musicianship by co-operating in the concerts of the society.

Brahms celebrated his fiftieth birthday by entertaining his friends Faber, Billroth, and Hanslick at a bachelor supper. He was occupied during the summer with the completion of a third symphony, on which he had worked the preceding year, and lived at Wiesbaden in a house that had belonged to the celebrated painter Ludwig Knaus, in whose former studio—Brahms' music-room for the nonce—the work was finished.

It was known to the composer that a delicate elderly lady inhabited the first-floor of the house of which Frau von Dewitz's flat, where he lodged, formed an upper story. Every night, therefore, on returning to his rooms, he took off his boots before going upstairs, and made the ascent in his socks, so that her rest should not be disturbed. This anecdote is but one amongst several of the same kind that have been related to the author by Brahms' intimate associates. Samples of another variety should not, however, be omitted.

A private performance of the new symphony, this time arranged for two pianofortes, was given as usual at Ehrbar's by Brahms and Brüll, and aroused immense expectations for the future of the work. Amongst the listeners was a musician who, not having hitherto allowed himself to be suspected of a partiality for the master's art, expressed his enthusiastic admiration of the composition. 'Have you had any conversation with X?' young Mr. Ehrbar asked Brahms; 'he has been telling me how delighted he is with the symphony.' 'And have you told him that he very often lies when he opens his mouth?' angrily retorted the composer, who could never bring himself to submit to the humiliation of accepting a compliment which he suspected—perhaps unjustly in this case—of being insincere.

A terrible rebuff was administered by him on the evening of a first Gewandhaus performance. It must be owned that Brahms was seldom in his happiest mood when on a visit to Leipzig; he was well aware that his music was not appreciated within the official 'ring' there, and suspiciously resented any well-meant efforts made to ignore this fact. 'And where are you going to lead us to-night, Herr Doctor?' inquired one of the committee a few minutes before the beginning of the concert, assuming a conciliatory manner as he smoothed on his white kid gloves; 'to heaven?' 'It is the same to me where you go,' rejoined Brahms.

The first performance of the Symphony in F major (No. 3) took place in Vienna at the Philharmonic concert of December 2, under Hans Richter, who was, according to Hanslick, originally responsible for the name 'the Brahms Eroica,' by which it has occasionally been called. Whether or not the suggestion is happy, a saying of the kind, probably uttered on the impulse of the moment, should not be taken very seriously.

Nothing of the quiescent autumn mood which we have observed in the master's chamber music of this period is to be traced in either of his symphonies, and the third, like its companions, represents him in the zenith of his energies, working happily in the consciousness of his absolute command over the resources of his art. Whether it be judged by its effect as an entire work or studied movement by movement, whether each movement be listened to as a whole or analyzed into its component parts, all is found to be without halt of inspiration or flaw in workmanship. Each theme is striking and pregnant, and, though contrasting with what precedes it, seems to belong inevitably to the movement and place in which it occurs, whilst the development of the thematic material is so masterly that to speak of admiring it seems almost ridiculous. The last movement closes with a very beautiful and distinctive Brahms coda. The third symphony is more immediately easy to follow than the first, and of broader atmosphere than the second. It is of an essentially objective character, and belongs absolutely to the domain of pure music.

The supreme and glorious pre-eminence which the great master had by this time attained in contemporary estimation naturally made it an object of competition with concert-givers and directors to announce the earliest performances of his works, and this was especially the case in the rare event of a new symphony which succeeded its immediate predecessor after an interval of six years. Brahms, however, had his own ideas on this matter, as on every other that he thought important, and after the first performance of the work in Vienna he sent the manuscript to Joachim in Berlin, and begged him to conduct the second performance when and where he liked. This proceeding would hardly have been noteworthy under the circumstances of intimate friendship which had so long united the two musicians, had it not been that the old relation between Brahms and Joachim had been clouded during the past year or two, during which there had been a cessation of their former affectionate intercourse. When, therefore, it became known that Joachim, acting on the composer's wish, proposed to conduct the symphony at one of the subscription concerts of the Royal Academy of Arts, Berlin, so much disappointment and heart-burning were felt and expressed that Joachim, although he had already replied in the affirmative to Brahms' request, consented to write again and ask what his wishes really were. The answer came without delay, and was clear enough to set the matter quite at rest. Brahms desired that the performance should be committed unreservedly to the care of his old friend.

The symphony was heard for the second time, therefore, on January 4 under Joachim at Berlin, and was enthusiastically received by all sections of the public and press. It was given again three times during the same month in the German imperial capital under the composer's bâton.

Detailed description of the triumphant progress of the new work from town to town is no longer necessary. The composer was overwhelmed with invitations to conduct it from the manuscript, and Bülow, convalescent from his illness, and determined not to be outdone in enthusiasm, placed it twice, as second and fourth numbers, in a Meiningen programme of five works. On publication, it was performed in all the chief music-loving towns of Germany, Great Britain, Holland, Russia, Switzerland, and the United States.

In an account of a performance of the symphony at a Hamburg Philharmonic concert under Brahms in December, which followed one under von Bernuth after three weeks' interval, the critic of the *Correspondenten* says:

'Brahms' interpretation of his works frequently differs so inconceivably in delicate rhythmic and harmonic accents from anything to which one is accustomed, that the apprehension of his intentions could only be entirely possible to another man possessed of exactly similar sound-susceptibility or inspired by the power of divination.'

The author feels a peculiar interest in quoting these lines, which strikingly corroborate the impression formed by her on hearing this and other of Brahms' works played under his own direction.

The publications of 1884 were, besides the third Symphony, Two Songs for Contralto with Viola and Pianoforte, the second being the 'Virgin's Cradle Song,' already mentioned as one of the compositions of 1865; two sets of four-part Songs, the one for accompanied Solo voices, the other for mixed Chorus *a capella*, and the two books of Songs, Op. 94 and 95.

At this date Brahms had entered into what we may call the third period of his activity as a song-writer—one in which he frequently chose texts that speak of loneliness or death. The wonderful beauty of his settings of these subjects penetrates the very soul, and by the mere force of its pathos carries to the hearer the conviction that the composer speaks out of the feeling of his own heart. Stockhausen, trying the song 'Mit vierzig Jahren' (Op. 94, No. 1) from the manuscript to the composer's accompaniment, was so affected during its performance that he could not at once proceed to the end. Our remarks are, however, by no means intended to convey the impression that Brahms only or generally chose poems of a melancholy tendency at this time.

WITH FORTY YEARS.

BY FRIEDRICH RÜCKERT (1788-1866).

With forty years we've gained the mountain's summit,
We stand awhile and look behind;
There we behold the quiet years of childhood
And there the joy of youth we find.
Look once again, and then, with freshened vigour,
Take up thy staff and onward wend!
A mountain-ridge extendeth, broad, before thee,
Not here, but there must thou descend.
No longer, climbing, need'st thou struggle breathless,
The level path will lead thee on;
And then with thee a little downward tending,
Before thou know'st, thy journey's done.

With the knowledge we have gained of the master's habit of producing his large works in couples, we are prepared to find him employed this summer on the composition of a fourth symphony. Avoiding a long journey, he settled down to his work at Mürz Zuschlag in Styria, not far from the highest ridge of the Semmering. Hearing soon after his arrival there that his old friend Misi Reinthaler, now grown up into a young lady, was leaving home under her mother's care to go through a course of treatment under a famous Vienna specialist, he wrote to place his rooms in Carlsgasse at Frau Reinthaler's disposal. The offer was not accepted, but when the invalid was sufficiently convalescent, he insisted that the two ladies should come for a few days as his guests to Mürz Zuschlag, where he took rooms for them near his own lodgings. He went over to see them also at Vienna, and spent the greater part of a morning showing them his valuable collection of autographs and other treasures. 'Yes, these would have been something to give a wife!' was his answer to the ladies' expressions of delight. Amongst his collection of musical autographs were two written on different sides of the same sheet of paper—one of Beethoven, the song 'Ich liebe dich'; the other of Schubert, part of a pianoforte composition. These, with Brahms' autograph signature 'Joh. Brahms in April 1872,' written at the bottom of one of the pages, constitute a unique triplet. The sheet now belongs to the Gesellschaft library, and is framed within glass.

The society of Hanslick, who came with his wife to stay near Mürz Zuschlag for part of the summer, was very acceptable to Brahms. The departure of his friends at the close of the season, in the company of some mutual Vienna acquaintances, incited the composer to an act of courtesy of a kind quite unusual with him, the sequel to which seems to have caused him almost comical annoyance that found expression in a couple of notes sent immediately afterwards to Hanslick.

'DEAREST FRIEND,

'Here I stand with roses and pansies; which means with a basket of fruit, liqueurs and cakes! You must have travelled through by the earlier Sunday extra train? I made a good and unusual impression for politeness at the station! The children are now rejoicing over the cakes....'

and, on finding that, mistaking the time of the train, he had arrived a quarter of an hour late:

'How such a stupid thing can spoil one's day and the thought of it recur to torment one. I hope you do not know this as well as I, who am for ever preparing for myself such vexatious worry....'

Later on, writing about other matters, he adds:

'... I hope Professor Schmidt's ladies do not describe my promenade with the basket too graphically in Vienna! Otherwise my unspoiled lady friends may cease to be so unassuming.'[68]

The journeys of the winter included visits to Bremen and Oldenburg, during which Hermine Spiess, one of the very favourite younger interpreters of Brahms' songs, sang dainty selections of them to the composer's accompaniment, with overwhelming success. The early death of this gifted artist, soon after her marriage, caused the master, with whom she was a great favourite, deep and sincere grief. Brahms went also to Crefeld, where the 'Tafellied,' dedicated on publication 'To the friends in Crefeld in remembrance of Jan. 28th 1885,' was sung on the date in question, with some of the new part-songs *a capella*, and other of the composer's works, at the jubilee of the Crefeld Concert Society. The manuscript score of the 'Tafellied' is in the possession of Herr Alwin von Beckerath, to whom it was presented by Brahms with an affectionate inscription.

CHAPTER XX
1885-1888

Vienna Tonkünstlerverein—Fourth Symphony—Hugo Wolf—Brahms at Thun—Three new works of chamber music—First performances of the second Violoncello Sonata by Brahms and Hausmann—Frau Celestine Truxa—Double Concerto—Marxsen's death—Eugen d'Albert—The Gipsy Songs—Conrat's translations from the Hungarian—Brahms and Jenner—The 'Zum rothen Igel'—Ehrbar's asparagus luncheons—Third Sonata for Pianoforte and Violin.

The early part of the year 1885 offers for record no event of unusual interest to the reader. The greater portion of it was spent by Brahms in his customary routine in Vienna. He was generally to be seen at the weekly meetings of the Tonkünstlerverein, a musicians' club founded by Epstein, Gänsbacher, and others, of which the master had consented to be named honorary life-president. The Monday evening proceedings included a short musical programme, sometimes followed by an informal supper. Brahms did not usually sit in the music-room, but would remain in a smaller apartment smoking and chatting sociably with friends of either sex. His arrival always became known at once to the assembled company, 'Brahms is here; Brahms is come!' being passed eagerly from mouth to mouth. His old love of open-air exercise had not diminished with increasing years, and the Sunday custom of a long walk in the country was still kept up. A few friends used to meet in the morning outside the Café Bauer, opposite the Opera House, and, taking train or tram to the outskirts of the city, would thence proceed on foot, returning in the late afternoon. Brahms, nearly always in a good humour on these occasions, was generally soon ahead of his companions, or leading the way with the foremost, and, as had usually been the case with him through life, was looked upon by his friends as the chief occasion of their meetings, allowed his own way, and admired as a kind of pet oracle. The excursions always commenced for the season on his return to Vienna in the autumn, and were continued with considerable regularity until his departure in the spring. They not infrequently gave opportunity for the employment of the composer's unfailing readiness of repartee, as on the occasion of a meeting in the train, on the return journey, with a learned but unmusical acquaintance of one of the party, between whom and Brahms an animated conversation arose. 'Will you not join us one day, Herr Doctor? Next Sunday, perhaps?' asked Brahms. 'I!' exclaimed the other. 'Saul among the prophets?' 'Na, so you give yourself royal airs!' instantly rejoined the master.

The fourth symphony was completed during the summer at Mürz Zuschlag, where Brahms this year had the advantage of Dr. and Frau Fellinger's society, and—indispensable for his complete enjoyment of a home circle—that of their children. Returning one afternoon from a walk, he found that the house in which he lodged had caught fire, and that his friends were busily engaged in bringing his papers, and amongst them the nearly-finished manuscript of the new symphony, into the garden. He immediately set to work to help in getting the fire under, whilst Frau Fellinger sat out of doors with either arm outspread on the precious papers piled on each side of her. Luckily, all serious harm was averted, and it was soon possible to restore the manuscripts intact to the composer's apartments.

Brahms paid a neighbourly call, in the course of the summer, on the author Rosegger, who was living in his small country house at Krieglach near Mürz Zuschlag, and tasted the unusual experience of a repulse. Absorbed in work at the moment when his servant announced 'a strange gentleman,' Rosegger, without glancing at the card placed beside him, desired his visitor to 'sit down for a moment.' Conscious only of the presence of a bearded stranger with a gray overcoat over his shoulder and a light-coloured umbrella in his hand, he vouchsafed but scant answer to the trifling remarks with which his caller tried to pave the way to cordiality, and before long Brahms composedly remarked that he would be on his legs again, and took leave. It was not till some minutes after his departure that it occurred to Rosegger to glance at the card, and he has himself described the feelings of despair with which he read the words 'Johannes Brahms' staring at him in all the reality of black on white. Not he alone, but the ladies of his family, were enthusiastic admirers of the composer's genius. He was so overwhelmed by his mistake as to be incapable of taking any steps to remedy it, and firmly declined to yield to the entreaties of his wife and daughter that he would return the visit and explain matters to Brahms. He published an amusing account of the misadventure in the year 1894 in an issue of the *Heimgarten*. Perhaps it may have fallen into the master's hands.

The honour not only of the first, but of several subsequent early performances of the Symphony in E minor, fell to the Meiningen orchestra. The work was announced for the third subscription concert of the season 1885-86, and shortly beforehand the score and parts of the third and fourth movements were sent by the composer to Meiningen for correction at a preliminary rehearsal under Bülow. Three listeners were, by Bülow's invitation, present on the occasion—the Landgraf of Hesse; Richard Strauss, the now famous composer, who had succeeded Mannstädt as second conductor of the Meiningen orchestra; and Frederic Lamond. The lapse of another day or so brought Brahms himself with the first and second movements, and the first public performance of the work took place on October 25.

That the new symphony was enthusiastically received on the occasion goes almost without saying. Persevering but unsuccessful efforts were made by the audience to obtain a repetition of the third movement, and the close of the work was followed by the emphatic demonstration incident to a great success.

The work was repeated under Bülow's direction at the following Meiningen concert of November 1, and was conducted by the composer throughout a three weeks' tour on which he started with Bülow and his orchestra immediately afterwards, and which included the towns Siegen, Dortmund, Essen, Elberfeld, Düsseldorf, Rotterdam, Utrecht, Amsterdam, the Hague, Arnheim, Crefeld, Bonn, and Cologne. A performance at Wiesbaden followed, and the work was heard for the first time in Vienna at the Philharmonic concert of January 17, 1886, under Richter. This occasion was celebrated by a dinner given by Billroth at the Hôtel Sacher, the guests invited to meet the composer being Richter, Hanslick, Goldmark, Faber, Door, Epstein, Ehrbar, Fuchs, Kalbeck, and Dömpke.

A new and important work by Brahms could hardly fail to obtain a warm reception in Vienna at a period when the composer could look back to thirty years' residence in the imperial city with which his name had become as closely associated as those of Haydn, Mozart, Beethoven, and Schubert; but though the symphony was applauded by the public and praised by all but the inveterately hostile section of the press, it did not reach the hearts of the Vienna audience in the same unmistakable manner as its two immediate predecessors, both of which had, as we have seen, made a more striking impression on a first hearing in Austria than the first Symphony in C minor. Strangely enough, the fourth symphony at once obtained some measure of real appreciation in Leipzig, where the first had been far more successful than the second and third. It was performed under the composer at the Gewandhaus concert of February 18. The account given of the occasion by the *Leipziger Nachrichten* is, perhaps, the more satisfactory since our old friend Dörffel, who might possibly have been suspected of partiality, had long since retired from the staff of the journal. Bernhard Vögl, his second successor, says:

'... The reception must, we think, have made amends to Brahms for former ones, which, in Bülow's opinion, were too cool. After each movement the hall resounded with tumultuous and long-continued applause, and, at the conclusion of the work, the composer was repeatedly called forward.... The finale is certainly the most original of the movements, and furnishes more complete argument than has before been brought forward for the opinion of those who see in Brahms the modern Sebastian Bach. The movement is not only constructed on the form displayed in Bach's Chaconne for violin, but is filled with Bach's spirit. It is built up with astounding mastery upon the eight notes,

[Listen]

and in such a manner that its contrapuntal learning remains subordinate to its poetic contents.... It can be compared with no former work of Brahms and stands alone in the symphonic literature of the present and the past.'

A still more triumphant issue attended the production of the symphony under Brahms at a concert of the Hamburg Cecilia Society on April 9. Josef Sittard, who had recently been appointed musical critic to the *Hamburger Correspondenten*, a post he has held to the present day, wrote:

'To-day we abide by what we have affirmed for years past in musical journals; that Brahms is the greatest instrumental composer since Beethoven. Power, passion, depth of thought, exalted nobility of melody and form, are the qualities which form the artistic sign manual of his creations. The E minor (fourth) Symphony is distinguished from the second and third principally by the rigorous and even grim earnestness which, though in a totally different way, mark the first. More than ever does the composer follow out his ideas to their conclusion, and this unbending logic makes the immediate understanding of the work difficult. But the oftener we have heard it, the more clearly have its great beauties, the depth, energy and power of its thoughts, the clearness of its classic form, revealed themselves to us. In the contrapuntal treatment of its themes, in richness of harmony and in the art of instrumentation, it seems to as superior to the second and third, these, perhaps, have the advantage of greater melodic beauty; a guarantee of popularity. In depth, power and originality of conception, however, the fourth symphony takes its place by the side of the first....'

After an interesting discussion of the several movements, the writer adds: 'In a word, the symphony is of monumental significance.'

Brahms' fourth symphony, produced when he was over fifty, is, in the opinion of most musicians, unsurpassed by any other achievement of his genius. It has during the past twenty years been growing slowly into general knowledge and favour, and will, it may be safely predicted, become still more deeply rooted in its place amongst the composer's most widely-valued works. The second movement, in the opinion of the late Philipp Spitta, 'does not find its equal in the symphonic world'; and the fourth, written in 'Passacaglia' form, is the most astonishing illustration achieved even by Brahms himself of the limitless capability of variation form, in which he is pre-eminent.[69]

It is with something of a mournful feeling that we find ourselves at the close of our enumeration of the master's four greatest instrumental works. Enough, we may hope, has been said to indicate that any comparison of the symphonies as inferior or superior is impossible, for the reason that each, while perfectly fulfilling its own particular destiny, is quite different from all the others, and such natural preference as may be felt by this or that listener for either must be considered as purely personal. The present writer may, perhaps, be allowed to confess that, with all joy in the dainty second and the magnificent third and fourth—emphatically the fourth—neither appeals to her quite so strongly as the first. There is here a quality of youth in the intensity of the soaring imagination that seems to search the universe, which, presented as it is with the wealth of resource that was at the command of the mature composer, could not by its nature be other than unique. The presence of this very quality may be the reason why the first symphony suffers even more lamentably than its companions from the dull, cold, cautious, 'classical' rendering which Brahms' orchestral works receive at the hands of some conductors, who seem unable to realize that a composer who founds his works on certain definite and traditional principles of structure does not thereby change his nature, or in any degree renounce the free exercise of his poetic gifts.

Perhaps the present is as good an opportunity as may occur for passing mention of a newspaper episode of the eighties, which was much talked of for a few years, but which, though it may have caused Brahms annoyance, could not possibly at this period of his career have had any more serious consequence so far as he was concerned.

Hugo Wolf, in 1884 a young aspirant to fame, seeking recognition but finding none, poor, gifted, disappointed, weak in health, highly nervous, without influential friends, accepted an opportunity of increasing his miserably small means of subsistence by becoming the musical critic of the *Salon Blatt*, a weekly society paper of Vienna, and soon made for himself an unenviable notoriety by his persistent attacks upon Brahms' compositions. The affair would not now demand mention in a biography of our master if it were not that the posthumous recognition afforded to Wolf's art gives some interest, though not of an agreeable nature, to this association of his name with that of Brahms. For the benefit of those readers who may wish to study the matter further, it may be added that Wolf's criticisms have been republished since his death. For ourselves, having done what was, perhaps, incumbent on us by referring to the matter, we shall adopt what we believe would have been Brahms' desire, by allowing it, so far as these pages are concerned, to follow others of the kind to oblivion.

The summer of 1886 was the first of the three seasons passed by Brahms at Thun, of which Widmann has written so charming an account. He rented the entire first-floor of a house opposite the spot where the river Aare flows out of the lake, the ground-floor being occupied by the owner, who kept a little haberdashery shop. According to his general custom, he dined in fine weather in the garden of some inn, occasionally alone, but oftener in the company of a friend or friends. Every Saturday he went to Bern to remain till Monday or longer with the Widmanns, who, like other friends, found him a most considerate and easily satisfied guest, though his exceptional energy of body and mind often made it exhausting work to keep up with him.

'His week-end visits were,' says Widmann, 'high festivals and times of rejoicing for me and mine; days of rest they certainly were not, for the constantly active mind of our guest demanded similar wakefulness from all his associates and one had to pull one's self well together to maintain sufficient freshness to satisfy the requirements of his indefatigable vitality.... I have never seen anyone who took such fresh, genuine and lasting interest in the surroundings of life as Brahms, whether in objects of nature, art, or even industry. The smallest invention, the improvement of some article for household use, every trace, in short, of practical ingenuity gave him real pleasure. And nothing escaped his observation.... He hated bicycles because the flow of his ideas was so often disturbed by the noiseless rushing past, or the sudden signal, of these machines, and also because he thought the trampling movement of the rider ugly. He was, however, glad to live in the age of great inventions and could not sufficiently admire the electric light, Edison's phonographs, etc. He was equally interested in the animal world. I always had to tell him anew about the family customs of the bears in the Bern bear-pits before which we often stood together. Indeed, subjects of conversation seemed inexhaustible during his visits.'[70]

Brahms' ordinary costume, the same here as elsewhere, was chosen quite without regard to appearances. Mere lapse of time must occasionally have compelled him to wear a new coat, but it is safe to conclude that his feelings suffered discomposure on the rare occurrence of such a crisis. Neckties and white collars were reserved as special marks of deference to conventionality. During his visits to Thun he used on wet Saturdays to appear at Bern wearing 'an old brown-gray plaid fastened over his chest with an immense pin, which completed his strange appearance.' Many were the books borrowed from Widmann at the beginning, and brought back at the end, of the week, carried by him in a leather bag slung over his shoulder. Most of them were standard works; he was not devoted to modern literature on the whole, though he read with pleasure new and really good books of history and travel, and was fond of Gottfried Keller's novels and poems. Over engravings and photographs of Italian works of art he would pore for hours, never weary of discussing memories and predilections with his friend.

Visits to the Bern summer theatre, a short mountain tour with Widmann, an introduction to Ernst von Wildenbruch, whose dramas the master liked, and with whom he now found himself in personal sympathy—events such as these served to diversify the summer season of 1886, which was made musically noteworthy by the composition of a group of chamber works, the Sonatas in A and F major for pianoforte with violin and violoncello respectively, and the Trio in C minor for pianoforte and strings. The Sonatas were performed for the first time in public in Vienna; severally by Brahms and Hellmesberger, at the Quartet concert of December 2, and by Brahms and Hausmann at Hausmann's concert of November 24; the Trio was introduced at Budapest about the same time by Brahms, Hubay, and Popper, in each case from the manuscript.

Detailed discussion of these works is superfluous; two of them, at all events, are amongst the best known of Brahms' compositions. The Sonata for pianoforte and violoncello in F is the least familiar of the group, but assuredly not because it is inferior to its companions. It is, indeed, one of the masterpieces of Brahms' later concise style. Each movement has a remarkable individuality of its own, whilst all are unmistakably characteristic of the composer. The first is broad and energetic, the second profoundly touching, the third vehemently passionate—in the Brahms' signification of the word, be it noted, which means that the emotions are reached through the intellectual imagination—the fourth written from beginning to end in a spirit of vivacity and fun. The work was tried in the first instance at Frau Fellinger's house. 'Are you expecting Hausmann?' Brahms inquired carelessly of this lady soon after his return in the autumn. Frau Fellinger, suspecting that something lay behind the question, telegraphed to the great violoncellist, who usually stayed at her house when in Vienna, to come as soon as possible, if only for a day. He duly appeared, and the new sonata was played by Brahms and himself on the evening of his arrival. They performed it again the day before the concert above recorded, at a large party at Billroth's.

The last movement of the beautiful Sonata in A for pianoforte and violin is sometimes criticised as being almost too concise. The present writer confesses that she always feels it to be so, and one day confided this sentiment to Joachim, who did not agree with her, but said that the coda was originally considerably longer. 'Brahms told me he had cut a good deal away; he aimed always at condensation.'

Dr. Widmann allows us to publish an English version of a poem written by him on this work, the original of which is published in the appendix to his 'Brahms Recollections.' We have desired to place it before our English-speaking readers, not only because it coincides remarkably with what we related in our early chapters of the delicate, fanciful tastes of the youthful Hannes, but because it gave pleasure to the Brahms of fifty-three, and even of sixty-three, and thus seems to illustrate the fact on which we have insisted, that if in any case then in our master's, the child was father to the man. Only a year before his death the great composer wrote to Widmann to beg for one or two more copies of the poem, which had been printed for private circulation.

THE THUN SONATA.

POEM ON THE SONATA IN A FOR PIANOFORTE AND VIOLIN, OP. 100,
BY JOHANNES BRAHMS,

WRITTEN BY
J. V. WIDMANN.

There where the Aare's waters gently glide
From out the lake and flow towards the town,
Where pleasant shelter spreading trees provide,
Amidst the waving grass I laid me down;
And sleeping softly on that summer day,
I saw a wondrous vision as I lay.

Three knights rode up on proudly stepping steeds,
Tiny as elves, but with the mien of kings,
And spake to me: 'We come to search the meads,
To seek a treasure here, of precious things
Amongst the fairest; wilt thou help us trace
A new-born child, a child of heav'nly race?'

'And who are ye?' I, dreaming, made reply;
'Knights of the golden meadows' then they said,
'That at the foot of yonder Niesen[71] lie;
And in our ancient castles many a maid
Hath listened to the greeting of our strings,
Long mute and passed amid forgotten things.

'But lately tones were heard upon the lake,
A sound of strings whose like we never knew,
So David played, perhaps, for Saul's dread sake,

Soothing the monarch curtained from his view;
It reached us as it softly swelled and sank,
And drew us, filled with longing, to this bank.

'Then help us search, for surely from this place,
This meadow by the river, came the sound;
Help us then here the miracle to trace,
That we may offer homage when 'tis found.
Sleeps under flow'rs the new-born creature rare?
Or is it floating in the evening air?'

But ere they ceased, a sudden rapid twirl
Ruffled the waters, and, before our eyes,
A fairy boat from out the wavelet's whirl
Floated up stream, guided by dragon-flies;
Within it sat a sweet-limbed, fair-haired may,
Singing as to herself in ecstasy.

'To ride on waters clear and cool is sweet,
For clear as deep my being's living source;
To open worlds where joy and sorrow meet,
Each flowing pure and full in mingling course;
Go on, my boat, upstream with happy cheer,
Heaven is reposing on the tranquil mere.'

So sang the fairy child and they that heard
Owned, by their swelling hearts, the music's might,
The knights had only tears, nor spake a word,
Welling from pain that thrilled them with delight;
But when the skiff had vanished from their eyes,
The eldest, pointing, said in tender wise:

'Thou beauteous wonder of the boat, farewell,
Sweet melody, revealed to us to-day;
We that with slumb'ring minnesingers dwell,
Bid thee Godspeed, thou guileless stranger fay;
Our land is newly consecrate in thee
That rang of old with fame of minstrelsy.

'Now we may sleep again amongst our dead,
The harper's holy spirit is awake,
And as the evening glory, purple-red,
Shineth upon our Alps and o'er our lake,
And yet on distant mountain sheds its light,
Throughout the earth this song will wing its flight.

'Yet, though subduing many a list'ning throng,
In stately town, in princely hall it sound,
To this our land it ever will belong,
For here on flowing river it was found.'
Fervent and glad the minnesinger spake;
'Yes!' cried my heart—and then I was awake.

Whilst our master had been living through the spring and summer months in the enchanted world of his imagination, coming out of it only for brief intervals of sojourn in earth's pleasant places amidst the companionship of chosen friends, certain hard, commonplace realities of the workaday world, which had arisen earlier at home in Vienna, were still awaiting a satisfactory solution. The death of the occupier of the third-floor flat of No. 4, Carlsgasse, the last remaining member of the family with whom Brahms had lodged for fourteen or fifteen years, had confronted him with the necessity of choosing between several alternatives almost equally disagreeable to him, concerning which it is only necessary to say that he had avoided the annoyance of a removal by taking on the entire dwelling direct from the landlord, and had escaped the disturbance of having to replace the furniture of his rooms by accepting the offer of friends to lend him sufficient for his absolute needs. Arrangements and all necessary changes were made during his absence. To Frau Fellinger Brahms had entrusted the keys of the flat and of his rooms, which under her directions were brought into apple-pie order by the time of his return, the drawers being tidied, and a list of the contents of each neatly drawn up on a piece of cardboard, so that everything should be ready to his hand. The greatest difficulty, however, still remained. Who was to keep the rooms in order and see to the very few of Brahms' daily requirements which he was not in the habit of looking after himself? His coffee, as we know, he always prepared at a very early hour in the morning, and he was kept provided with a regular supply of the finest Mocha by a lady friend at Marseilles. Dinner, afternoon coffee, and often supper, were taken away from home. The master now declared he would have no one in the flat. To as many visitors as he felt disposed to admit he could himself open the door, whilst the cleaning and tidying of the rooms could be done by the 'Hausmeisterin,' an old woman occupying a room in the courtyard, and responsible for the cleaning of the general staircase, etc. In vain Frau Fellinger contested the point. Brahms was inflexible, and this kind lady apparently withdrew her opposition to his plan, though remaining quietly on the look-out for an opportunity of securing more suitable arrangements. By-and-by it presented itself. In Frau Celestine Truxa, the widow of a journalist, whose family party consisted of two young sons and an old aunt, Frau Fellinger felt that she saw a most desirable tenant for the Carlsgasse flat, and after a renewed attack on the master, whose arguments, founded on the immaculate purity of his rooms under the old woman's care, she irretrievably damaged by lifting a sofa cushion and laying bare a collection of dust, which she declared would soon develop into something worse, he was so far shaken as to say that if she would make inquiries for him he would consider her views. Frau Fellinger wisely abstained from further discussion, but after a few days Frau Truxa herself, having been duly advised to open the matter to Brahms with diplomatic sang-froid, went in person to apply for the dwelling. After her third ring at the door-bell, the door was opened by the master himself, who started in dismay at seeing a strange lady standing in front of him.

'I have come to see the flat,' said Frau Truxa.

'What!' cried Brahms.

'I have heard there is an empty flat here, and have come to look at it,' responded Frau Truxa indifferently; 'but perhaps it is not to let?'

A moment's pause, and the composer's suspicious expression relaxed.

'Frau Dr. Fellinger mentioned the circumstances to me,' she continued, 'and I thought they might suit me.'

By this time Brahms had become sufficiently reassured to show the rooms and to listen, though without remark, to a brief description of Frau Truxa's family and of the circumstances in which she found herself.

'Perhaps, Dr. Brahms, you will consider the matter,' she concluded, 'and communicate with me if you think further of it. If I hear nothing more from you, I shall consider the matter at an end.'

After about a week, during which Frau Truxa kept her own confidence, her maid came one day to tell her a gentleman had called to see her. Being engaged at the moment, she asked her aunt to ascertain his business, but the old lady returned immediately with a frightened look.

'I don't know what to think!' she exclaimed; 'there is a strange-looking man walking about in the next room measuring the furniture with a tape!'

'The things will all go in!' exclaimed the master as Frau Truxa hurried to receive him.

The upshot was that the master gave up the tenancy of the flat, returning to his old irresponsible position as lodger, whilst Frau Truxa, bringing her household with her, stepped into the position of his former landlady, thereby giving Brahms cause to be grateful for the remainder of his life for Frau Fellinger's wise firmness. He was, says Frau Truxa, perfectly easy to get on with; all he desired was to be let alone. He was extremely orderly and neat in his ways, and expected the things scattered about his room to be dusted and kept tidy, but was vexed if he found the least trifle at all displaced—even if his glasses were turned the wrong way—and, without making direct allusion to the subject, would manage to show that he had noticed it. Observing, after she had been a little time in the flat, that he always rearranged the things returned from the laundress after they had been placed in their drawer, she asked him why he did so. 'Only,' he said, 'because perhaps it is better that those last sent back should be put at the bottom, then they all get worn alike.' A glove or other article requiring a little mending would be placed carelessly at the top of a drawer left open as if by accident. The next day he would observe to Frau Truxa, 'I found my glove mended last night; I wonder who can have done it!' and on her replying, 'I did it, Herr Doctor,' would answer, 'You? How very kind!'

Frau Truxa came to respect and honour the composer more and more the longer he lived in her house. She made his peculiarities her study, and after a short time understood his little signs, and was able to supply his requirements as they arose without being expressly asked to do so. It is almost needless to say that he took great interest in her two boys, and once, when she was summoned away from Vienna to the sick-bed of her father, begged that the maid-servant might be instructed to give all her attention to the children during their mother's absence, even if his rooms were neglected. 'I can take care of myself, but suppose something were to happen to the children whilst the girl was engaged for me!' Every night whilst Frau Truxa was away, the master himself looked in on the boys to assure himself of their being safe in bed. For the old aunt he always had a pleasant passing word.

The fourth Symphony and two books of Songs were published in 1886, and the three new works of chamber music, Op. 99, 100, 101, in 1887. Of the songs we would select for particular mention the wonderfully beautiful setting of Heine's verses:

'Death is the cool night,
Life is the sultry day,'

Op. 96, No. 1, and Nos. 1 and 2 of Op. 97.

Brahms' Italian journey in the spring of 1887 was made in the company of Simrock and Kirchner. The following year he travelled in Widmann's society, visiting Verona, Bologna, Rimini, Ancona, Loretto, Rome, and Turin. Widmann sees in Brahms' spiritual kinship with the masters of the Italian Renaissance the chief secret of his love for Italy.

'Their buildings, their statues, their pictures were his delight and when one witnessed the absorbed devotion with which he contemplated their works, or heard him admire in the old masters a trait conspicuous in himself, their conscientious perfection of detail ... even where it could hardly be noticeable to the ordinary observer, one could not help instituting the comparison between himself and them.'

Brahms had an interview when on this journey with the now famous Italian composer Martucci, who displayed a thorough familiarity with the works of the German master.

Amongst the friends and acquaintances whom the composer met at Thun during his second and third summers there were the Landgraf of Hesse, Hanslick, Gottfried Keller, Professor Bächthold, Hermine Spiess and her sister, Gustav Wendt, the Hegars, Max Kalbeck, Steiner, Claus Groth, etc. One day, as he had started for a walk, he was stopped by a stranger, who asked if he knew where Dr. Brahms lived. 'He lives there,' replied the master, pointing to the haberdasher's shop. 'Do you know if he is at home?' 'That I cannot tell you,' was the reply. 'But go and ask in the shop; you will certainly be able to find out there.' The gentleman followed this advice, sent his card up, and received the answer that the Doctor was at home, and would be pleased to see him. To his surprise, on ascending the stairs, he found his newly-formed acquaintance waiting for him at the top.

Brahms' Lodgings near Thun.
Photograph by Moegle, Thun.

The rumour revived in the summer of 1887 that Brahms was engaged on an opera. This came about, perhaps, from his intimacy with Widmann. 'I am composing the entr'actes,' he jestingly replied to the Landgraf's question as to whether the report had any foundation. As a matter of fact, the subject of opera was not mentioned between the composer and his friend at this time.

The works which really occupied Brahms during the summer of 1887 were the double Concerto for violin and violoncello, with orchestral accompaniment, and the 'Gipsy Songs.'

The Concerto was performed privately, immediately on its completion, in the 'Louis Quinze' room of the Baden-Baden Kurhaus. Brahms conducted, and the solo parts were performed by Joachim and Hausmann. Amongst the listeners were Frau Schumann and her eldest daughter, Rosenhain,

Lachner, the violoncellist Hugo Becker, and Gustav Wendt. The work was heard in public for the first time in Cologne on October 15, Brahms conducting, and Joachim and Hausmann playing the solos as before; and the next performances, carried out under the same unique opportunities for success, were in Wiesbaden, Frankfurt, and Basle, on November 17, 18, and 20.

In the autumn of this year one of the few remaining figures linked with the most cherished associations of Brahms' early youth passed away. Marxsen died on November 17, 1887, at the age of eighty-one, having retained to the end almost unimpaired vigour of his mental faculties. The last great pleasure of his life was associated with his beloved art. In spite of great bodily weakness, he managed to be present a week before his death at a concert of the Hamburg Philharmonic Society to hear a performance of the 'ninth' Symphony. 'I am here for the last time,' he said, pressing Sittard's hand; and he passed peacefully away fourteen days later.

A few years previously his artistic jubilee had been celebrated in Hamburg, and his dear Johannes had surprised him with the proof-sheets of a set of one hundred Variations composed long ago by Marxsen, not with a view to publication, but as a practical illustration of the inexhaustible possibilities contained in the art of thematic development. Brahms, who happened to see the manuscript in Marxsen's room during one of his subsequent visits to Hamburg, was so strongly interested in it that in the end Marxsen gave it him, with leave to do as he should like with it after his death. The parcel of proof-sheets was accompanied by an affectionate letter, in which Brahms begged forgiveness for having anticipated this permission and yielded to his desire of placing the work within general reach during his master's lifetime; and perhaps no jubilee honour of which the old musician was the recipient filled him with such lively joy as was caused by this tribute. Marxsen's name as a composer is, indeed, now forgotten without chance of revival, but his memory will live gloriously in the way he would have chosen, carried through the years by the hand that wrote the great composer's acknowledgment to his teacher on the title-page of the Concerto in B flat.

Four more performances from the manuscript of the double concerto of interest in our narrative remain to be chronicled—those of the Leipzig Gewandhaus, under Brahms, on January 1, 1888; of the Berlin Philharmonic Society, under Bülow, of February 6; and of the London Symphony Concerts, under Henschel, on February 15 and 21. The work, published in time for the autumn season, was given in Vienna at the Philharmonic concert of December 23 under Richter. On all these occasions the solos were played, as before, by Joachim and Hausmann.

Bülow, having at this time resigned his post at Meiningen, had entered on a period of activity as conductor in some of the northern cities of Germany, and particularly in Hamburg and Berlin. His future programmes, in which our master's works were well represented, though not with the conspicuous prominence that had been possible at Meiningen, do not fall within the scope of these pages, since, with the mention of the double concerto, the enumeration of Brahms' orchestral works is complete. Bülow's successor at Meiningen, Court Capellmeister Fritz Steinbach, carried on the traditions and preferences of the little Thuringian capital as he found them, until his removal to Cologne a year or two ago, and has become especially appreciated as a conductor of the works of Brahms, whose personal friendship and artistic confidence he enjoyed in a high degree.

The name of Eugen d'Albert, whose great gifts and attainments were warmly recognised by Brahms, should not be omitted from our pages, though detailed account of his relations with the master is outside their limits. D'Albert's fine performances of the pianoforte concertos helped to make these works familiar to many Continental audiences, and certainly contributed, during the second half of the eighties, to the better understanding of the great composer which has gradually come to prevail at Leipzig.

But little needs to be said about the double concerto. This fine work, which may be regarded as in some sort a successor to the double and triple concertos of Mozart and Beethoven, exhibits all the power of construction, the command of resource, the logical unity of idea, characteristic of Brahms' style, whilst its popularity has been hindered by the same cause that has retarded that of the pianoforte concertos; the solo parts do not stand out sufficiently from the orchestral accompaniment to give effective opportunity for the display of virtuosity, in the absence of which no performer, appearing before a great public as the exponent of an unfamiliar work for an accompanied solo instrument, has much chance of sustaining the lively interest of his audience in the composition. Of the three movements of the double concerto, the first is especially interesting to musicians, whilst the second, a beautiful example of Brahms' expressive lyrical muse, appeals equally to less technically prepared listeners. On the copy of the work presented by Brahms to Joachim the words are inscribed in the composer's handwriting: 'To him for whom it was written.'

Widely contrasted in every respect was the other new work of 1887, introduced to the private circle of Vienna musicians at the last meeting for the season of the Tonkünstlerverein in April, 1888. The eleven four-part 'Gipsy Songs,' published in the course of the year as Op. 103, were sung from the manuscript by Fräulein Walter, Frau Gomperz-Bettelheim, Gustav Walter, and Weiglein of the imperial opera, to the composer's accompaniment. Brahms obtained the texts of this characteristic and attractive work from a collection of twenty-five 'Hungarian Folk-songs' translated into German by Hugo Conrat, and published in Budapest, with their original melodies set by Zoltan Nagy for mezzo-soprano or baritone, with the addition of pianoforte accompaniment. Conrat's translations have been done in masterly fashion. Literal as far as possible, slight modifications of the original have been admitted here and there in order to obtain a natural flow of the lines; and to some single-strophe songs, including Nos. 3 and 4 of Brahms' work, a second verse, developing the idea of the first, has been added. The German texts, in which the national Hungarian character is admirably preserved, appealed irresistibly to our master, and are well adapted to the four-part setting with pianoforte accompaniment which had proved so successful in the two books of Liebeslieder Walzer.

One of the earliest public performances of the Gipsy Songs was that of the Monday Popular concert of November 26 by Mr. and Mrs. Henschel, Miss Lena Little, and Mr. Shakespeare, with Miss Fanny Davies as pianist. They were repeated at the Saturday Popular of December 1, and again on Monday and Saturday, December 22 and 28. The first public performance in Vienna—by the executants who had already given the work privately—took place at Walter's concert in the Börsendorfer Hall on January 18, 1889.

The Gipsy Songs had an immediate widespread, and enormous success, and were soon heard in all parts of the musical world. They were sung in Paris in a French translation, and many times in Budapest, where the composer's art had become popular, in Hungarian retranslated from Conrat's version. Great though their popularity has remained, however, it has not equalled that of the Liebeslieder, and of these the demand for the first book has continued to exceed that for the second.

A graphic picture of Brahms as he was in the year 1888 and onwards is to be found in an article by Dr. Jenner.[72] This gentleman made the master's acquaintance under particularly interesting circumstances. When still a very young man, resident at Kiel, and a favourite of Claus Groth, the manuscripts of some of his songs came under Brahms' notice, and so much engaged his sympathy as to induce him to say he would be happy to receive the composer during his visit to Leipzig on the occasion of the above-recorded performance of the new double concerto.

'My friend Julius Spengel joined me in Hamburg and we went together to Berlin,' says Dr. Jenner. 'There I was present for the first time at a Joachim Quartet evening. Immediately after the concert we travelled with the Quartet to Leipzig, arriving in the middle of the night at the Hôtel Hauffe.

Never shall I forget the feeling that came over me as I read in the visitors' list, "Johannes Brahms from Vienna." He had already retired. By a strange chance I was shown into the room next his and as I entered it a sound of healthy snoring proclaimed the proximity of the mighty one. Moving about quietly, I went to rest with a strange mixed feeling of awe, pride and anxiety. When I came down the next morning Brahms had already breakfasted. Comfortably smoking, he was reading the papers.... He received me with pleasant, simple kindness, intimated that he knew why I had come, and took pains to help me over my first embarrassment and shyness by every now and then putting to me some short, direct question, so that I was soon convinced of his good-nature and felt unlimited confidence in him....

'It was past 3 o'clock when we returned that night to the Hôtel Hauffe. How delighted but also astonished I was when Brahms, as he said good-night, announced that he would expect me in his room at 7 o'clock in the morning to speak to me about my compositions. I presented myself punctually at the appointed time and found him at breakfast, fresh, rosy and the picture of equanimity....

'I had brought a trio for pianoforte and strings, a chorus with orchestral accompaniment, unaccompanied choruses for women's voices, and songs; and found that he had made himself acquainted with them down to the smallest detail, and, indeed, later he never looked through work with me which he had not thoroughly examined beforehand. After a few introductory remarks, in which he said that he had formed a generally favourable impression of my compositions, he gave me back the accompanied chorus with the words "Pity for the beautiful little poem." It was Claus Groth's "Wenn ein müder Leib." The *a capella* choruses met with the same fate; I received them back with the remark "Such things are very difficult to make....'"

For the sequel the reader must be referred to the article itself, which amusingly describes the tranquil and ruthless methods by which the master reduced his young friend to the verge of despair. All ended well, however, and the middle of February saw the arrival in Vienna of Herr Jenner and his introduction to Mandyczewski, under whom he was to go through a course of study in strict counterpoint, whilst his work in free composition was to be carried on under the master's personal supervision. After making Mandyczewski's acquaintance,

'I dined with Brahms at the "Zum Rothen Igel" and afterwards he went with me to find a lodging, giving preference to the old houses. Whilst we were on this expedition, he took every opportunity of making me acquainted with the sacred places of the city. Before one house it was "This is the Auge Gottes," before another "Look, Figaro was written there." At length a suitable room was found near his own dwelling. "The young man likes music" said Brahms to the landlady, "will he be able to hear a little pianoforte playing or singing here sometimes?" This she could not offer. "Never mind, it does not matter." Then he gave me one of his coffee-machines, plates, cups, forks, knives and spoons, so that I was comfortably settled the first day. The use of his library was at my disposal; his purse also. I could have as much money as I needed from him, but I was never obliged to take any and never did so....

'I think with deep melancholy of the glorious evenings when Rottenberg and I sat alone with him in the low back room of the Igel and the silent Brahms thawed and showed us glimpses of a great and strong soul. But he never spoke on such occasions of his works, very rarely of himself and his life. I have, indeed, often had the good fortune of hearing him speak of himself whilst he was giving me a lesson; it was nearly always with some excitement. I was unfortunately obliged to give up the pleasure of dining with him every day during my second winter, as the Igel was too dear for me. Brahms always declared it was the cheapest house in Vienna and in fact he understood so well how to choose that he always had to pay less than I and yet got a better dinner. He was quite extraordinarily moderate in his daily life; 70-80 kreuzers was the most that he spent for his dinner and this included a glass of Pilsener beer or a quarter of a litre of wine. In the evening he drank but little more. It is only because the contrary has been so often affirmed that I think it my duty to tell the truth in such detail.'

The old-fashioned restaurant Zum Rothen Igel, where Brahms was for many years a 'Stammgast'—*i.e.*, a daily customer—is situated in a corner of the Wildpret Markt close to the Augustinestrasse. Brahms did not frequent the regular dining-room of the house, but took his dinner in a low, dark, vaulted chamber at the back, on the ground-floor, ordinarily used by waiters, coachmen, and similar guests. Here, at a table near a door leading to a small, gloomy courtyard, many a distinguished guest, the Landgraf of Hesse, Joachim, and many another, has partaken in our master's company of the homely but well-cooked dishes that he preferred. In fact, but few prominent musical visitors to Vienna quitted the imperial city without making the acquaintance, under Brahms' auspices, of the dingy apartment in the Wildpret Markt now called 'the Brahms room' and decorated with a photograph of the master. He was very often joined at his mid-day meal by resident friends and acquaintances, and often supped at the Igel after a concert with a party of musicians. Amongst those most frequently seen with him were his old friends Epstein and Door and a circle of the young men in whom he took an interest; at the date now reached by our narrative, Mandyczewski and Rottenberg were his almost daily companions. If he supped alone at the Igel, he preferred to take his place in a corner behind the house-door, which was screened from the taproom by a red curtain and was just large enough to hold a table and bench, occupied in slack hours by the manager. During the short time that the weather permitted, he dined, after his return to Vienna at the beginning of October, in the 'garden'—*i.e.*, at one of the two or three tables placed outside the house, and flanked by large pots of ever-greens which were carried away when the days became cold.

During the last ten years of his life Brahms allowed himself to accept more invitations than formerly to dine or sup with one and another of the small group of families forming his immediate circle, and when invited out he liked, and even expected, to be asked to a good table and to have good wine put before him. He retained the notion, universal in a former generation, but now out of date, that it was incumbent on a bidden guest, not only to appreciate, but to show appreciation, of the hospitality of his host and hostess. 'There are people,' he used to say, 'who are afraid of showing that they like a good dinner.' Brahms was certainly not one of these. He was prepared to do ample justice to the recherché cookery and excellent wines with which his friends liked to regale him, but he was at no period of his life either a glutton or a wine-bibber, and, indeed, never varied from the abstemious habits which the early circumstances of his life had made incumbent on him as a young man.

One of the annual Brahms festivities was the asparagus luncheon always given by Ehrbar on, or as near as possible to, May 7, in honour of the master's birthday. About twelve or sixteen people were invited, amongst whom the Hanslicks and Billroth and his daughter were regularly included. The luncheon hour was twelve o'clock, and the menu, which never varied, consisted of oysters, caviare, cold meat, then the *pièce de résistance*, asparagus, which was always provided in the proportion of two bundles to each person. This was followed by cheese and dessert, and there was a free flow of fine champagne.

The summer of 1888, the last one passed by Brahms at Thun, did not reach the end of its course in such unbroken tranquillity as the two previous ones. A heated political discussion with Widmann, in which neither disputant would give way, threatened to put a sudden end to the intimacy which had been a source of pleasure and advantage to both friends. Fortunately this catastrophe was averted by the good sense of the two men and the cordial affection existing between them, and when Brahms left Switzerland in October they looked forward to renewing the experience of a journey to Italy together which had brought them a succession of delights in the spring of the year.

The third Sonata for pianoforte and violin, in D minor, was composed during the summer, and was played for the first time in public from the manuscript by Brahms and Joachim at Joachim's Vienna concert of February 13, 1889. It was published in the spring, with Brahms' dedication to 'his friend Hans von Bülow,' and was performed immediately afterwards in London by Miss Fanny Davies and Ludwig Straus at Miss Davies' concert of May 7. The three sonatas for pianoforte and violin were played one summer's day at Gmünden, by Brahms and Joachim, before the Queen and royal family of Hanover, an incident which carries the memory back to the year 1853, when Johannes, having come safely through the first stages of his concert-journey and taken Joachim's heart by storm, appeared with Reményi for the first time before King George and his circle at Hanover.

The other publications of 1889 were a book of five Songs for mixed Chorus *a capella*, and three books of five Songs each, for a single voice with pianoforte accompaniment. Of these 'Wie Melodien,' 'Auf dem Kirchhofe,' and 'Verrath' (Nos. 1, 4, 5 of Op. 105), and 'Serenade' (No. 1 of Op. 106), are great favourites of the author's. Brahms' songs, however, offer such rich choice of beauty that the selection of one or another, even of the more celebrated, for particular mention must be regarded as little more than the indication of a personal preference.

CHAPTER XXI
1889-1895

Hamburg honorary citizenship—Christmas at Dr. Fellinger's—Second String Quintet—Mühlfeld—Clarinet Quintet and Trio—Last journey to Italy—Sixtieth birthday—Pianoforte Pieces—Billroth's death—Brahms' collection of German Folk-songs—Life at Ischl—Clarinet Sonatas—Frau Schumann, Brahms, and Joachim together for the last time.

From the year 1889 onward Brahms chose for his summer dwelling-place the charming town of Ischl, the central point of the beautiful region of the Salzkammergut, and a favourite watering-place of the Viennese. He rented rooms, as on one or two former visits, in a cottage prettily situated on the outskirts of the town near the rushing river Traun, away from the visitors' quarter and convenient for his favourite walks about the picturesque mountains which surround the valley. A strong note of affectionate regret, very characteristic of the composer, is observable in the letter in which he announced to Widmann his arrangements for the open-air season of 1889. His extreme attachment, however, to his Vienna friends, to whom he may be said to have belonged almost entirely during the closing years of his life, probably determined his choice of Ischl, which was well within the reach of any of them who wished to visit him, whilst several had villas for summer residence in the immediate neighbourhood. Johann Strauss always lived at Ischl during the summer, the Billroths' delightfully situated home at St. Gilgen could be reached by train or the lake boat service in an hour, whilst the house and grounds of Herr and Frau Victor von Miller zu Aichholz at Gmünden, and Goldmark's rooms, also at Gmünden, were not much further off, and so on with other friends.

'I have heard by chance,' writes Billroth from St. Gilgen to Brahms at Ischl on June 16, 'that Mandyczewski and Rottenberg are with you ... make up your mind quickly therefore and come over with them to St. Gilgen and invite Brüll or Goldmark also in my name....'

Brahms always dined when at Ischl in the 'Keller' of the Hôtel Elisabeth, which was reached by a flight of steps leading downwards from the street, and is thus described by Billroth:

'I passed a couple of pleasant hours with Brahms at Ischl. We dined in a damp, underground room belonging to the Hôtel Elisabeth. The same dishes are served there as in the better class dining-room but at rather cheaper prices; it is very cool in the summer and no toilet is required; everything as if made for Brahms.'

The city of Hamburg this year conferred its honorary citizenship on Brahms, a distinction he shared with Bismarck and Moltke. Greatly touched by this recognition, the master let himself go for once, and immediately telegraphed his thanks to the mayor in natural, impulsive fashion that he seems to have regretted when he saw his words in print.

'... You will find me here,' he wrote to Hanslick from Ischl, 'until—I must go to the music festival at Hamburg! I must, for my honorary citizenship, with all that is associated with it, has been too pleasant and gratifying. I dread it, however, for I see that my telegram to the mayor has been printed! It sounds too foolish; "the best that could have come to me from men"—as though I had been thinking of eternal bliss; whereas all that I had in my mind was that when a melody occurs to me it is more welcome than an order, and that if it lead to my succeeding with a symphony, it gives me more pleasure than all honorary citizenships!...'[73]

In acknowledgment of the honour bestowed on him, Brahms composed three eight-part choruses *a capella*, which he entitled 'Fest and Gedenksprüche' (Festival and Commemoration Sayings) and dedicated to the mayor of Hamburg, Herr Oberbürgermeister Dr. Petersen. Patriotic remembrances and hopes were vividly present to his mind as he composed them, and the work is to be accepted as a second great musical memorial and glorification of the events of 1870-71. The texts are again selected from the Bible: from Deuteronomy, the Psalms, and the Gospels of St. Matthew and St. Luke. The choruses were studied by the Cecilia Society, and performed under Spengel at the first of three festival concerts arranged by Bülow for the opening of the Hamburg Industrial Exhibition. Sittard calls them 'a splendid musical gift,' and places them amongst the best and finest of the composer's works.

'The "Sayings" do not address themselves to a particular nation or creed, but speak to every thoughtful mind, to every human heart susceptible to earnest, ideal influences, and striving after the high and the beautiful. There lives in these movements something of that strong confidence which we find—expressive of another period of thought and of art—in Handel's works, and which acts like a tonic on every faithful mind. Brahms is the only composer of the present day who can sufficiently control his own individuality to be capable of expressing his texts in a musical language universally applicable and intelligible.'

The work was received with immense enthusiasm, and the master was obliged to come forward to acknowledge the long-continued plaudits which followed its conclusion. It was the last time that he stood on a concert platform of his native city.

Spengel, who witnessed with Bülow the presentation of the citizens' document, which took place at Dr. Petersen's house, relates that Brahms gave warm verbal expression to the deep feeling animating the written acknowledgment by which he had supplemented his telegram of thanks. This letter ran as follows:[74]

'YOUR MAGNIFICENCE
'MOST HONOURABLE HERR BÜRGERMEISTER

'I feel with my whole heart the need to add a few words to my hasty, short telegram. Kindly permit me again to assure your magnificence that my fellow-citizens have delighted and honoured me beyond measure by the bestowal of the honorary citizenship. As the artist is rejoiced by such a distinguished token of recognition, so also is the man by the glorious feeling of knowing himself so highly esteemed and loved in his native city. A feeling doubly proud when this native city is our beautiful, ancient, noble Hamburg!... The precious gift of my citizen's letter ... becomes more precious and dear to me as I place it by the side of my father's citizen's document (still in Low-German). My father was, indeed, my first thought in connection with the pleasant event, and one wish only remains, that he were here to rejoice with me....'

This was not the only mark of the esteem felt for him in high places by which the master was this year honoured. The news that the Emperor Francis Joseph had conferred upon him the distinguished 'Leopold's' order reached him in Ischl, taking him completely by surprise, and was followed by an inundation of letters, cards, and telegrams of congratulation, to all of which he replied individually.

'I was so pleased that the Austrians, as such, were glad that I was obliged to reply prettily,' he wrote to Hanslick.[75]

Another of the distinctions bestowed upon Brahms late in his career, which gave him, as a German musician, extraordinary pleasure, was that of his election as foreign member of the Académie française. He endeavoured to write his letter of acknowledgment in French, but, not being able to satisfy himself, was obliged to be content with expressing his gratification in his own language.

It seems appropriate to record, with the mention of these pleasant incidents, the fact of Brahms' warm admiration of the opera 'Carmen,' the work of the French composer Bizet.

A visit to Cologne—the last—in February is noteworthy as having furnished opportunity for the first (private) performance from the manuscript of three Motets for four and eight part chorus *a capella.* They were sung by the students' choral class of the conservatoire, and on the same occasion Brahms played—also from the manuscript—with two of the professors, the revised edition of his early B major Trio for the first time outside Vienna. We have already, in the early pages of our narrative, expressed our preference for the original version of this lovely work.

A visit to Italy in the spring with Widmann, which included Parma, Cremona, Brescia, and Vicenza, afforded Brahms opportunity of deriving pleasure from the most varied sources. The sight of the cathedral of Cremona by moonlight, upon which he and Widmann came suddenly the night of their arrival, as they turned a street corner, quite overpowered him. He could not gaze long enough at the wonderful scene, and was obliged to return with his friend to look at it once again before he could persuade himself to go in for the night. He was able, on the other hand, to derive amusement from the trifling incidents of each day's adventures, and was always ready to meet the passing difficulties and embarrassments of the traveller with laudable equanimity and resource. He used, later on, to describe, with some zest, an opera performance which he attended at Brescia. The work, he declared, consisted entirely of final cadences, but was so beautifully sung that he had great pleasure in listening to it.

His appearance and manner, which at this period of his life made an irresistible impression of nobility and, generally, of benevolence on strangers, in spite of his short stature and careless dress, attracted the constant admiration of his casual fellow-travellers and of the people of the country with whom he had to do; and amongst other anecdotes related by Widmann is one of a guide at Palermo who had fought under Garibaldi:

'Our refined and amiable guide suddenly stopped short in the midst of his flowing discourse, and, with a look at Brahms, exclaimed involuntarily: "Ah! mi pare di parlare al mio venerabile generale Garibaldi!" at which the master's eyes lightened enthusiastically.'

Brahms was frequently asked to officiate as godfather to his friends' children, and this summer he acceded to the request of Frau Dr. Marie Janssen, eldest daughter of his first teacher, Cossel, that he would stand sponsor to her little son. A few months later Frau Janssen sent him a photograph of two of her children, which he acknowledged in the following words:

'DEAR AND ESTEEMED LADY,

'I am not able to write a real letter however strongly your kind and welcome packet tempts me to do so. Let me, however, briefly express my thanks and believe that my most cordial thoughts go out to you at Kiel, and again to Hamburg to your unforgettable father, whose memory is amongst those most sacred and dear to me. Only one thing were to be wished as to the charming little packet—that it could have smiled at him.

'In warm remembrance and with best greetings

'Yours sincerely,

'J. BRAHMS.'

When the Janssens settled at Kiel, Brahms wrote to ask Groth to call upon them, saying:

'... The lady is the daughter of my first pianoforte teacher Cossel of whom I must have told you. And when I began to speak of him I was certainly unable to leave off again....'

At the period we have now reached, Brahms had given up his solitary Christmas evenings. The home of Dr. and Mrs. Fellinger became every year more and more a substitute to him in some sort for that home of his own which he imagined, perhaps, with longing and regret till the last year of his life. Each Christmas Eve of his last seven winters found him amongst the Fellinger family group, rejoicing in the joy of the young people, stimulating their fun, happy in feeling himself truly one in the midst of a family circle whose greatest delight it was to know that their friend of friends liked to be amongst them. Frau Fellinger always contrived some charming practical joke in the matter of the Christmas presents prepared for the master, by which he was annually and unfailingly taken in. One year—the first Christmas he passed at the house—part of her own gift table, labelled with his name, was tastefully arranged with toilet accessories. In front of a burnished mirror two candlesticks stood, holding lighted candles; between these was a pincushion, on to which was pinned a black silk necktie; some parcels with pink paper wrappings, tied with ribbon and labelled 'Finest perfume,' lay near. The only uncovered articles were packets of writing-paper of the kinds most used by Brahms, supplied in sufficient quantities to last some time.

The usual general survey of the gift-laden tables took place, and Brahms evinced much sympathetic interest during the tour of inspection, but presently he walked silently away to the other end of the room, passing his hand over his beard, then sauntered back carelessly, only to retire again and pace about apart, the picture of quiet dismay. 'But won't you look at your things, Dr. Brahms?' inquired Frau Fellinger by-and-by, when her guest had summoned sufficient courage to mingle again with the party and admire the young people's presents, though he carefully avoided glancing at his own. Poor Brahms allowed himself to be led to the table, and stood mute and dazed before it. 'Ah! *here* is mine,' he cried, suddenly catching sight of the paper; 'this is for me!' 'But all is for you,' returned his hostess kindly but firmly. 'But these things are all for you,' said the master, pleading; 'they are not for me, they are yours.' 'But why, Dr. Brahms?' insisted the lady; 'pray look at your things; do you not like scent?' By little and little the master was persuaded to handle his presents, gingerly enough, it is true. And now ensued the transformation scene. Each dainty trifle turned into some useful article suited to Brahms' needs. The two candlesticks became cream-jugs, the pincushion a sugar-basin, the packets of perfume proved to be tablets of unscented soap. A bread-basket containing bundles of English quills such as Brahms always used for writing music, and a clothes-brush, stood in bare, attractive reality before his astonished eyes. Soon nothing remained but the mirror. 'But this really does belong to you,' he implored, still deceived. 'Look behind it,' said Frau Fellinger; and the mirror became a nickel coffee-tray, chosen because of its smooth, brilliantly-polished back, which had well served the Christmas Eve purpose. 'Now I really must sit down,' said Brahms, drawing a long breath, his kind face shining; and he insisted on carrying away all his things in a cab the same evening.

But though Brahms was persuaded, in the later years of his life, to join the family festivities of these kind friends, he kept up to the last his custom of showing himself at his landlady's Christmas Eve party. Frau Truxa used to light up her tree an hour or two earlier than formerly, so that he should feel quite happy in setting out for Dr. Fellinger's. Of course her two boys were always remembered by the master, and his gifts to them, generally books, were found punctually on the table at the hour appointed for the commencement of the festivity.

The publications of the year 1890 were the 'Fest und Gedenksprüche,' as Op. 109, and three Motets for four and eight part Chorus *a capella*, Op. 110.

The writer of these pages was present at a supper-party given in Vienna in January, 1890, after a concert of the Joachim Quartet, at which Brahms with Joachim and his colleagues were the chief guests. 'What shall we have next?' said Joachim to Brahms in the course of supper; 'a quintet; we have one, a very fine one; we will have another.' A second string quintet, with two violas, composed during the summer at Ischl, was the next work produced by Brahms, and was heard for the first time in public from the manuscript in Vienna at the Rosé Quartet concert of November 11 (Rosé, Bachrich, Hummer, Jenek, and Siebert). An anecdote which appears to the author worth preserving, as expressive of Brahms' appreciation of his friend's incomparable playing, may find a place here. At a period when the two men had not met for a couple of years an occasion came when Brahms heard Joachim play. 'Now,' he said afterwards to the lady who related the story to the author, 'now I know what it is that has been wanting in my life during the past two years. I felt something was missing, but could not tell what. It was the sound of Joachim's violin. How he plays!'

Brahms' Quintet in G major is, in the opinion of most competent judges, one of the most powerful and fascinating of his works of chamber music for strings. If there is, in one or two of his late compositions for pianoforte and other instruments, something that suggests the feeling that in this domain the elasticity of his imagination was approaching its limits, nothing of the sort can be said of either of the works for strings only, and the Quintet in G is certainly second to none of them in wealth of spontaneous melody, in vigour and variety of inventive power, in all, in short, that is included in the word 'vitality.' To the present writer it appears quite clear and easy to follow, but that there may be two impressions on this point is proved in a remarkable way by two letters written by Billroth, the first to Brahms himself after the work had been performed for the first time from the manuscript at a party at Billroth's house, the second a few months later to Hanslick.

In the letter to Brahms, dated November 6, the famous surgeon, writing evidently under the influence of the great artistic excitement of the day, tells the master that he cannot rest without sending him word of his delight.

'Lately I have been silent, for I know not what more to say than, wonderfully fine and now clear to me at first hearing, clear as the blue sky!... Could one compare the various works of Michael Angelo, Raphael, Beethoven, Mozart when they were at the height of their powers? Only in the sense of a limited personal sympathy.... I have often wondered what human happiness is—now I was happy to-day when listening to your music. That is quite clear to me.'

The following March, however, Billroth wrote to Hanslick that he found the quintet one of the most difficult of Brahms' works.

'The form, when one has found it out, is simple and clear; but the length of the first bass theme and the rhythmic and harmonic over-rich, I might say overladen, five-part development make enjoyment of the movement [the first] impossible except under great mental strain. One must be fresher and better in health for it than I am at present.... But it is easy to talk; we are always wanting something new, something which interests us more than the last; no one can quite satisfy us.'[76]

Billroth heard the work the first time under the most favourable imaginable conditions, when his own powers of receptivity were strongly stimulated. He was depressed and out of health when he wrote the second letter. The majority of music-lovers would, we fancy, range themselves on the side of his original impression. The power and loveliness of the first movement, the romance of the second (the wonderful adagio), the plaintive daintiness of the third, the vivacity of the fourth, tinged with Hungarian colouring, all seem to foretell a continued prolongation of the composer's creative force and impulse. That Brahms himself, however, in the beginning of the nineties was conscious of needing rest is well known. Billroth says of him in a letter dated May 28, 1890, after visiting him at Ischl:

'He rejected the idea that he is composing or will ever compose anything. He is deep in Sybel's "Foundation of the German Empire," three thick volumes and the fourth to come.'

To another friend Brahms said in 1891: 'I have tormented myself to no purpose lately, and till now I never had to do so at all; things always came easily to me.' He professed his intention of giving his creative activity a rest, and employing his time in reading, going excursions, and seeing his friends, but did not at once persevere in the resolution.

In the early part of the year 1891 he paid a visit to Meiningen. His enjoyment was the greater since the Duke, to whom the master had often spoken of Widmann, had invited this gentleman to meet his friend. Several delightful details of the time are related by Widmann. For us, however, the fact of particular interest is that it was now that Brahms' admiration of the performances of the clarinettist Mühlfeld, of the Meiningen orchestra, culminated in the determination to write for his instrument. Mühlfeld had gained particular reputation as a soloist by his performances of Weber, whose Concertino for clarinet and orchestra had been introduced by him at Meiningen on December 25, 1886, the hundredth anniversary of the composer's birth. Our master, who since that date had had many opportunities of listening to Mühlfeld's wonderful tone and execution, now asked for a private recital with only himself as audience, in the course of which the clarinettist played to him one piece after another from his répertoire, and discussed his instrument with him. The sequel was the composition by Brahms, during his annual residence at Ischl, of a trio for pianoforte, clarinet, and violoncello and a quintet for clarinet and strings. These works were performed from the manuscripts before the ducal circle at Meiningen Castle on November 24 of the same year, the Trio by Brahms, Mühlfeld, and Hausmann, the Quintet by the same musicians, Joachim, and two members of the Meiningen orchestra.

Brahms remained on as the Duke's guest for some little time after the performance, and then followed his friends to Berlin in order to take part in the Joachim Quartet concert of December 12, when his new works were heard for the first time in public. This occasion was, and has remained, unique in the history of the famous party of artists. The Joachim Quartet concerts in Berlin, occupying a position in the forefront of the musical life of the city, have now taken place annually for nearly forty years; but into no other programme than that of December 12, 1891, has a work not written exclusively for strings been admitted. That Brahms was much gratified by the compliment paid him is evident from a letter written by him on December 1 to Hanslick, in which he says:

'... I shall not be able to tell you about it [a performance of Strauss' opera, 'Ritter Paynim'] for another fortnight. This is because Joachim has sacrificed the virginity of his Quartet to my newest things. Hitherto he has carefully protected the chaste sanctuary but now, in spite of all my protestations, he insists that I invade it with clarinet and piano, with trio and quintet. This will take place on the 12th of December, and with the Meiningen clarinettist. Tell Mandyczewski (or let him read) that the quintet "adagio con sordini" was played as long and often as the clarinettist could hold out.'[77]

The visit to Berlin resulted in a phenomenal triumph. A public rehearsal was held on the 10th, when every seat was occupied, and at the conclusion of the quintet, the last number of the programme, the audience indulged in an overwhelming demonstration to composer and executants. They went so far as to demand a repetition of the entire work, and Joachim and his colleagues at length consented to repeat the adagio. A similar scene was enacted at the concert on the 12th. Both new works were favourably noticed by the Berlin press, which waxed enthusiastic over the quintet, and especially the adagio.

The trio was played in Vienna the same month at a Hellmesberger concert; the quintet on January 5, 1892, by the Rosé Quartet party, with the clarinettist Steiner. Both works were heard again in the Austrian capital a fortnight later at a concert given there by the Joachim Quartet party, with the co-operation of Brahms and Mühlfeld. The quintet was introduced to a London audience at the Monday Popular concert of March 28 by Mühlfeld, Joachim, Ries, Straus, and Piatti, and repeated at the Saturday concert of April 2, when the trio was also played by Miss Fanny Davies, Mühlfeld, and Piatti.

The Clarinet Trio appears to us one of the least convincing of Brahms' works, and this in spite of the fact that it bears its composer's name writ large on every page. No one could fail to recognise his handwriting in either of the four movements, and to true Brahms lovers the handwriting must always be dear; but if one may compare the composer with himself, the inspiration of this work seems to us to halt, the spirit to want flexibility. Far otherwise is it with the beautiful and now favourite quintet, which contains, as Steiner says, richest fruits of the golden harvest of the poet's activity. Here 'the brooks of life are flowing as at high noon,' though the tone of gentle, loving regret which pervades the four movements, and holds the heart of the listener in firm grip, suggests the composer's feeling that the evening is not far away from him in which no man may work. A fulness of rich melody, a luscious charm of tone, original effects arising from the treatment of the clarinet, 'olympian' ease and mastery, distinguish every movement of this noble and attractive work, which, taking its hearers by storm on its first production, has grown more firmly rooted into the hearts of musicians and laymen with each fresh hearing. In the middle section of the second movement Brahms has written for the clarinet a number of quasi-improvisatory passages embracing the entire extent of its compass, which are supported by the strings, and which, when competently performed, are of surprisingly attractive effect. A fancy that suggested itself to one of the Berlin critics, as to the position assigned in this movement to the clarinet, seems to have commended itself to Brahms, who was ever afterwards in the habit of introducing the distinguished artist for whom it was written, to intimate friends, as 'Fräulein von Mühlfeld, meine Primadonna.'

In 1891 were published the String Quintet in G, Op. 111; six Vocal Quartets, the last four being additional Gipsy Songs set to Conrat's texts, Op. 112; and thirteen Canons for women's voices, the appearance of which forms a direct link between the composer's late maturity and early youth.

The Clarinet Trio and Quintet and three books of short Pianoforte Pieces, Op. 116, Nos. 1 and 2, and Op. 117, appeared in 1892.

Brahms departed in good time in the spring of 1893 for what was to be his last holiday in the south, meeting Widmann and two Zürich friends (Friedrich Hegar and Robert Freund) in Milan and proceeding with them to Sicily, whose scenery and general romantic charm had made an indelible impression on his mind when he had travelled in the country with Billroth some fifteen years previously. He had an additional and weighty reason for desiring to leave Vienna in April. The coming 7th of May, his sixtieth birthday, could not fail to be made the occasion, not only of friendly rejoicings, but, if he were at home, of formal congratulatory functions in which he would be asked to take part. To his mind, such a predicament left but one course open to him—flight; and for this he had made arrangement months beforehand. As early as the year 1892 he had refused Hegar's invitation to celebrate his birthday by some festival performances at Zürich in the following terms:

'VIENNA, *September 29th, 1892.*

'DEAR FRIEND

'I hasten to place this pretty sheet of paper before me and will endeavour approximately to express my gratitude to you and your society for your extremely kind and friendly project for the next 7th May. To-day I will only say that I have for some time been intending to make a proposal to you. My indolence in writing is the only cause that you have been beforehand with me. I wished to ask you and Widmann if you would not like, as I should, to go for a little while to Italy?

'When and where is all one to me; if on the 7th of May we are only safe in the Abruzzi or somewhere else where no one can find us; if we can only devote ourselves to touching (and preferably jovial) meditation. You see my plans and ideas are quite different from yours and my next letter will contain only many thanks for your very kind thought....'[78]

To Herr Ehrbar's annual invitation to the asparagus luncheon, therefore, which was sent as usual about the middle of April to No. 4, Carlsgasse, and which contained a special request that in this particular year the festivity should be celebrated on May 7 itself, a telegraphic reply was received from Genoa. The master was very sorry that he would not be able to be present this year, but sent his kindest greetings to all friends who should assemble on the occasion. Instead of postponing the party on account of this disappointment, Herr Ehrbar decided not only to gather the old friends about him as usual, but to hold the festivity at the Hôtel Sacher, and to invite some additional guests to drink the health of the absent composer, bringing up the number to about thirty.

Widmann, who had an accident during the return journey which injured his knee and obliged him to remain for two days at Naples under the surgeon's care, has thus described how Brahms spent May 7:

'And so it happened that Brahms passed his sixtieth birthday in the most quiet seclusion, remaining to watch faithfully by my bed after we had persuaded our two friends to make an excursion to Pompeii. The doctor's performances, which gave me little pain, excited him fearfully, though he tried to conceal this by making jesting remarks, as when he muttered grimly between his teeth, "If it should come to cutting, I am the right man; I was always Billroth's assistant in such cases." When we were alone he provided for my comfort like a deaconess and took pains to keep up my spirits by chatting cheerfully, saying for instance, "You have already tramped about so much in the Swiss Alps and Italy. Even if, at the worst, this should not again be possible, you are much better off than a hundred thousand others who have not had such opportunity." ... Every now and then whilst he was sitting with me, congratulatory telegrams arrived from intimate friends who had obtained intelligence from one or other of us as to our whereabouts.'

It was rumoured in Vienna, nevertheless, that Brahms was present at Herr Ehrbar's luncheon; that he was seen in the Augustinestrasse in the evening of the 6th; that he astonished his friends by joining them at the Hôtel Sacher at twelve o'clock on the 7th, just as they were about to sit down to table; and that he vanished from the city immediately after the festivity, to come back no more until the usual time of his return in October.

The sixtieth birthday of its honorary president was celebrated by a special meeting and musical performance in the club-rooms of the Tonkünstlerverein, and the Gesellschaft had a gold medal cast in the master's honour.

A note to Frau Caroline, written in June from Ischl, headed by a diminutive photograph of himself in walking dress, is suggestive of Brahms' happy mood at this time:

'Here I come, dear mother, and thank you for your dear letter.

'I am delighted that Fritz [Schnack] is making a nice tour which shows that you are both well—let him only make further plans, and travel!... I will be careful that you get a cast of the medal. It will interest Fritz as a connoisseur—he must imagine the gold. I am very well and the summer becomes finer every day. In the autumn or winter I really must look in upon you myself and not merely in a portrait.

'Have you a great deal too much money, or may I send some? I should like Fritz to spend plenty in travelling and he can afterwards entertain you and himself again with his sufferings!...

'Your JOHANNES.'[79]

Years before this date, Frau Caroline had, at the urgent and oft-repeated wish of Johannes, given up her boarding-house in the Anscharplatz, and retired to enjoy the remainder of her life as mistress of her son's quiet home in Pinneberg. Johannes kept his stepmother supplied with the necessary funds, which were regularly transmitted to her through his publisher, Herr Simrock of Berlin; but he was never tired of urging upon her his readiness to meet intermediate demands as they might arise, and particularly of suggesting holiday journeys for Fritz Schnack as a good way of spending extra money. Frau Caroline and her son, who both worshipped Johannes, frequently incurred his displeasure on account of the moderation with which they availed themselves of his generosity.

He never went to Hamburg after his stepmother's retirement without reserving a few hours to visit her at Pinneberg, and there, in the modest little dwelling he had provided, felt himself, as it were, in the old family home. He would sit in a corner of the sofa in the room by the side of the shop filled with clocks whose hands pointed to the right time and whose pendulums swung cheerily to and fro, and chat happily with her and Fritz, hearing little items of domestic news, asking after this and the other acquaintance; then would suddenly relapse into silence and reverie, which were unfailingly respected by the two people to whom he was so dear. By-and-by, after he had arranged his thoughts, he would come out again from his musing to continue the pleasant chit-chat where it had been left.

Brahms always expected his stepmother to be present at his public appearances in Hamburg, and continued to stay with her, when visiting the city, until she went to live at Pinneberg. On an occasion of his coming, after her retirement, to conduct a symphony at one of Bülow's Hamburg concerts, he took a room for her next his own at the Hôtel Moser, that they might be as much as possible together during the few days of his stay, and led her on his arm to her seat at rehearsals and concert. Frau Caroline did not, perhaps, entirely fathom the depths and intricacies of her stepson's fourth symphony, but she loved the work, and shared in the joy of it with her whole heart. Fritz, too, came over from Pinneberg, and greeted his stepbrother in the artist's room before the concert began. The master's sister, Elise Grund, died in 1892, and his visit to Hamburg after her death seems to have been the last known by his friends to have been paid by him to his native city. He was at Pinneberg, however, after this date.

Some of Brahms' time at Ischl this summer was given to the editing of the supplementary volume of Frau Schumann's complete edition of her husband's works. One cannot but read in this deeply-interesting book our master's desire to associate his name once more with those of Schumann and his wife, especially as he has taken the, for him, altogether exceptional course of writing and signing the introductory sentences of its first page. It contains, to quote Brahms' words,

'a few things found amongst Robert Schumann's papers which, on account of their value, or of some special interest, ought not to be omitted from this collection.... The theme with which the volume concludes is, in a quite peculiar sense, Schumann's last musical thought. He wrote it on the 7th of February, 1854, and afterwards added five variations which are withheld here. It speaks to us as a kindly greeting spirit [genius] about to depart and we think with reverence and emotion of the glorious man and artist.

'JOHANNES BRAHMS.

ISCHL, *July 1893.*'[80]

Of the composer's original work of the season Billroth writes a few months later to a friend:

'Brahms has, so far as I know, composed a dozen pianoforte pieces during the summer. I do not know the cause of this sudden passion. I like him least of all in this style, the G minor Rhapsody excepted. He does not sufficiently diversify his form in these little works.... He ought to keep to the great style.'

The pieces in question were published in the autumn in two books—Op. 118 and 119. The other publications of the year, issued without opus number, were the two books of Technical Exercises for Pianoforte.

Billroth's expression of feeling about the Pianoforte Pieces will probably be endorsed by many even of the most faithful admirer's of Brahms' art, whilst all will certainly agree as to his one exception. Beautiful as many of the intermezzi, fantasias, etc., are, it is to be doubted whether Brahms' short compositions for the pianoforte will ever gain such universal and unreserved affection as has long since been accorded to those of Schumann and Chopin. The manner in which the thoughts are expressed sometimes seems out of proportion to the moderate length of their development, the height of the structure to be, as it were, too great in comparison with the superficial area allotted to it. In several instances at all events, however, this impression is due to the unusualness of the pieces, and passes away as they become really familiar. It is as yet too soon to form any definite opinion as to the place they may ultimately take.

True appreciation of Brahms' small as of his great works is sometimes slow in coming, even to those who love his music with deepest affection. When, however, from time to time, the spirit dwelling within his inspirations reveals itself unsought as in a sudden flash, the whole heart is apt to go out with complete acceptance to the reception of its beauty and truth. Only in one instance (Op. 117, No. 1) has the master given any clue as to the sources which may have stirred his fancy during the composition of his thirty short pieces for the pianoforte from Op. 76 onwards, and where he has been reticent it would ill beseem others to stamp any particular piece with a definite suggestion. It may, however, be surmised that many of the little compositions are expressions derived from his passion for nature. The mountain storm swept up by the wind and bursting with a sudden crash, the approaching and retreating roll of its thunder, with the ceaseless pattering of rain on the leaves; the gay flitting of butterflies; the lazy hum of the insect world on a hot summer day; the long sweep of gray waves breaking into foam on the shore—all may be found in them. The music of the spheres, also, too ethereal for the perception of ordinary mortals, has been caught by our master's ear, and, woven into gossamer sound-textures, has been conveyed by him to the appreciation of organizations less delicate than his own. Some of the pieces have certainly grown up around the fancies of a legend or a poem. In these we may hear the weird footsteps of the spirit world, the dread strike of the bell of fate, the catastrophe of human lives. In no case, however, except in the one mentioned, are the several works to be taken as having been associated with this or that in the mind of the composer. The same one may mean different things to different people, and Brahms has carefully guarded against the possibility of being suspected of programme-music by giving to the Fantasias, Rhapsodies, Ballades, Intermezzi, the vaguest of all possible titles.[81] The book Op. 117 has become really popular, and is sold in the United Kingdom alone in its thousands. One of the first persons—perhaps the first—to hear books Op. 116 and 117 was Frau Schumann's pupil, Fräulein Ilona Eibenschütz (now Mrs. Carl Derenberg), to whom Brahms played them on their completion, inviting her especially to hear them.

Asking Brahms to be present in October at a festival meeting of the Imperial and Royal Society of Physicians, Billroth says:

'I should like to see you for once in evening dress [*schön decorirt*]. If, however, you object to this, you will find a place among the younger doctors in the (not high) gallery in walking costume.'

It was one of the last semi-public functions in which the famous surgeon took part. His health had for some time been declining, and he died on February 6, regretted by all ranks of Vienna citizens. The funeral procession was witnessed by crowds of people, especially of the poorer classes.

'We do not wear such open hearts,' writes Brahms afterwards to Widmann, 'nor show such pure and warm affection as they do here (I mean the people, the gallery).... In the whole innumerable concourse no inquisitive or indifferent face was to be seen, but upon each countenance the most touching sympathy and love. This did me much good when passing through the streets and at the cemetery.'[82]

Brahms could not trust himself to remain too close a spectator of the last scene. Whilst the relatives and friends of the departed surgeon remained standing round the open grave, he quietly strolled to a side-walk and paced up and down, talking with an acquaintance of other matters.

The thought of death had, indeed, a power over the master which probably held him in its clutch at times throughout his life. He could not bring himself to face the enemy with resolute front, especially during his later years, when the iron hand laid claim to one of his friends, but would speak of the matter as little as might be, and no doubt kept it as much as possible at bay in his thoughts. 'I do not mean to drink any more coffee,' he said one day to his landlady in Carlsgasse. 'Why, Herr Doctor, you enjoy your coffee so much!' exclaimed Frau Truxa, who had gained an insight into his character, and felt sure that something lay behind this announcement. 'I have taken coffee for a long time,' returned Brahms. 'I am going to leave it off, and drink something else.' A few days later Frau Truxa heard by chance of the death of a lady living in Marseilles who had for years kept the master supplied with Mocha. Nothing more was said, but an arrangement was made, without Brahms' knowledge, by which the same supply was to be despatched at the same interval by her daughter. Coming as it were from the same hand, Brahms continued to drink the coffee, but without further comment.

Death had, however, till now been kind to our master, sparing him the agony of many severe partings. We have seen his deep grief at the loss of the parents who had loved him with the entire devotion of their simple, affectionate hearts. By the nature of things, his sense of bereavement on the deaths of brother and sister had been less enduring in its sting. His friend Pohl, librarian of the Gesellschaft, died in 1887, but with this exception the old circle of chums remained as it had been. Joachim, Stockhausen, Grimm, Dietrich, Kirchner, Hanslick, Faber, Billroth, Goldmark, Epstein, Gänsbacher, all had continued with him, whilst in Frau Schumann's presence he was at the age of sixty-one still young, with youthful feelings of veneration in his heart. The death of Billroth dealt him a severe blow. Who shall say that even at this time he had not a presentiment that before very long he was to follow?

If this were so, but little change showed itself in his outward habits. The pedestrian excursions near Vienna took place every second or third Sunday as before, and if Brahms, growing every year heavier, found the ascent of the surrounding heights more fatiguing than in past years, he did not openly allude to the fact, but would invite his companions to pause for a few moments to look at the country, whilst they, at once acceding to his wish, always carefully avoided perceiving that he was short of breath. Hugo Conrat frequently made one of the party of walkers at this period, and the master was often a guest at his house, where it is to be feared that Frau Conrat, in no way behind the rest of his friends, sadly spoiled him. He had become in these years a complete autocrat in the circles in which he moved. His comfort was studied, his desires were anticipated, his witticisms appreciated, his tempers accepted, and his utterances recognised as final. Brahms enjoyed his position, and, it must be confessed, did not hesitate to avail himself of his privileges. On one occasion of a dinner-party, being asked to escort one of the principal lady guests to the dining-room, he turned sharply round and offered his arm to the young governess. On another—a party at the Conrats' country house—finding on his arrival that the cloth had been laid in the dining-room, and not in the veranda, he went up to the hostess, saying: 'But it is still fine weather. I always dine out of doors in October.' The lady sent word to the kitchen that the dinner was to be put back for twenty minutes, and, begging her visitors to walk in the garden meanwhile, gave orders for the alteration of her arrangements. 'But what did Brahms say when he found he was causing such trouble?' someone asked Fräulein Conrat afterwards. 'Then he was good again,' she replied. Such incidents could be multiplied from the experiences of many of

Brahms' friends. They serve chiefly to prove that the master's mind lost its pliancy as he grew older, and that he became incapable of adapting himself to circumstances outside his ordinary routine. His friends accepted his whims as a part of himself, and, knowing his sensitiveness to contradiction, did not contradict him. They were aware that the sterling nature had not really changed, and did not trouble themselves to criticise the outer crust of irritability and roughness that sometimes concealed it from the appreciation of less indulgent observers.

Silhouette by Dr. Böhler.
Photograph by R. Lechner (Wilh. Müller), Vienna.

'All that you tell me is very nice,' said Brahms one day to Herr Conrat's two gifted young daughters, who, paying the master a visit in his rooms, had been encouraged by him to talk about the progress of their studies. 'You must know these things, which are very important; but I will show you something to be learnt of still greater consequence;' and he fetched from a drawer an old, worn, folded table-cloth. 'Look here,' said he, showing the two girls some exquisite darning, 'my old mother did this. When you can do such work you may be prouder of it than of all your other studies.'

After the completion of the Clarinet Quintet and Trio in 1892, Brahms allowed his mind the refreshment of change of work. The only original compositions belonging to the following year are the two books of 'Clavierstücke,' Op. 118 and 119, the appearance of which we have already chronicled. He was, however, engaged with his collection of German Folk-songs, arranged with pianoforte accompaniment, six volumes for one voice, and the seventh for leader and small chorus.

The publication of this valuable work in 1894, almost at the end of the life of the great musician who compiled it, adds yet another and most striking illustration to those on which we have commented, of the general continuity of the lines on which Brahms' career was shaped. As he began, so he ended. The boy of fifteen who arranged folk-songs for practice by his village society, the youth of twenty who used them in his first published works, the mature master who returned to them again and again for inspiration and delight, all live in the veteran of sixty-one, who, as he busies himself in preparing the unique collection, every page of which bears mark of his insight, skill, and sympathetic tact, seems to be looking back over the years of the past with longing to leave behind him a final sign of his love for his great nation and all belonging to it. 'It is the only one of my works from which I part with a feeling of tenderness,' he said on its completion for the press. A child of the people by birth, Brahms remained, with all his literary and artistic culture, a child of the people by sympathy. He loved, and ever had loved, the simple peasant folk of the country places where he dwelt, as part of the great life of nature which was his delight. His partiality for them had in it something which resembled his feeling for children. He was pleased with their naïveté, valued their confidence, and perhaps, idealist as he was, gave them credit for a genuineness and simplicity not always theirs. In their songs, it was this same naturalness that attracted him, and whether in his original settings of national texts, or in his arrangements of the people's melodies, nearly always, as we have seen, left the words as he found them in their spontaneous directness of expression. Writing to Professor Bächtold, to whom he sent a copy of his collection, he says:

'... I think you will find some things new to you, for if you have been interested in the music of our folk-songs, Erk and now Böhme will have been your guides? These have hitherto led the (very Philistine) tone, and my collection stands in direct opposition to them. I could and should like to gossip more if I knew that you were interested and especially if we were sitting together comfortably....'[83]

Brahms at one time contemplated changing his rather confined quarters at Ischl, but a feeling of loyalty to the good folks in whose house he had spent several summers, and who regarded themselves as having a prescriptive right to their lodger, asserted its sway over his kind heart. He returned to them as each succeeding spring came round, and the little signs that heralded his approach—the opening of shutters, the cleaning of windows, and other preparations visible from outside—were eagerly looked forward to by the country people near as the first tokens of the approaching season.

Frau Grüber's little house, of which Brahms occupied the first-floor, was built on a mountain slope, and a short flight of steps at the side led to a small garden furnished with a grass plot, a garden bench, and a summer-house. Visitors had to mount the steps, cross the garden, find a second entrance-door at the back of the house, go in, and knock at the door of the composer's sitting-room. Sometimes he would cross the room, open the door, and peep cautiously out; but more often than not he called out, 'Come in!' and the visitor stepped at once into his presence. He laid strict injunctions on his landlady, however, that the door of his rooms was to be kept locked and the key in her possession whenever he was out, and that on no account was she to allow anyone even to peep into the room containing his papers and piano. If he once found out that she had disregarded this rule, once would be enough for him; that very day he would pack up and leave her, never to return. It was a most necessary precaution to take, for numerous visitors of either sex who were unknown to him found their way to the house, and would gladly have sought consolation for their disappointment at not seeing him by inspecting some of his belongings.

One or other of his friends frequently called for him about half-past eleven, and soon afterwards he would start out and gradually make his way to the Hôtel Kaiserin Elisabeth. Between two and three o'clock he usually made his appearance on the promenade by the side of the river. Stopping at Walter's coffee-house, he would seat himself at a table under the trees outside, where a cup of black coffee and the daily papers were at once brought to him. Here he generally remained for at least an hour, and sometimes it was much longer, to be joined by one friend and another till his party numbered a dozen or more. Walter's became, indeed, at this hour of the day, a rendezvous not only for Brahms' personal friends, but for many musical visitors to Ischl who did not know him, but who heard that they could easily get a sight of him there. He was very particular in acknowledging the greetings of his numerous acquaintance as they passed along the promenade, and, owing to his anxiety to be courteous and his near-sightedness combined, he sometimes made a mistake and bowed to people whom he did not know.

'Oh, if you had only been with us this afternoon!' a friend and fellow-lodger said to the author one day in the summer of 1894. 'Paula and I were walking on the promenade, and we met Brahms, who greeted us so kindly. He waved his hand, and looked round, saying, "Good-day! good-day!" Of course I returned his greeting. I wonder if it could have been because he was pleased with my little Paula? He takes so much notice of children.' Frau F. was far too much gratified by the incident to accept the author's opinion that it was a case of mistaken identity, as Brahms was not in the habit of consciously bowing to strangers.

Herr Oberschulrath Wendt, of Carlsruhe, when staying at Ischl, was daily to be seen in the master's company, and the two men, both of striking appearance, presented a singular contrast as they paced side by side along the promenade. Wendt, tall, thin, and pale, was delicate-looking, and walked with a slight stoop. Brahms, rather short, very stout, with a good deal of colour, probably acquired by exposure to the weather, that seemed the more pronounced from its contrast with his white hair and beard, went along with head well thrown back, the very personification of vigour. On leaving Walter's he generally betook himself to a friend's house, most frequently that of Johann Strauss. To his intimacy there the world is indebted for some of the best of his late photographs—those of Krziwanek, of Vienna and Ischl—which were taken one afternoon in the summer of 1895 as he was sitting at ease with his friends.

Brahms knew, and was well known to, all the children of the neighbourhood, and when starting on his country walks would fill his pockets with sweetmeats and little pictures, and amuse himself with the eagerness of the small barefooted folk, who knew his ways and would run after him as he passed, on the look-out for booty. 'Whoever can jump gets a gulden,' he would say; and, displaying beyond reach of the little ones a handful of sweetmeats made in imitation of the Austrian coin, he would increase his speed, and raise his hand higher and higher, drawing after him the flock of running, leaping children, until he allowed one and another to gain a prize.

Two Sonatas for clarinet and pianoforte, the last works of chamber music composed by Brahms, were completed during the summer of 1894, and towards the end of September Mühlfeld arrived at Ischl to try them with the composer. The first private performance took place very soon afterwards, when the two artists played them before the ducal circle of Meiningen at the palace of Berchtesgarten.

A reunion at Frankfurt in November is of pathetic interest. It carries us back to the very early pages of our narrative, and is the last complete one of the kind we shall have to record. For the last time we find Frau Schumann and her husband's and her own two dearest musician-friends assembled and making music together. Brahms arrived at her house on a few days' visit on the 9th of the month; on the 10th Mühlfeld spent the evening there, having come from Meiningen at the composer's especial request, and the new works were played to the illustrious lady, 'the revered Frau

Schumann,' as Brahms used to call her to his younger friends, who had now completed her seventy-fifth year. The next day Joachim, prince of violinists at sixty-three as at twenty-one, the age at which he entered these pages, gave a concert with his colleagues of the Quartet, and on the 12th there was a party at Herr and Frau Sommerhoff's, when Brahms and Mühlfeld again played the two Sonatas, and Frau Schumann, Joachim, and Mühlfeld, Mozart's beautiful Clarinet Trio, a favourite work of Brahms. The reunion of old friends was completed by the presence of Stockhausen, who, like Frau Schumann, had been resident in Frankfurt since 1878. On the 13th, the third Frankfurt performance of the Clarinet Sonatas by Brahms and Mühlfeld took place at a large music-party at Frau Schumann's, and another memorable item of the evening's pleasures was the playing by Frau Schumann and Mühlfeld of Schumann's Fantasiestücke for pianoforte and clarinet. Joachim had left to fulfil other engagements before the evening, and Brahms departed on the 14th.

The master's journeys and performances with Mühlfeld gave him extraordinary pleasure, and the publication of the two sonatas, which in the usual course of things would have taken place in the autumn of 1894, was delayed until the summer of 1895, that his possession of the manuscripts might be prolonged. Both works were performed at the Rosé concerts, Vienna, by the composer and his friend—No. 2 in E flat on January 8, 1895, when the Clarinet Quintet was also played; and No. 1 in F minor at an extra concert on January 11, the programme of which included the G major String Quintet. Amongst other towns visited by Brahms and Mühlfeld in the month of February were Frankfurt, Rudesheim, and Meiningen, and the master was seen for the last time in public by his Frankfurt friends on the 17th, when he listened to a performance of his D major Symphony, and conducted his Academic Overture at a Museum concert. The two sonatas were performed for the first time after publication at Miss Fanny Davies' concert of June 24 in St. James's Hall, London, by the concert-giver and Mühlfeld, engaged expressly to come to England for the occasion. The manuscripts of both works are in the possession of Mühlfeld, to whom the composer presented them on publication, with an appreciative autograph inscription.

With the publication of the two Clarinet Sonatas, our master's career is all but closed, and closed as we would have it. The more familiar they become, the more firmly will they root themselves, as we believe, in the affection of the lovers of his music. The fresh, bounding imagination of youth is, indeed, not in them, nor would we wish it to be there; but both works are pervaded by a warmth and glow as of sunset radiance, which, reflecting the spirit of the composer as he was when he wrote them, fill the mind of the listener with a sense of the mellow beauty, the rich pathos, the unwavering sincerity of his art. To compare the two sonatas one with the other is unnecessary. We prefer simply to commend them to the study of those of our readers to whom they are not entirely familiar, holding them, as we do, to be amongst the especially lovable examples of the late period of Brahms' art.

CHAPTER XXII
1895-1897

The Meiningen Festival—Visit to Frau Schumann—Festival at Zürich—Brahms in Berlin—The 'Four Serious Songs'—Geheimrath Engelmann's visit to Ischl—Frau Schumann's death—Brahms' illness—He goes to Carlsbad—The Joachim Quartet in Vienna—Brahms' last Christmas—Brahms and Joachim together for the last time—The Vienna Philharmonic concert of March 7—Last visits to old friends—Brahms' death.

But few events remain for record in the life which we have now followed step by step nearly to the end of its progress. Of these few, several have the pathetic interest of last visits to dear and familiar places made, so far as appears, without presentiment that they were final. The composer was present at a three days' festival held in Meiningen September 27-29; 'the Festival of the three B's,' as it has sometimes been called, from the circumstance that the programmes were devoted to works by Bach, Beethoven, and Brahms. Those of Brahms selected for performance included the Song of Triumph, the fourth Symphony, the B flat Pianoforte Concerto, with d'Albert as pianist, the Clarinet Sonatas performed by the same artist with Mühlfeld, some of the Vocal Quartets, amongst them the early favourite 'Alternative Dance Song,' and others.

The festival was an immense success, and the pleasure which the master derived from the concerts is evident in the following lines written to Steinbach immediately after the last one:

'DEAR FRIEND,

'However tempted I may feel, I dare not break in upon your well-deserved rest; but you shall find my hearty greeting awaiting you on your happy awakening; how hearty and grateful it is there is no need to tell you in detail. You must have perceived each day that you gave me and all who took part in your splendid festival, a quite exceptional pleasure....'[84]

Brahms was, of course, a guest at the castle, and he remained on for a few days after the last concert. Leaving Meiningen on October 3, he proceeded to Frankfurt on a flying visit to Frau Schumann. Professor Kufferath of the Brussels Conservatoire, with Mr. and Mrs. Edward Speyer, accompanied him on the short journey, and were, by his particular suggestion, invited to spend the evening at Frau Schumann's house. Professor Kufferath, a pupil of Mendelssohn at Leipzig, and on a very old footing of intimacy at the Schumanns', had been for more than twenty years on terms of cordial friendship with Brahms also, though the two men met but seldom. Frau

Schumann's daughters Marie and Eugénie, and Stockhausen, were the only others present. The hours were spent in pleasant chat as between old friends, and music was represented only by a few of Brahms' folk-songs sung by Mrs. Speyer (Fräulein Antonia Kufferath) to the master's accompaniment.

Brahms left the next morning, but before his departure he requested his old friend to play to him. Forty-two years had passed since Schumann had desired him to play for the first time to her, marking both musicians with inevitable outward signs. The traces of suffering and sorrow had deepened of late on Frau Schumann's countenance, but those who were happy enough to listen to her playing at this period, in the privacy of her home, knew that her spirit was still young, and Brahms' last remembrance of the great artist, the remembrance of an old age which had left the poetry of her genius untouched, will have fitly completed the long chain of personal associations begun when Schumann called his wife to rejoice with him in the daring power and romantic enthusiasm of Johannes' inexperienced youth. When she rose from the piano on that October morning, the final link had been added. Frau Schumann and Brahms were not to meet again on earth.

A four days' festival in October (19-22) to celebrate the inauguration of the new concert-hall at Zürich seems to carry us more than one stage nearer the end. It brought Brahms for the last time to Switzerland to conduct his Triumphlied; a fine close—for as such it may almost be regarded—to a noble career.

Let us pause for a moment to picture the robust figure of the composer as he stands before the vast audience completely filling the brilliantly lighted hall, and leads with sure, quiet dignity the 'masses of chorus and orchestra' that swell out in proud tones of thankfulness for his country's glory. Listen! for with the sounds of the grand old hymn 'Now thank we all our God' the bells of victory are pealing, and a sensation of happiness spreads through the mass of hearers, a vibration that stirs something of the feeling which roused the great German audience at Cologne to enthusiasm as they listened twenty years ago to the same jubilant tones. Who so fitted to raise the strain as the patriot citizen of ancient Hamburg, the unique descendant of the mighty Bach, the musician of true, rich, loving spirit, conqueror of life and of himself, our Johannes Brahms? Conqueror, too, of death; for surely we cannot be mistaken in accepting the likeness of the master, that looks down with those of the greatest of his art from the painted ceiling of the new hall, as the symbol of a further life to be his even here on earth, when he has entered the darkness that is soon to cover him from our sight.

Brahms was in overflowing spirits during the entire festival, enjoying the concerts, the private gatherings, the meetings with old friends, in a mood of harmless gaiety that recalls the Detmold days.

'We have seen Brahms and Joachim together again, both in full vigour; may we not hope for a prolongation of this happy state of things?' writes Steiner a few days after the festival.

Widmann was, of course, there, and stayed with Brahms at Hegar's house. When he bade the master farewell on the day after the concert, the two friends clasped hands in a final grasp.

One of Brahms' late public appearances was on the occasion of the concert given in the Börsendorfer Hall, Vienna, by Signorina Alice Barbi (now the Baroness Wolff Homersee) shortly before her marriage. He pleased himself by acting as accompanist to the distinguished cantatrice, whose programme included a number of his songs. He held the bâton for the last time on a Vienna platform when he directed the performance of his Academic Overture by the students of the conservatoire at the festival concert given to celebrate the twenty-fifth anniversary (1895) of the opening of the present home of the Gesellschaft der Musikfreunde. He officiated for the last time in public at d'Albert's concert in Berlin of January 10, 1896, conducting his two Pianoforte Concertos and the Academic Overture, and was received with the usual enthusiasm. Stanford speaks of being present at a dinner-party given by Joachim during Brahms' brief visit.

'Joachim, in a few well-chosen words, was asking us not to lose the opportunity of drinking the health of the greatest composer— when, before he could say the name, Brahms started to his feet, glass in hand, and calling out "Quite right; here's to Mozart's health," walked round clinking glasses with us all. His old hatred of personal eulogy was never more prettily expressed.... The last vision I had of him was as he sat beside the diminutive form of the aged Menzel, drinking in, like a schoolboy, every word the great old artist said with an attitude as full of unaffected reverence as of unconscious dignity.'

Of all modern painters, Adolph von Menzel was the most admired by Brahms. He visited him on several occasions, and spoke of him and his works with unfailing enthusiasm.

That the master had realized a competence some years before his death—more than a competence for one of his extraordinarily simple habits—is generally known. How he regarded it, how he used it, may have been but little suspected outside a small circle. His friend and publisher, the late head of the firm of Simrock, shared his confidence on the subject more than anyone else, for it was often through his agency that Brahms' munificence was applied to its object; the substantial help, perhaps, of a needy musician, or a promising talent. He contributed more than one large donation to the 'Franz Liszt Pensionsverein' of Hamburg, a society founded by Liszt in 1840 for the benefit of aged or disabled members of the Stadt Theater orchestra. Several authentic stories are told by accidental witnesses of some of his particular acts of generosity. One has been related to the author by the Landgraf of Hesse, who was sitting with the master one morning when a caller appeared with a tale of distress which touched his heart. He listened quietly, asked some questions, then went to his writing-table, and, handing his visitor the entire sum of money towards which he was asked for a contribution, said quietly, 'Take this from me; I do not need it. I have more money than I want for myself.' This was his usual formula on such occasions, 'I do not need it,' to which was sometimes added, 'If you should ever have it in your power, you can pay me back.'

Brahms' heart was of gold, if ever such existed. He was rough sometimes—often, perhaps—let it be freely granted. The spoiled humours of his last two or three years have already been noted; they do not amount to much. He permitted himself deliberately to repulse strangers or slight acquaintances when he felt so disposed; necessarily, if his time and tranquillity were to be protected. Now and then he was inconsiderate or blunt to his friends. The concentration of mind, the sacrifice of immediate inclination, the devotion of energy, involved in the fulfilment of the career of genius are often but imperfectly realized even by the friends of a famous man. The great poet, the great painter, the great musician, has his brilliant rewards. He has also his bitter disappointments, and one of the hardest of these—which is especially apportioned to the lot of the creative musician—is the discovery that, as in the case of other princes and sovereigns of the world, his path in life must be solitary. Brahms may sometimes have imagined he had reason for his impoliteness; more frequently a gruff manner, an awkward joke, was the result of a constitutional want of presence of mind in trifling matters, which frequently caused him to be misunderstood. His real attitude is expressed in a note published after his death by Hanslick in the *Neue Freie Presse* article from which we have already more than once quoted.[85] Hanslick had sent him a packet of letters to read, and had inadvertently enclosed in it one from a mutual friend which contained a comparison of Beethoven and Brahms. In it were these words:

'He is often offensively rough to his friends like Beethoven, and is as little able as Beethoven was to free himself entirely from the effects of a neglected education.'

Hanslick was very much upset on remembering what he had done, and immediately wrote to Brahms to throw himself on his mercy and beg his silence on the matter. The master immediately answered:

'DEAR FRIEND

'You need not be in the least uneasy. I scarcely read ——'s letter, but put it back at once into the cover, and only gently shook my head. I am not to say anything to him—Ah, dear friend, that happens, unfortunately, quite of itself in my case! That one is taken even by old acquaintances and friends for something quite different from what one is (or, apparently, shows one's self in their eyes) is an old experience with me. I remember how I, startled and confounded, formerly kept silence in such cases; now however, quite calmly and as a matter of course. That will sound harsh or severe to you, good and kind man—yet I hope not to have wandered too far from Goethe's saying, "Blessed is he who, without hate, shuts himself from the world."'

Brahms was ready for another journey to Italy in the spring, but Widmann was unable to accompany him, and he passed his sixty-third birthday anniversary in Vienna. When it dawned, the work that was for a short time generally accepted as his swan-song had been completed. Deiters writes that the immediate occasion of the composition of the 'Four Serious Songs' was the death of the artist Max Klinger's father, which occurred earlier in the year. The not unnatural assumption that has sometimes seen in these solemn utterances of the great composer a presentiment of his own fast-approaching end may or may not represent a fact. It has not been accepted by those of his friends amongst whom he passed the last few months of his life, and certainly nothing that is known of his individuality lends likelihood to the notion of his going out, as it were, to meet the thought of his death. On the other hand, his repeated assertion that the songs had been composed for his own birthday points to the possibility that his mind may have been under the influence of forebodings of which he was, perhaps, but vaguely conscious. 'Yes, Grüber, we are in the front line now,' he said to his landlord on hearing of the death of some of the old people in the course of one of his last summers at Ischl.

The 'Four Serious Songs' were published in the summer of 1896 with a dedication to Max Klinger, his personal friend, of whose work, including that inspired by his own compositions, he became a warm admirer, though he at first disliked the painter's 'Brahms Fantasie.'

Three of the songs deal grimly with the thought of death (Eccles. iii. 19-22, iv. 1-3; Ecclus. xli. 1, 2); the fourth has for its text St. Paul's beautiful glorification of love (1 Cor. xiii. 1-3, 12, 13):

'For that which befalleth the sons of men befalleth beasts; as the one dieth, so dieth the other, for all is vanity....

'Though I spake with the tongues of men and of angels, and had not love, I should be as sounding brass or a tinkling bell....

'We see now through a glass, in a dark word, but then face to face. Now I know it partly, but then I shall know it as I am known.

'Now remain faith, hope, love; but the greatest is love.'

It is certain that Brahms speaks to us in the songs from the depth of his convictions. Herr Geheimrath Dr. Engelmann arrived one evening in the course of the summer on a day's visit to Ischl. Brahms called at his hotel at six o'clock the next morning, and after breakfast brought his friend back to his rooms, where they spent several hours together. The composer was in delight over some lately-arrived volumes of the complete edition of Schubert's works, then in progress, and could not sufficiently express his joy in their contents. 'See here,' he said, with his energetic enthusiasm, as he pointed to one place after another with beaming face and lightening eyes—'see here, what a splendid fellow he was! People talk of him as a mere melodist, but look what material he had even in his early works; look what the melodies are, how they grow.' By-and-by, taking up a copy of the 'Four Serious Songs,' he said: 'Have you seen my protest? I wrote these for my birthday.'

The explanation of these words is that the master viewed with mistrust, or even dislike, modern efforts to revivify and popularize the services of the Evangelical Church by the introduction of sacred musical works composed for the purpose, of which those of Heinrich von Herzogenberg may be taken as the type. Brahms, who subscribed to no church dogmas, regarded this tendency as artificial, and therefore as weak and unhealthy, and much as he admired Herzogenberg's powers, he regretted that they were dominated during the last ten years of his creative activity by his strong ecclesiastical bias.[86] Brahms' love of the Bible and his preference for Scriptural texts was, as we know, not that of what is conventionally called a 'pietist.' He spoke in the language of the people's book as a realist who was at the same time an idealist. He has so arranged the texts of his German Requiem that it would be difficult to construe the work as the embodiment of a definite belief, and he expressly refused to enlarge it into an account of the Passion, Death, and Resurrection of Christ; and yet, as we have endeavoured to show, it contains the presentiment, the inspiration, of something positive. From Brahms' standpoint the attempt to go behind the mysteries of life and death, to construct the unspeakable, the unthinkable, into verbal formulæ, is not only predoomed to failure, but is almost irreverent. Yet, as we may remember, 'he had his faith,' and if anything may be judged of it from the story of his life, the spirit of his works, this faith lay in acceptance of the immutability of truth, the sacredness of life, and the sovereignty of love.

Brahms had been settled in his rooms at Ischl scarcely a fortnight, when he was profoundly shaken by the tidings of Frau Schumann's death. She passed away peacefully at her home in Frankfurt on May 20, in the seventy-seventh year of her age, and was laid to rest by her husband's side at Bonn on Whit Sunday, May 24. The story of her life, triply crowned by fame, love, and sorrow, remains amongst the ideal possessions of the world.

A great crowd of musicians and friends assembled at the funeral, those of Frankfurt, Bonn, and Cologne being strongly represented. The custom of the ceremony had changed with time since Johannes had borne Frau Clara's laurel-wreath to Schumann's grave, and on the conclusion of the service, which consisted of the singing of chorales and an address by Dr. Sell of Bonn University, more than two hundred floral tributes were piled up around the spot. Joachim with Herzogenberg, bound by Italian engagements, had attended a service held in the Schumanns' house at Frankfurt. Woldemar Bargiel and Bernhard Scholz were at the cemetery, and of our own particular musicians, Stockhausen and Brahms. Another last meeting.

On the termination of the service, Brahms, whose agitation had been very unpleasantly heightened during his journey from Ischl by the delay of a train, and his consequent anxiety lest he should be late, went to Honnef to stay till the next day with Herr and Frau Wehermann, the near relatives of his Crefeld friends, the von Beckeraths and von der Leyens, who were at the time on a visit there. Professor Richard Barth and his wife, Dr. Ophüls, and two of the Meiningen musicians, Concertmeister Eldering and Herr Piening, were also of the party. The master was very much excited and overcome on his arrival at Honnef, but the soothing influence of the Rhine country, so closely associated with the recollections of his youth, did him good, and he prolonged his visit to nearly a week. Confiding to Barth the day after his arrival that he had with him something new, which he would like to play very quietly to one or two chosen listeners, his three most intimate friends retired with him to a room secure from interruption, impressed by his manner with the feeling that something unusual was about to ensue. When the little party had taken their places, Brahms, with every sign of the most profound emotion, which communicated itself to his companions, played through the 'Four Serious Songs' from the manuscript. 'I wrote them for my birthday,' he said in the same words which he afterwards used to Dr. Engelmann. He then played some new organ preludes.

He was agreeably interested in Dr. Ophüls' project of arranging a collection of his composed texts. 'I have often wished for such a thing, for though I do not care to look closely at my music, it would be quite pleasant to recall it now and then by reading the texts.' The collection was completed during the ensuing months, and the manuscript placed in the master's hands.[87]

BRAHMS AT DR. FELLINGER'S, JUNE 15, 1896.
Photograph by Maria Fellinger.

Brahms appeared unannounced in Vienna in the middle of June to take part in the family celebration of Dr. and Frau Fellinger's silver wedding day. Returning immediately to Ischl, he spent the next few weeks in his usual fashion, though neither mind nor body really recovered the double shock of Frau Schumann's death and of the anxious journey to Bonn. He occupied himself still with his art, and on June 24 had completed seven organ preludes, which he played to Heuberger on that date at Ischl. 'Splendid pieces,' says Heuberger's diary; and in another entry, dated July 5: 'Brahms' things must have been sent away already, for he has promised to show me *new* compositions.'[88] These were, no doubt, some more preludes. Eleven were found after Brahms' death, the last four being written on a different kind of paper from that used for the first seven.

The 'Elf Chorale-Vorspiele' (Eleven Chorale-Preludes) for organ are instrumental movements founded, as their name implies, upon some of the grand old church tunes for which Germany is famous. They are worked in florid counterpoint in a style which may be studied, also, in the organ preludes contained in the third volume of the Leipzig Society's edition of Bach's works, and are written with an ease to which no other composer than Brahms has attained in this style since Bach's day. That the great modern master had studied it during the years of his retirement in the fifties, before he was in possession of the Society's volumes, seems certain, from the fact that three old books of Bach's Chorale-Preludes once belonging to Brahms are still in existence. One, bearing Brahms' pencil autograph, is in manuscript, possibly that of his father or brother; the others are early published editions.[89]

The majority of the chorales selected for treatment in 1896 have death for their subject, and are written in the profoundly serious vein to which we are accustomed in the composer's sacred works. The fourth prelude, 'Herzlich thut mich erfreuen,' is in a somewhat lighter vein than the others, but is, none the less, absolutely and distinctly Brahms. One of the most delicately touching is the eighth, 'Es ist ein Ros' entsprungen.' 'Herzlich thut mir' is the subject of two of the movements, 'O Welt ich muss dich lassen' of two, of which one is the eleventh and last.

It is impossible that we can be mistaken in accepting the Chorale-Preludes, together with the 'Four Serious Songs' which immediately preceded them, as indicating the bent of the composer's thoughts during his last year of life, and we involuntarily apply to them the words, quoted in the preceding chapter, used by Brahms in reference to Schumann's theme. They speak to us 'as the message of a spirit about to depart, and we think with reverence and emotion of the glorious man and artist.' Nevertheless, a note written by the composer to Frau Caroline on August 13 contains little sign of his depressed condition. It opens with charming, simple comments on his stepmother's last little budget of home news, urges a tour in Norway and Sweden on Fritz Schnack—'it would give me real pleasure if he would do it, and tell me all about it afterwards'—and ends:

'The summer is not exactly fine, but whoever, like myself, rises early and can go out walking when he will, may be content and there are innumerable beautiful walks here. I hope you will continue so well and write sometimes to

'Your heartily greeting JOHANNES.'[90]

It had not escaped the notice of Brahms' friends, however, that his ruddy complexion had changed to a yellow colour, and some of them were courageous enough to speak to him about his health, and urge him to consult a doctor. At first he showed much annoyance when the subject was broached, and turned it off impatiently with the reply that, as he never used a glass, he did not know how he looked. But the uneasiness felt about his condition increased, and he was at length persuaded to seek medical advice in Vienna. The doctor whom he consulted did not issue an alarmist report, but, pronouncing him to be suffering from jaundice, ordered him to Carlsbad for the 'cure.' Much against his will, the master, who hated the very idea of waters and cures, and who prided himself on never having being ill in his life, gave up some pleasant Ischl engagements, and started on September 2 for Carlsbad. He was met at the station by two friends of Hanslick, Herr Emil Seling and Musikdirektor Janetschek, who took him to the 'Stadt Brussels,' near the Hirschensprung. Here, during the fine autumn days which succeeded the wet summer, he made himself content, and even wrote cheerful reports to his friends, in which he expressed satisfaction at having been obliged to make the acquaintance of the celebrated watering-place. He was the object of much considerate and respectful attention, which seemed to cheer him; and Faber came to be near him, accompanied him in his daily walks, and took tender care of him.

The report written to Hanslick by the distinguished Carlsbad physician Dr. Grünberger, after three weeks' careful observation, was ominous. There was considerable swelling of the liver, with complete blocking of the gall-passages, and the inevitable results—jaundice, indigestion, etc. The eminent medical authority could not but regard the condition of his patient as 'very serious.'

No more definite name was given to the malady on the master's return to Vienna after some six weeks' treatment at Carlsbad, and his request that he should be told 'nothing unpleasant' was scrupulously observed. He went about as before, dining more frequently, however, with his most intimate friends the Fellingers, Fabers, Millers, Conrats, Strauss' and von Hornbostels, and often accepting the offer from one and another of a seat in a box at the Burg Theater. He became very testy if asked how he was or if told that he looked better, and answered to every inquiry, 'Each day a little worse,' but continued in letters to his stepmother and other friends at a distance to keep up the fiction that he was suffering from an ordinary jaundice which only needed patience. Those who loved him, however, looked with dismay at the alteration that was taking place in his appearance. The yellow colour, which had been the first striking symptom of his condition, was changing gradually to a darker hue, the bulky figure shrinking to terrible emaciation; the firm gait was beginning to falter, the head was no longer held erect. A visit to Vienna, early in December, of Joachim and his colleagues of the Quartet gave him touching pleasure; he was with them as much as possible during the day, and generally remained with them, after attending their concerts, until late at night. He continued to take interest in important new compositions, and begged Hausmann to come to his rooms to play him Dvořák's Violoncello Concerto. He accompanied the entire work on the piano, and broke into enthusiastic admiration at the end of each movement, exclaiming after the last one, 'Had I known that such a violoncello concerto as that could be written, I would have tried to compose one myself!'

He not only spent Christmas Eve with the Fellingers, but invited himself to dine with them also on December 25, 26, and 27. Frau Fellinger gave him a 'secco,' a soft, short coat, as one of her Christmas presents, and it seemed a sort of comfort to him to put it on when he was at the house, where it was kept in readiness for his use, and to sit quietly in the family sitting-rooms without need of exerting himself. After dinner on the 27th he raised his glass, saying, 'To our meeting in the New Year,' but by-and-by added, pointing downwards, 'But I shall soon be there.' He dined again on New Year's Day with the same dear friends, whose joy it was to feel that they were privileged to afford him some solace in his weakness and suffering.

The Joachim party returned to Vienna after a tour in the Austrian provinces, and gave two concluding concerts in the Börsendorfer Hall on January 1 and 2, 1897. Ill as he was, Brahms not only attended both concerts, but came on the morning of the 2nd to Joachim's rooms at the Hôtel Tegethof to listen to the rehearsal of his G major Quintet, which was in the evening's programme. He derived peculiar pleasure from hearing it. 'That is not a bad piece,' he said, as though half ignoring that it was his own. The scene which took place after the performance of the work in the evening is remembered with emotion by those who took part in it. It was the final one in the friendship of Brahms and Joachim—a friendship as striking and interesting as any contained in the history of art. Its character may be suggested to the reader's imagination in a few words written to the author by the great musician whose love and recognition Brahms enjoyed from beginning to end of his career.

'He had great pleasure that evening in the G major Quintet. It was touching to see him come before the public to acknowledge the enthusiasm aroused by his work. The tears were in his eyes and he was very weak. The people cheered and cheered endlessly.'

Thus the master's state gradually changed for the worse. He dined with the Fellingers in the middle of the day on February 7, and seemed excited and restless throughout the meal. When it was at an end, he intimated that he wished to be alone with Dr. and Frau Fellinger, and, retiring with them, began to speak about his affairs. He desired, he said, to make a new will, but dreaded the necessary formalities to such a degree that he knew not how to resolve to go through them. Would it not be possible to arrange his affairs quietly without having to speak about them with strangers? Dr. Fellinger said it could be done, and that by the Austrian law things could be so managed that there need not even be witnesses. The master remained for four hours—from two till six o'clock—with Dr. and Frau Fellinger, discussed his affairs in minute detail, and asked Dr. Fellinger to be his curator. He seemed relieved at the end of the conversation, and stayed on with the family, chatting about other topics. The following morning Dr. Fellinger took to the composer at his rooms in Carlsgasse the copy of a will which he had drawn out to meet Brahms' expressed desires, and explained to him that he had only to write it out himself, date and sign his name to it, and it would be valid according to Austrian law. Brahms, who was on the point of starting out to his dinner, expressed himself as glad and relieved, and placed the paper in a drawer of his writing-table; and Dr. Fellinger, pleased to have cheered him, returned home with the conviction that he would copy it without delay. The master did not return to the subject at any future meeting with his friends, whilst they, believing the matter to have been finally settled, did not again allude to it.

February passed, and Brahms grew continually worse. Every day he spent a good deal of time in looking through and destroying old letters and other papers. 'It is so sad,' he would say, when one or other intimate friend called and found him thus employed, his stove filled with ashes. He attended the Philharmonic concert on March 7, when Dvořák's Violoncello Concerto, played by Hugo Becker, and his own fourth Symphony in E minor were in the programme. Going into the concert-room he met his old friend Gänsbacher. 'Ah,' he said, 'you have been so often to see me, and I cannot go to you, I am so suffering;' then, rousing himself a little, went on, 'You will hear a piece to-day, a piece by a man!' (Dvořák's concerto).

The fourth symphony had never become a favourite work in Vienna. Received with reserve on its first performance, it had not since gained much more from the general public of the city than the respect sure to be accorded there to an important work by Brahms. To-day, however, a storm of applause broke out at the end of the first movement, not to be quieted until the composer, coming to the front of the 'artists'' box in which he was seated, showed himself to the audience. The demonstration was renewed after the second and the third movements, and an extraordinary scene followed the conclusion of the work. The applauding, shouting house, its gaze riveted on the figure standing in the balcony, so familiar and yet in present aspect so strange, seemed unable to let him go. Tears ran down his cheeks as he stood there shrunken in form, with lined countenance, strained expression, white hair hanging lank; and through the audience there was a feeling as of a stifled sob, for each knew that they were saying farewell. Another outburst of applause and yet another; one more acknowledgment from the master; and Brahms and his Vienna had parted for ever.

Brahms appeared after the concert at a luncheon-party given by Excellenz Dumba, a distinguished protector of art in Vienna. About twenty-five gentlemen, chiefly artists and art-lovers, and the ladies of the house were present. Brahms was placed near to several of his intimate friends—Epstein, Conrat, Hanslick, Gänsbacher, and Mandyczewski—but he was not able to remain long. Within a few days of this date his Ischl landlady received a postcard from him announcing his intention of going to Ischl earlier than usual, and desiring that his rooms might be got ready. The last opera he heard was his friend Goldmark's 'Das Heimchen'; he entered a theatre for the last time on March 13, sitting with Hanslick at the production of Johann Strauss' 'Die Göttin der Vernunft,' but was obliged to leave at the end of the second act, and, much against his will, suffered a friend to accompany him home in a cab.

From this time he grew rapidly worse. He complained that he could no longer remember what he read, but wished for Busch's 'Bismarck,' the last book with which he tried to occupy himself. He soon became unable to take a walk even in a friend's care, and Dr. Victor von Miller called every day in his carriage to take him to drive in the Prater, where the fresh air somewhat revived him. His strength of will remained phenomenal to the last. He dragged himself to a rehearsal of the Roeger-Soldat Quartet party held at Frau Wittgenstein's less than a fortnight before his death, to hear Weber's Clarinet Quintet with Mühlfeld's co-operation. A performance of the work at Meiningen had particularly pleased him, and its inclusion in the Soldat programme was by his suggestion. In the same week he paid his last visit to the Fabers, and, whilst ascending the staircase to their flat, nearly fainted with pain. Herr Faber revived him, and got him on to the drawing-room sofa, where he sat exhausted, his head on his breast. He was obliged to leave the family dinner-table of some other intimate friends, and, retiring to the next room, sank down in agony. Frau Fellinger was ill at this time, and unable to leave her room. Brahms' last call of inquiry at her house was made on March 19.

The master was very gentle during the last months of his life, and touchingly grateful for every attention shown him. His evenings were of necessity passed in his rooms, for he firmly refused all the entreaties of his friends that he would take up his abode in one or another house. Every evening at dusk he used to place himself at the piano, and improvise softly for about half an hour, and when too tired to continue, would sit by the window gazing out on the familiar scene till long after darkness had set in. On March 24 Frau Door, who had always been a favourite with him, called to take him a bunch of violets. She was not admitted, but, observing Dr. von Miller's carriage before the house door, waited near the entrance, hoping to see Brahms pass out. He came down in about half an hour leaning on his friend's arm, and, noticing Frau Door, gave her his hand. 'I am very ill' (Mir geht es sehr schlecht), he answered faintly to her inquiry. He did not go out again. The next day Conrat was admitted, and was sitting talking quietly with him, when Brahms, who was on the sofa smoking, suddenly dropped his head. 'There must be something in it,' he muttered. Conrat gently left the room without disturbing him. On the 26th the physician wrote word to Frau Fellinger that all chance of moving him was over. Brahms did not leave his bed again. His two or three closest friends were constantly at his side, whilst his landlady, Frau Truxa, was his faithful and devoted nurse. He spoke little during the last days, and was too weak to notice much of what was passing in his room, but he managed on the 29th to write a few pencil lines from his bed to Frau Caroline:

'D. M. For the sake of change I am lying down a little and cannot, therefore, write comfortably. Otherwise there is no alteration and as usual, I only need patience.

'Affectionately your JOH.'[91]

A few more weary days and nights, during which the beloved master's life ebbed rapidly away, bring us to the early morning of April 3. He had lost consciousness several times in the night and been restored, and had recognised Faber, who, calling at about six o'clock and performing some slight service for him, caught the whispered words, 'Du bist ein guter Mensch' (You are a kind man). It is now nearly nine o'clock, and Brahms has fallen asleep. Early messages of inquiry have been answered, and the doctor, who has been at hand during the night, has departed, promising soon to return. The day has begun with the bright spring promise that the master was wont to greet year after year with joyful welcome; the sun shines, a soft breeze enters through the open window; outside there is a twittering of birds. Near the bed sits the untiring nurse, noticing the signs of the fast-approaching end. A movement from the bed claims her assistance. Brahms has opened his eyes, and tries to raise himself. With Frau Truxa's help he attains a sitting posture, and, looking at her, tries to speak. The lips move, but the tongue has lost its power, and he can only utter an inarticulate sound. Great tears roll down his cheeks; a last sigh, a last breath, and he sinks back, supported by gentle hands, on to his pillow, rid of his sufferings, passed quietly to his rest.[92]

Dr. von Miller, whose house was in the vicinity, was the first of the friends to receive intelligence of the master's decease. He hurried at once to Carlsgasse, and was immediately joined by Dr. Fellinger and Herr Faber. Many others called during the morning, some of whom were admitted to look at the still features, smoothed by the caress of death into an expression of noble serenity. A sketch was taken by the painter Michalek, a mask by

Professor Kundemann, a photograph by a private friend. The cause of death was certified, after a medical examination of the remains, as degeneration of the liver. The body, in evening dress, was placed the same afternoon in the coffin, and the room arranged with candelabra containing lighted candles; on a crimson cushion were displayed the various orders of the deceased composer. The next day the arrival began of the flowers, wreaths, crosses, and other floral tributes that transformed the room into a temple of beauty.

On the afternoon of the 4th General-Secretary Koch, Dr. Fellinger, and Herr Faber met in the dwelling, and searched for a will in the presence of a notary, but only found one written in May, 1891, on two sheets of paper, the last of them signed and dated, in the form of a letter to Simrock. This, a legally competent document in its original form, except for the slight omission of the signature on the first sheet of paper—which, under the indisputable circumstances establishing the authenticity of the will, would not have rendered it invalid—had been returned to the master at his own request by Simrock some time subsequent to the death of his sister, Elise Grund, in 1892. It was found, however, to have been marked by Brahms in pencil, some of the clauses lined out, whilst notes in the margin indicated designed alterations. These were in exact correspondence with the wishes expressed by Brahms in February to Dr. and Frau Fellinger, and embodied by Dr. Fellinger in the paper he had delivered into the hands of the composer to be copied by himself and signed. Another search was made the next day, therefore, but it proved fruitless. Only Dr. Fellinger's manuscript was found, and it must be presumed that Brahms had put off the dreaded task from day to day in the hope of feeling more capable of it, until his strength was no longer equal to its fulfilment. Nothing remained, therefore, but to apply to the proper authorities for the nomination of a curator in order that the necessary arrangements might be proceeded with. This was done; Dr. Fellinger was appointed, and on the afternoon of the 5th the sitting-room which, with the small inner room leading from it, contained Brahms library, manuscripts, and other possessions, was formally sealed. The coffin was closed the same day.

As soon as the master's death became known, the offer of an honorary grave was made by the city of Vienna. There was no hesitation in accepting it, but a deliberation was held as to whether the remains should be taken direct to the Central Friedhof or should be cremated at Gotha, according to directions contained in the letter to Simrock, and the ashes only deposited in Vienna. The remembrance of a few words dropped by Brahms himself when speaking of the 'sacred spot' which contains the graves of Beethoven and Schubert decided the point. It was felt that he would have chosen to rest in the place selected for him: the particular garden of the Friedhof in which the remains of Beethoven and Schubert lie, and which is sacred also to the memory of Mozart.

'All musical Vienna accompanied the great dead to the grave on the afternoon of April 6 and a stranger not knowing the man's greatness might have measured it by the number of prominent artists mingling in the great assemblage of the funeral procession, by the celebrated men and women who came from afar to show the last honour to Brahms.'

Till the hour appointed for the commencement of the ceremony deputations continued to arrive, from various parts of Europe, from the numerous societies of which the composer had been an honorary member, and telegrams and messages to pour in. At one o'clock a deputation from the Hamburg Senate was admitted to the house to lay a magnificent wreath on the coffin side by side with that from the Corporation of Vienna. Wreaths had been sent by the Queen of Hanover, the Duke of Cumberland, the Princess Marie of Hanover, Duke George of Saxe-Meiningen, the Princess Marie of Saxe-Meiningen, Helene, Baroness von Heldburg, and innumerable private friends known and unknown to Brahms; by the Society of Plastic Arts, Committee of the Opera, Gesellschaft, and other societies of Vienna; by the Philharmonic Society, Society of Music-lovers, Cecilia Society of Hamburg; by the Royal Academy of Arts, Berlin; by the various musical societies of Berlin, Leipzig, Budapest, Cologne, Salzburg, Mannheim, Frankfurt, Jena, Laubach, Lemberg, Graz, St. Petersburg, Brussels, Amsterdam, Cambridge, Basle, Zürich, and many other towns. Six cars scarcely sufficed to hold them.

The arrangements of the public funeral with which the city of Vienna honoured the remains of the great composer formed a singular contrast to the simplicity which had marked the daily habits of his life. Details may be read in the journals of the time. We shall confine ourselves to the record of a few of those appropriate to our narrative. The cortège, followed by the long train of mourners, started from Carlsgasse about half-past two, and, proceeding to the building of the Gesellschaft der Musikfreunde, halted before the principal entrance, where arrangements had been made for a short ceremony, consisting of an address by Herr Direktor J. R. Fuchs, of the conservatoire, and the singing of Brahms' part-song 'Fahr'wohl,' for unaccompanied chorus, under the direction of Richard von Perger, conductor of the Singverein. The procession then passed on to the Evangelical Church in Dorotheenstrasse, where the clergy and choir and several of the city dignitaries were assembled. After the coffin had been carried into the church, the choir sang Mendelssohn's 'Es ist bestimmt in Gottes' Rath.' The funeral address was delivered by Dr. von Zimmermann, who especially dwelt on the inspiration derived by the deceased composer's art from the pages of the Bible, on his love for children and the childlike spirit, and on his sympathy with distress.

'Wherever he could bring support to the unknown sufferer, the laborious striver, the helpless, the dying, there, in the man who, in his own habits, was frugal to the verge of parsimony, was found the most eager benefactor. The master Johannes Brahms is not dead. His spirit has conquered death and has entered into the light and blessed world of the pure harmonies of peace.'

At the entrance to the Friedhof the coffin was surrounded by personal friends of the deceased composer, carrying lighted wind-torches, and was accompanied by them to the grave. They were Ignaz Brüll, Anton Dvořák, Arthur Faber, Dr. Fellinger, Robert Fuchs, Richard Heuberger, Max Kalbeck, Ludwig Koch, Eusebius Mandyczewski, Dr. von Miller-Aichholz, Richard von Perger. At the grave-side Dr. von Perger spoke a few words of last farewell:

'This sacred place is now to receive the mortal remains of our great contemporary. He who has so enriched and blessed the whole world, what has he been to us musicians! In the light which streamed from his creative genius, his penetrating art-comprehension, we were able to look up confidently to his incomparable mastership, to his lofty, unbending artistic intelligence. Amid the countless paths and by-paths which to-day intersect the domain of musical art, we were guided by the torch held high and secure by the hand of her first priest. He has met his worthy spiritual brothers, indeed, for the first time to-day in this resting-place, but he was always a simple, sympathetic friend to his living colleagues in art, in spite of the great distance which raised him above them; always a helper of uprising talent, a sure and faithful friend in adversity and suffering.... Here thou restest now, thou blessed of heaven, in this vast, awful world-solitude; clouds of light float above thee and that of thee which is immortal floats with them through eternal spaces. Ade Meister Johannes, fahr'wohl, fahr'wohl.'

Joachim was in England at the time of Brahms' death, fulfilling long-contracted engagements. Stockhausen, now a man of seventy-three, and not in strong health, was at this period unequal to a hurried and distressing journey from Frankfurt to Vienna.

Memorial performances were given by the Cecilia Verein, Hamburg, on April 5, the day preceding the funeral; by the Vienna Gesellschaft on the 11th; by the Beethoven-Haus Verein, Bonn, in May; by the Royal High School for Music, Berlin, in the summer; and by innumerable musical societies of Europe and America during the season 1897-98. In nearly all instances the German Requiem formed part of such concerts as were orchestral.

A clause in Brahms' will provided that any of his unpublished works found in his rooms after death should be the property of Simrock. There was one opus only—the eleven Organ Preludes. With them were the arrangements, as pianoforte duets, of Joachim's two overtures referred to in an earlier chapter. All three works were published in 1902, a delay of five years having been caused by difficulties that arose in connection with the will. Apart from detail, these may be generally stated as follows:

Brahms is said to have left, besides his library, which included valuable autograph musical manuscripts, and a very few personal possessions, about £20,000 in investments. In the original will three societies—the Liszt Pensions-Verein of Hamburg, the Czerny Verein and the Gesellschaft der Musikfreunde of Vienna—were named as the inheritors, subject to the payment of a legacy to the composer's landlady, Frau Truxa, and of two life-annuities—one to his stepmother, Frau Caroline Brahms, to be continued after her death to her son, Fritz Schnack, for his life; the other to Brahms' sister, Elise Grund. These would practically account for the time being for the income arising from the investments.

In the absence of any legally valid document, about twenty cousins of various degrees of kinship came forward, in answer to advertisements in the newspapers, as claimants to the property. Litigation ensued, and was protracted through several years. The original process and the first appeal were determined in favour of the societies; the second appeal reversed these decisions, and declared the blood relations to be the heirs. To prevent the further expense and delay of another appeal, a compromise was now arrived at by the contending parties, and the general results of the will, the law-processes, and the compromise have been that the blood relations have been recognised as the heirs to all but the library, which is now in the possession of the Gesellschaft der Musikfreunde; that Frau Truxa's legacy has been paid; and that certain sums accepted by the societies, by which they will ultimately benefit, have been invested, and the income arising from them secured for the payment of the life-annuity to Herr Schnack. (Frau Caroline Brahms died in the spring of 1902.)

Projects for the erection of memorials to the master in Hamburg, Vienna, and Meiningen, were set on foot soon after his death. The first to be completed has been that now standing in the 'English Garden' at Meiningen, the unveiling of which was made the occasion of a Memorial Festival in October, 1899. The bust of the master which it displays is the work of Professor Hildebrandt.

The memorial erected at the grave by the heirs, after the final settlement of the property, designed and executed by Fräulein Ilse Conrat, was unveiled on May 7, 1903, the seventieth anniversary of Brahms' birth. It consists of a marble bust and pedestal in front of a marble headstone, on which are allegorical figures in bas-relief.

Memorial tablets have been placed by the respective municipalities on the houses in which Brahms lived in Vienna, Ischl, and Thun, and the garden of the house at Mürz Zuschlag has been bought by the town and made into a music-garden. A bronze bust of the master by Frau Dr. Fellinger stands in the musicians' pavilion.

A Brahms-Haus has been erected by Dr. von Miller-Aichholz in his private grounds at Gmünden, the rooms of which are constructed to the exact dimensions of those occupied by Brahms in Ischl, and furnished with the Ischl furniture as it used to stand. They contain an interesting collection of musical and other autographs of the master, photographs, programmes, and other mementos.

A Brahms Society has been formed in Vienna for the purpose of collecting and preserving all available mementos in a special museum.

Our task is now completed. If it should prove to have been so far successfully accomplished as to suggest to our readers at all a true conception of the character and individuality of Brahms, to throw some additional light upon the spirit which dictated the composition of his works, our aim will have been achieved. It is as yet far too soon to attempt any surmise as to the exact ultimate place that he will occupy amongst the great ones of his art. Schumann's words, however, spoken rather more than half a century ago, which proclaimed Johannes as the prophet destined to give ideal presentment to the highest spirit of his time, have, even now, been surely proved true. Brahms stands immovable in his position as the representative of the musical thought of the ages as it has gradually developed through three hundred and fifty years from Palestrina's day to his own; and in his works dwells the high and beautiful spirit—the essential spirit of life—which, whilst it knows no compromise with truth, works out its appointed course in 'faith and hope and love, these three; and the greatest of them is love.'

THE END

---

[1] Head of the celebrated Vienna firm of pianoforte-makers.

[2] The *Deutsche Musikzeitung* of November 29, the very day of the concert, announces vocal duets and choruses by Brahms as part of the programme. The review of the concert in the same paper concludes: 'Frau Passy-Cornet and Herr Fürchtgott assisted the concert-giver, whose programme was altered, by performing songs and ballads.'

[3] Egg-punch was a birthday institution in the family. The Wednesday in question was probably the birthday of Brahms' mother.

[4] Reimann's 'Johannes Brahms.' Published in facsimile opposite p. 28.

[5] Moser's 'Joseph Joachim,' p. 177.

[6] 'Aus meinem Leben.'

[7] Probably a private performance. Hellmesberger's published programmes give the first concert performance of the work by his quartet party as on December 27, 1863.

[8] 'Brahms Erinnerungen,' by Franz Fribberg (*Berliner Tagblatt*, December 18, 1898).

N.B.—Fribberg was a member of the Philharmonic orchestra of Vienna at the period in question.

[9] The collection is now in the Imperial Gallery on the Burg Ring.

[10] This and the extract immediately following are from some letters first published by Hanslick in the *Neue Freie Presse* of July 1, 1897, and republished in *Am Ende des Jahrhunderts* ('Der Modernen Oper,' Part VIII.): 'Johannes Brahms.'

[11]

'Josef lieber, Josef mein,
hilf mir wieg'n mein Kindlein fein.
Gott der wird dein Lohner sein
in Himmelreich der Jungfrau Sohn, Maria.'

(Joseph dearest, Joseph mine,
Help me rock the babe divine.
Heaven's blessing shall be thine
In th' kingdom of the Virgin's Son, Mariè.)

[12] Personally communicated to the author by Herr Hofcapellmeister Dietrich.

[13] From a letter published by Richard Heuberger (*Beilage zur Allg. Musikzeitung*, 1899, No. 260).

[14] Brahms, by giving to the variations the second title of Studies for the Pianoforte, has sufficiently indicated the intention with which he placed them before the world.

[15] The date of the publication of the Horn Trio is given in Simrock's Thematic Catalogue as 1868.

[16] See Vol. I., p. 167.

[17] 'Briefe von Theodor Billroth' (sixth enlarged edition).

[18] 'Neujahrsblatt der Allgemeinen Musikgesellschaft in Zürich,' 1898.

[19] The author is indebted for this and a few other extracts from Frau Schumann's diary to the kindness of Fräulein Marie Schumann.

[20] The date assigned to this letter in Dietrich's 'Recollections' is one amongst several similar mistakes that occur in the volume. They are to be explained by the circumstances that Brahms rarely put dates to his letters, and that those in question were supplied from memory.

[21] 'Briefe u. Schriften von Hans von Bülow.' Published by Marie von Bülow.

[22] Dietrich.

[23] A pedal point is a sound sustained, according to conditions prescribed by the rules of art, during a succession of varying harmonies of which it need not form an essential part.

[24] Matt. v. 4; Ps. cxxvi. 5, 6; 1 Pet. i. 24; James v. 7; 1 Pet. i. 25; Isa. xxxv. 10; Ps. xxxix. 4-7; Wisd. iii. 1; Ps. lxxxiv. 1, 2, 4; John xvi. 22; Ecclus. li. 27; Isa. lxvi. 13; Heb. xiii. 14; 1 Cor. xv 51-55; Rev. iv. 11; Rev. xiv. 13.

[25] The cadences of music are somewhat analogous to the punctuation of literature. A 'final cadence' has the effect of closing a musical period.

[26] Dated April 4 in Dietrich's 'Recollections.'

[27] Schumann.

[28] Communicated in a letter to the author by Dr. Deiters.

[29] See Vol. I., p. 207.

[30] *Cf.* Dietrich, p. 54 *et seq*. The dates in the text are given on the authority of Frau Schumann's diary.

[31] The strict strophic form is that in which voice-melody and accompaniment are the same in each verse. It admits, however, of several kinds of modification, as by varied accompaniment, slight variation of voice-melody, and so forth. The 'durchcomponirtes' Lied, for which there

is no technical English term, is that of which the text is set throughout to fresh musical thoughts and developments.

[32] Those who wish to study Brahms' treatment of folk-music in detail are referred to Hohenemser's articles, 'Brahms und die Volksmusik,' in *Die Musik*, Nos. 15 and 18, 1903.

[33] Dated 1866 in the Thematic Catalogue.

[34] Sir C. Villiers Stanford remembers being present at a public performance of the German Requiem in London earlier than that of the Philharmonic Society. This was at a students' concert of the Royal Academy of Music under John Hullah, the then conductor of the orchestra, the date of which, however, the author has not succeeded in ascertaining.

[35] 'Johannes Brahms in Erinnerung,' p. 37.

[36] 'Meine Bekanntschaft mit Brahms,' *Die Musik*, No. 5 of 1902.

[37] A few words that occur in a letter of Mendelssohn to his sister Fanny Hensel are of interest here. 'Yesterday I read "Nausikaa" to Cécile in Voss' translation.... This poem is really irresistible when it becomes sentimental. I always felt an inclination to set it to music, of course not for the theatre, only as an epic, and this whole day I feel renewed pleasure in the idea' (p. 148 of Lady Wallace's translation of Mendelssohn's letters, 1833-1847).

[38] The entire letter is published by Richard Heuberger in the supplement to the *Allgemeine Musikzeitung*, 1899, No. 260.

[39] 'Franz Liszt's Briefe an Carl Gille,' with a biographical introduction by Adolph Stern.

[40] Numbers 1, 3, 10, were published in 1874 as arranged by the composer for orchestra, and were frequently conducted by him about that date.

[41] The full programme was as follows:

A German Requiem (under Reinthaler's direction).

Arie from Handel's 'Messiah' and Graun's 'Der Tod Jesu.'

'Hallelujah, Heil and Preis sei Gott.' A song of Triumph for eight-part Chorus and Orchestra lately composed by Johannes Brahms (under the composer's direction).

Soprano, Frau Wilt from Vienna, Imperial chamber singer.

Baritone, Herr Schelper, of the Berlin Court Opera.

(The chorus of the Singakademie was augmented for the occasion to about 300 voices.)

The general (public) rehearsal took place on Thursday evening, April 6.

[42] The following were, as the author believes, first performances in this country:

Quartet in A major for Pianoforte and Strings: May 23, 1871. St. James's Hall, Musical Union (John Ella), by Jaell, Heermann, Wäfelghem, Lasserre.

Pianoforte Concerto, D minor: March 9, 1872. Crystal Palace (A. Manns), by Miss Baglehole (pupil of the pianist W. H. Holmes, one of the first English musicians to appreciate the significance of Brahms' art). The concerto was played for the second time in London by Jaell at the Philharmonic concert of June 23, 1873.

Sextet for Strings, G major: November 27, 1872. St. George's Hall, Musical Evenings, by Henry Holmes, Folkes, Burnett, Hann, C. Ould, Pezze.

Ballades for Pianoforte, Op. 10, Nos. 2 and 3: March 17, 1873. St. James's Hall, Monday Popular Concerts (S. Arthur Chappell), by Frau Schumann.

Handel Variations and Fugue for Pianoforte: November 12, 1873. Crystal Palace, by Florence May.

Hungarian Variations for Pianoforte: March 25, 1874. Crystal Palace, by Florence May.

Schumann Variations (Pianoforte Duet): March 30, 1874. St. James's Hall, Monday Popular Concerts, by Miss Agnes Zimmermann and Mr. Franklin Taylor.

Serenade in A major (small Orchestra): June 29, 1874. St. James's Hall, Philharmonic Society. Conductor: W. G. Cusins.

Liebeslieder, Op. 52: January 15 and 27, 1877. St. James's Hall, M. and S. Popular Concerts. Pianists: Fräulein Marie Krebs and Miss A. Zimmermann. Singers: Fräulein Sophie Löwe, Fräulein Redeker, William Shakespeare, G. Pyatt.

Neue Liebeslieder, Walzer, Op. 65: May 18, 1877. Cambridge University Musical Society's Concerts. Pianists: C. Villiers Stanford and Raoul C. de Versan. Singers: Fräulein Thekla Friedländer, Fräulein Redeker, Rev. L. Borrisow, Gerard F. Cobb.

N.B.—The *Quartet in G minor* and the *Quintet in F minor*, both for *Pianoforte and Strings*, were played for the first time at the Popular Concerts respectively on January 26, 1874, by Hallé, Madame Norman-Néruda (now Lady Hallé), Ludwig Straus, and Piatti; and on February 27, 1875, by Hallé, Joachim, L. Ries, and Piatti, but may have been previously given in England elsewhere.

The *Pianoforte Concerto in D minor* was played for the first time in Vienna at one of the Philharmonic Concerts of the season 1870-71, by the composer, and for the second time in March, 1873, by Anton Door.

[43] The author has followed the date given in the published catalogue of the issue of these two books of songs. By their opus numbers they would rather belong to the year 1873 or 1874. Brahms' well-known arrangement for Pianoforte of Gluck's Gavotte in A was published in 1871 by Senff.

[44] P. 278 of Vol. I.

[45] Dietrich, p. 42.

[46] Allgeyers, 'Life of Feuerbach.'

[47] From the article in the *Gegenwart* already referred to.

[48] Steiner's 'Johannes Brahms.'

[49] Reimann's 'Johannes Brahms,' p. 117.

[50] See Vol. II., pp. 77 and 138.

[51] Schumann's essay, 'New Paths.'

[52] The variations for orchestra on Haydn's theme and six of Brahms' songs, sung by Henschel, were included in the programme of the concert.

[53] Goethe's song, 'Unüberwindlich,' set by Brahms and published in 1877 as No. 6 of Op. 72: 'Though a thousand vows I've taken.'

[54] Article in the *New York Outlook*, July 25, 1903.

[55] See Vol. I., Appendix No. 1.

[56] *Die Musik*, in the article referred to in a previous chapter.

[57] Fräulein Ettlinger informs the author that it was she herself who put the question to the master and received his answer. For the article on Levi see 'Biographisches Jahrbuch und Deutscher Nekrolog,' 1902.

[58] Widmann's 'Brahms Recollections,' p. 38 and following.

[59] Kalbeck's 'Johannes Brahms,' p. 187 and following.

[60] *Die Musik*, No. 5 of 1902.

[61] First published with others by Hanslick in the *Neue Freie Presse* of July 1, 1897.

[62] Hanslick, *Neue Freie Presse*, as before.

[63] Claus Groth, in the Brahms Recollections to which we have several times referred, speaks of the festival banquet as having taken place at the

Hamburger Hof, Hamburg, and 'as I think' after the performance of Brahms' symphony. Groth's articles were written in the year 1897, when he was at an advanced age—he was much Brahms' senior—and his memory has misled him in one or two of his details. As regards those here referred to, the author has, in the above description, followed the accounts given in the *Hamburger Correspondenten* of the time, with which that of Hanslick, in his very interesting 'Essays on Music and Musicians,' is in strict accord.

[64] See p. 29 of this volume.

[65] Widmann, p. 43.

[66] Steiner's 'Johannes Brahms,' i., p. 25.

[67] Allgeyer's 'Feuerbach': Introduction to the second edition.

[68] Published by Hanslick in the *Neue Freie Presse*, July 1, 1897.

[69] The scope of these pages does not permit the author to yield to the temptation of presenting an analysis of the means by which Brahms has produced the romantic, mysterious atmosphere which pervades the 'andante moderato.' They will be found strangely simple and intelligible by those inclined to examine for themselves the harmonic material; in the first place of the introductory bars (which consists of the chromatic major concord on the minor sixth of the key, E major, and a couple of passing notes); and in the second place of the full statement of the opening theme (which includes the chords of the dominant minor ninth and the tonic seventh and minor thirteenth, all chromatic).

[70] Widmann's 'Johannes Brahms in Erinnerungen,' p. 58 and following.

[71] A mountain near Thun.

[72] *Die Musik*, first May number of 1902.

[73] *Neue Freie Presse*, June, 1897.

[74] Spengel's 'Johannes Brahms,' p. 8.

[75] *Neue Freie Presse*, June 29, 1897.

[76] Billroth's Briefe.

[77] *Neue Freie Presse*, July 1, 1897.

[78] Published in Steiner's 'Johannes Brahms,' p. 29.

[79] Published in Reimann's 'Johannes Brahms,' p. 117.

[80] The theme is the one alluded to on p. 156 of our first volume.

N.B. On the occasion of Schumann's opera 'Genoveva' being put into rehearsal at the Hanover court theatre in 1874, Brahms, with Frau Schumann's approval, added a few bars to the close of Siegfried's song in the third act. These do not appear, however, in the pianoforte score of the work included in the complete edition.

[81] See Appendix No. I.

[82] Widmann's 'Recollections.'

[83] Steiner, p. 33.

[84] Reimann, p. 109.

[85] *July 1, 1897.*

[86] See for an account of Herzogenberg's church music 'Heinrich von Herzogenberg und die evangelischen Kirchenmusik,' by Friedrich Spitta. Reprint from the *Monatschrift für Gottesdienst und kirchliche Kunst*, 1900, No. 11.

[87] Preface to the 'Vollständige Sammlung der von Johannes Brahms componirten und musikalisch bearbeiteten Dichtungen,' by Dr. G. Ophüls.

[88] 'Der musikalische Nachlass von Johannes Brahms,' by Ludwig Karpath. *Signale*, March 26, 1902.

[89] In the author's possession.

[90] First published by Reimann, p. 118.

[91] Reimann, p. 118.

[92] See 'Am Sterbebett Brahms,' by Celestine Truxa, *Neue Freie Presse*, May 7, 1903.

[93] The dates of publication here printed are those given in Simrock's published Thematic Catalogue of Brahms' works, excepting in the few instances especially indicated in the main narrative.

[94] Unless otherwise described, all songs for a single voice are composed with pianoforte accompaniment only.

CPSIA information can be obtained
at www.ICGtesting.com
Printed in the USA
LVHW040958020323
740706LV00008B/746

9 789356 900264